The
First Battle for
Petersburg

The Attack and Defense
of the Cockade City, June 9, 1864

William Glenn Robertson

SB

Savas Beatie
California

Library of Congress Control Number: 2014958739

Savas Beatie First edition, first printing
ISBN: 978-1-61121-214-3

Published by
Savas Beatie LLC
989 Governor Drive, Suite 102
El Dorado Hills, CA 95762

Phone: 916-941-6896
(E-mail) sales@savasbeatie.com

Digital edition by Savas Publishing Company
ISBN: 978-1-94066-945-8

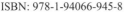

FSC
www.fsc.org
MIX
Paper from
responsible sources
FSC® C011935

Savas Beatie titles are available at special discounts for bulk purchases in the United States by corporations, institutions, and other organizations. For more details, please contact Special Sales, P.O. Box 4527, El Dorado Hills, CA 95762, or you may e-mail us at sales@savasbeatie.com, or visit our website at www.savasbeatie.com for additional information.

Proudly published, printed, and warehoused in the United States of America.

To The Memory of William C. Banister

And Those Who Fell With Him In the Defense of their City,

June 9, 1864

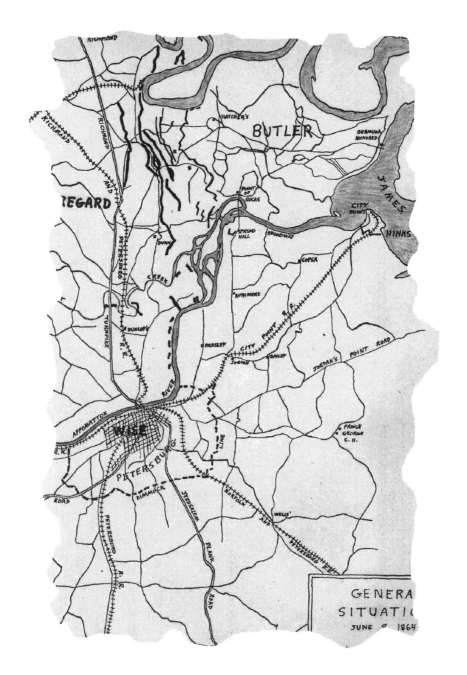

Table of Contents

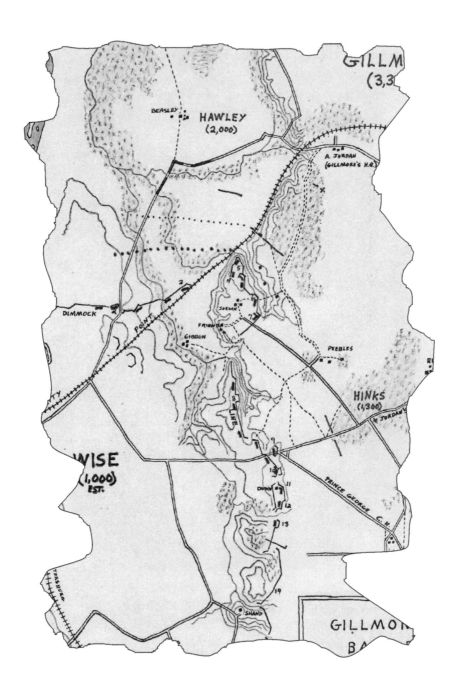

Preface

History does not link the date of June 9, 1864 with any significant battle of the American Civil War nor, in the same context, does the name of Petersburg, Virginia bring to mind much more than tales of valor and incompetence at the Crater and the privations of a long and dreary siege. In fact, the Cockade City and its inhabitants seldom are noted, except in passing references to Richmond's transportation system, until the arrival of U. S. Grant and his veterans in front of the city's outer defenses on June 15, 1864. Yet there was another, earlier attempt to seize Petersburg, six days before the arrival of the Army of the Potomac, and that attempt led to what Douglas Southall Freeman called "perhaps the unique battle of the entire war." The story of that battle and the events immediately surrounding it are the subject of this study.

A major reason for the uniqueness of the Battle of June 9, 1864 is the fact that the citizens of Petersburg themselves contributed heavily to the successful defense of their city—and paid a disproportionate share of the cost. Another reason is the possibility that there might never have been a ten-month Siege of Petersburg if the results of the Battle of June 9 had been reversed. Still another reason, and one important to all Americans, is the fact that the great national day of remembrance known as Memorial Day indirectly stemmed from ceremonies begun at Petersburg in 1866 commemorating the heroes of "The Ninth of June." For one hundred and twenty-five years Petersburg has remembered that day both in fact and in legend, but the nation at large is unfamiliar with the events of June 9. It is an important story, a story of heroism and sacrifice which belongs to all Americans, and which the Cockade City is proud to share with the rest of the nation. Perhaps the present work may contribute in some small measure to that sharing.

In its initial form this study began as a master's thesis at the University of Virginia more than twenty years ago. As such it benefitted from the gracious assistance of a large number of people. Foremost among them are two individuals, Willie Lee Rose and Martin Conway. Although not a devotee of military history, Professor Rose graciously consented to serve as thesis adviser and gave unstintingly of her time during what was officially a year's sabbatical whenever advice and encouragement were requested. Martin Conway of the National Park Service, Historian at what then was called Petersburg National Military Park, was another source of inspiration. Mr. Conway and his associates gladly opened their extensive library and other facilities to the author without restrictions and never failed to meet any number of bothersome requests. As always, the staffs of the manuscript repositories listed in the bibliography provided timely, professional assistance. Other individuals who assisted the author in various important ways were Cullen Sherwood, Harrell Pratt, Curtis Williams, Thaddeus Williams, Nelson Linaburg, Rodger Plaster, Ada R. Bailey, and Linwood Duck. At every step of the way, the author's parents, Mr. and Mrs. William S. Robertson provided unflagging encouragement and support.

In the twenty years following the completion of the thesis, the author continued to amass new evidence relating to the action on June 9, 1864, but made no overt effort to get the manuscript to a wider audience. It comes before the public today largely because of the interest shown in it by another pair of individuals, Chris Calkins and Harold E. Howard. Like Martin Conway before him, Petersburg National Battlefield Historian Chris Calkins believed the story of June 9 to be an important one, worthy of publication, and he recommended it to publisher Harold Howard. Mr. Howard believed the study would fit into a new series on Virginia Civil War Battles and Leaders he was launching, and he urged the author to revise the original thesis manuscript for publication. With financial assistance from Roy L. Vaught, who made purchase of a word processor possible, and with devoted proofreading and advice from Janet Vaught Robertson, the revision was completed in a timely fashion. To one and all the author extends his deepest and most heartfelt thanks!

William Glenn Robertson
Leavenworth, Kansas
January 16, 1989

Preface to the New Edition

Although two scholarly histories of Civil War Petersburg and a similar volume on the Army of the James have been published since the original publication of this work nearly a quarter of a century ago, the details of the Battle of June 9, 1864 and its analysis remain virtually the same as when the author first recounted them. The recent availability of electronic editions of the Compiled Service Records of Confederate Soldiers and the United States Federal Census, however, now permits a much more extensive analysis of the casualties among the "Old Men and Young Boys" than was previously attempted. Presentation of that analysis, detailed in Appendix 3, plus a desire to keep the story of this "unique" Civil War event current in historical memory has led to the publication of this new edition.

In addition to those individuals noted in the original preface, the author wishes to thank: Hal Jespersen for the new maps, Janet Robertson for tireless work on the illustrations, Stewart Robertson for invaluable technical assistance at a critical moment, and the staff at Savas Beatie LLC for excellence in presentation. I am in their debt.

William Glenn Robertson
Leavenworth, Kansas
April 20, 2015

William Glenn
Robertson

The
First Battle for
Petersburg

The Attack and Defense
of the Cockade City, June 9, 1864

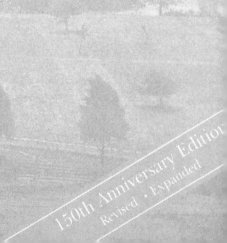

150th Anniversary Edition
Revised · Expanded

Chapter I

Petersburg Goes to War

Like all Americans in the year 1860, the 18,266 residents of Petersburg, Virginia, were caught up in the great national controversy that would soon lead to civil war. Most of Petersburg's citizens initially favored remaining in the Union, though their representative in the Virginia legislature, John Herbert Claiborne, was a secessionist. Claiborne's views were supported by the younger men in the city, who often attempted to raise "secession poles" on Petersburg's streets. In turn, these poles were cut down and destroyed by Unionists, who represented a majority of the older and more influential residents. When Governor Letcher called a convention to determine Virginia's course of action, Petersburg chose Thomas Branch, a successful merchant and conservative elder statesman of the city, to cast its vote for Union.[1]

Gradually, sentiment in the city began to change. A citizen's letter dated March 23, 1861, noted "Tom" Branch's selection, but the writer believed that if the election were to be held again, a secessionist representative would be chosen. In the end, President Abraham Lincoln's request for Virginia troops to join in suppressing the states which had already seceded made Petersburg's, and Virginia's, Unionist position untenable. Following Lincoln's call, the Virginia Convention voted to take the state out of the Union, and Petersburg by this

---

1 George S. Bernard, Diary, 1860, microfilm copy, University of Virginia Library; James G. Scott and Edward A. Wyatt, IV, *Petersburg's Story: A History* (Richmond, VA, 1960), 169; "Senate Speech of John Herbert Claiborne on Appropriation for Arms and Armory, January 19, 1860," in John H. Claiborne Papers, University of Virginia; J. Pinckney Williamson, *Ye Olden Tymes, History of Petersburg* (Petersburg, VA, 1906), 50. For descriptions of Petersburg and its citizens in 1860, see William D. Henderson, *Petersburg in the Civil War: War at the Door* (Lynchburg, VA, 1998), 1-18, and A. Wilson Greene, *Civil War Petersburg: Confederate City in the Crucible of War* (Charlottesville, VA, 2006), 3-14.

time agreed with the delegates' decision. Remembering the city's contribution to the nation and knowing that war would jeopardize all the progress that had been made in Petersburg's 112-year history, the respectable citizens of the Cockade City had stood for Union as long as they could. With Lincoln's action they could resist no longer and were forced to join the rising tide of secessionist sentiment. Petersburg residents risked more than many rural Southerners by going to war in 1861, but in the last analysis they had no other choice.[2]

Once the decision for war was reached, the citizens of Petersburg immediately took steps to serve the cause. The first resource to be mobilized was manpower. Most of the young men who had clamored so strongly for war enlisted at once, if they were not already members of militia companies which joined the Confederate army en masse. Altogether Petersburg furnished 17 separate units for Confederate service—11 infantry companies, three cavalry companies, and three artillery batteries. Added to this number were the men who enlisted in units formed in other localities. Petersburg residents proudly boasted that they sent more men to war than the total number of registered voters in the city. As if this were not contribution enough, in the fall of 1863 the fear of a Federal assault led to the formation of a City Battalion of reserves commanded by Maj. Peter V. Batte. The few remaining prewar militia companies were joined by several new ones at a camp of instruction located at the head of Washington Street. There instructors furnished by the Confederate government drilled the troops for over a month before allowing them to return to their homes. Exempt from conscription because of their age or skills, these men remained ready for instant mobilization should an enemy threat appear.[3]

Petersburg's industry was also drafted into the war effort. Most of the tobacco factories closed their doors but the cotton mills operated at capacity from the beginning, producing tent cloth, sheets, and uniform material for the

---

2   L. W. Britten to Joseph P. Gilliam, March 23, 1861, in Gilliam Family Papers, University of Virginia Library; Williamson, *Ye Olden Tymes*, 51; Scott and Wyatt, *Petersburg's Story*, 169; Henderson, *Petersburg in the Civil War*, 19-20; Greene, *Civil War Petersburg*, 14-30. The "Cockade City" designation was conferred upon Petersburg by President James Madison following the War of 1812, in honor of the service of Petersburg troops under William Henry Harrison. Scott and Wyatt, *Petersburg's Story*, 126.

3   Scott and Wyatt, *Petersburg's Story*, 170; Fletcher H. Archer, "The Defense of Petersburg on the 9th of June, 1864," in George S. Bernard, ed., *War Talks of Confederate Veterans* (Petersburg, VA, 1892), 110-11; Lee A. Wallace, *A Guide to Virginia Military Organizations, 1861-1865*, rev. 2d ed. (Lynchburg, VA, 1986), 125. Batte's unit was designated the 44th Battalion (Petersburg City Battalion) Virginia Infantry and was assigned to Virginia's reserve forces.

Confederacy. Uriah Wells and William Tappey ceased production of agricultural implements and iron railings, and turned their foundries into repair shops for light artillery and army wagons. The old rope walk that in prewar days had served the river trade now became the Naval Rope Works and turned out cordage for the Confederate navy. Just west of the city an entirely new industry, a powder mill, sprang up almost overnight. Near the head of Halifax Street, Col. Josiah Gorgas, Chief of Ordnance of the Confederate army, established a large lead smelter which processed ore from as far away as Wytheville. Even the productive capacity of Petersburg's women was utilized with the formation of a sewing society to make uniforms. Receiving their orders from the Quartermaster Department in Richmond and their cloth from the local mills, the ladies rented a store in front of the court house and made thousands of shirts and pairs of trousers. The weekly payroll of this organization alone often amounted to over $1000 in Confederate currency.[4]

With the coming of hostilities Petersburg's railroad network assumed even greater significance than it had had in peacetime. Unfortunately the Confederate government soon discovered that the rails of the Richmond and Petersburg Railroad did not join any of the lines coming into the city from the south, east, and west. This peculiar situation was the result of constant lobbying by the local draying interests, who opposed the loss of the highly lucrative transfer business. Such narrow self-interest could not be allowed to hinder the war effort, and because both the military authorities and the railroads favored closing the gap, countervailing pressure was soon applied. In May 1861 the Richmond city engineer, Washington Gill, made preliminary surveys and after Gen. R. E. Lee spoke in favor of the proposal the Virginia General Assembly formally approved the project. Under the direction of Maj. William S. Ashe, the job was finally completed in late August 1861.[5]

Another new feature in wartime Petersburg was the establishment of military hospitals within the city. The first hospital opened early in the war, soon

4 Scott and Wyatt, *Petersburg's Story*, 224; Jennings C. Wise, *The Long Arm of Lee* (1915; reprint, New York, NY, 1959), 49; Frank E. Vandiver, *Ploughshares into Swords: Josiah Gorgas and Confederate Ordnance* (Austin, TX, 1952), 136; Bessie Callender, "Personal Recollections of the Civil War," typescript, Petersburg National Battlefield; Henderson, *Petersburg in the Civil War*, 24.

5 Robert C. Black, III, *The Railroads of the Confederacy* (Chapel Hill, NC, 1952), 9, 72-73, 311; George Edgar Turner, *Victory Rode the Rails* (Indianapolis, IN, 1953), 69-70; Angus James Johnston, II, *Virginia Railroads in the Civil War* (Chapel Hill, NC, 1961), 19; Henderson, *Petersburg in the Civil War*, 25-26. Because of gauge differences, only the north-south lines were connected.

after the ladies of Bollingbrook Street found an ill soldier resting in a doorway. Funds which were to have gone toward the construction of a gunboat were diverted to the hospital cause and from these modest beginnings Petersburg's system of hospitals developed rapidly. As the war progressed the machinery was removed from idle tobacco factories and replaced by hospital beds. The prevailing practice was to establish separate hospitals for the wounded of each state, staffing them with doctors and nurses from that state as much as possible. Petersburg, therefore, had a Virginia Hospital as well as hospitals for patients from North Carolina, South Carolina, and Georgia. Apparently Southerners from other states were treated at the Confederate States Hospital, which was also located in Petersburg. Dr. John Herbert Claiborne was the Chief Surgeon of the city and was responsible for the management of all of Petersburg's several hospitals. By the spring of 1864, his patients numbered around 3,000 men.[6]

The first three years of the war carried with it significant changes for the city's residents. The absence of so many of Petersburg's sons, coupled with the pitiful condition of the wounded convalescing in the city's hospitals piled heavy emotional burdens upon the populace. Unlike the capital of Richmond, there was little gaiety to be seen on the faces of the citizens of the Cockade City. Still, its citizens withstood the constant strain and gradually became conditioned to the new situation. Such inconveniences as martial law and obstructions in the Appomattox River could be easily accommodated into one's life, if a small amount of effort were applied. The effects of the war could be seen only in a more "serious and thoughtful" manner adopted by most citizens and which was noted by many visitors. The resident acting company still trod the boards at Phoenix Hall, for example, but such amusements no longer represented the spirit of the city.[7]

More and more the citizens began to turn their energies to philanthropic activities. Whenever a troop train passed through the city in daylight, some residents were always on hand to offer the soldiers flowers, fruit, and food if such items were available. Petersburg had too many of its own men in the army

---

6 Scott and Wyatt, *Petersburg's Story*, 172; John H. Claiborne, *Seventy-Five Years in Old Virginia* (New York, NY, 1904), 200-01, 206; Henderson, *Petersburg in the Civil War*, 32-33; Greene, *Civil War Petersburg*, 111-13.

7 Mrs. Roger A. Pryor, *Reminiscences of Peace and War* (New York, NY, 1904), 259; Scott and Wyatt, *Petersburg's Story*, 172.

Sycamore Street, Petersburg
Library of Congress

not to be kind to their comrades.[8] The local troops themselves were partially supported by the efforts of the Common Council, Petersburg's governing body. The Council often appropriated large sums to buy shoes and blankets for the 17 units serving with the main armies, but the needs of the troops were never fully met. Nor were the city's resources adequate to alleviate the suffering of the poor. The wives and widows of soldiers could not support their families in the absence of the head of the household. In addition, industrial employment had been curtailed in some areas of production, leaving many more people in a destitute condition. The problem was compounded by the presence in the city of a number of refugees from areas under Federal control. Initially the city tried

8   Pryor, *Peace and War*, 257-58. Others passing through did not receive such favors. In the month of February, 1864, 12,000 Federal prisoners moved through Petersburg on their way to Andersonville, Georgia, 400 prisoners per train, one train per day. This southward traffic never ceased thereafter. Black, *Railroads of the Confederacy*, 234.

to care for all of these people, but city officials soon found that most refugees and the families of known deserters had to be excluded from the relief rolls. The Common Council established the position of Salt Agent to ration that precious commodity and made similar arrangements in regard to food and fuel. A Board of Relief and a General Board of Charities attempted to coordinate the city's efforts, which by 1863 had come to include a soup kitchen. Nevertheless, none of these stopgap measures was more than moderately successful.[9]

By the fall of 1863 the citizens of Petersburg had begun to feel the economic pinch. The city was so clogged with refugees that the wife of Brig. Gen. Roger Pryor was compelled to search for days before finding accommodations in an abandoned overseer's cabin. Many of the original residents had moved away temporarily and their houses were occupied by strangers, tenants in some instances and squatters in others. Food was extremely scarce and prices reflected the scarcity. In January of 1864 Donnan and Johnston, Petersburg commission merchants, listed flour at $200 per barrel, butter at $6 per pound, sugar and lard at $4 per pound, beans at $30 per bushel, wheat at $25 per bushel, and tea not available. According to Mrs. Pryor, Petersburg had been "drained by its generous gifts to the army; regiments were constantly passing, and none ever departed without the offer of refreshment." Already residents were turning to substitutes for items that in peacetime had been regarded as necessities.[10]

As if the absence of local men, the passage of troop trains, and the overwhelming scarcity of food were not enough to remind Petersburg's citizens of the war, another reminder was located just outside the city. If anyone's business carried him a mile or so beyond the corporate limits, he passed through a system of fortifications that served as the main line of Petersburg's defenses. Begun in 1862 by slaves under the direction of a Confederate engineer, Capt. Charles Dimmock, the works had been completed in 1863. This "Dimmock Line," as it was called in Petersburg, extended for 10 miles in a flattened horseshoe around the city, with the points of the horseshoe firmly resting against the Appomattox River east and west of town. The line consisted of long trenches or rifle-pits connecting 55 batteries, redans, and lunettes scattered atop commanding hills or where roads and railroads passed through

9   Scott and Wyatt, *Petersburg's Story*, 222-23; Greene, *Civil War Petersburg*, 120-21.

10   Pryor, *Peace and War*, 251, 261; Nora F. M. Davidson, *Cullings From the Confederacy* (Washington, DC, 1903), 125-26; Greene, *Civil War Petersburg*, 118-19.

the system. Within these batteries positions had been prepared for 352 heavy guns, but in the spring of 1864 only a few were in position. On paper the Dimmock Line appeared to be a strong defense, but reality was something different, for time and the elements had not been kind to it. Wind and rain had attacked the parapets and little by little they had crumbled, slowly filling up the ditches. In early 1863 the earth had been freshly turned and the outlines sharply defined, but by the spring of 1864 nature had had her way and the contours of the walls and ditches had become gently rounded. Once the Dimmock Line had been a formidable obstacle; now a horseman could ride over it with ease in more places than not.[11]

Although the war had measurably altered daily life in Petersburg by the spring of 1864, the city had not experienced the physical devastation that had been the fate of other Southern towns like Fredericksburg and Vicksburg. No hostile armies had menaced Petersburg's gates, no shells had exploded within its corporate limits, and no barricades impeded traffic on its streets. In 1861 a few citizens claimed they heard the guns roaring at Big Bethel, but this was generally discounted because that hamlet was more than 60 miles away. Malvern Hill was something else entirely—there was no question that the dull rumbling heard northeast of the city in July 1862 was anything but cannon firing.[12] Nevertheless, while operating on the Peninsula the Federals had at all times been separated from Petersburg by the broad expanse of the James River. The overland approach to the city had long been barred by Confederate troops stationed 50 miles to the southeast along the line of the Blackwater River. These defenses had never really been tested when the Federals had been strong at Suffolk. With the Federal withdrawal to Portsmouth in the summer of 1863, Petersburg seemed doubly secure from a land attack.[13]

11 Richard W. Lykes, *Petersburg Battlefields* (Washington, DC, 1951), 6-7; Calvin D. Cowles, comp., *Atlas to Accompany the Official Records of the Union and Confederate Armies* (Washington, DC, 1891-1895), plate XL; Raleigh E. Colston, "Repelling the First Assault on Petersburg," in Robert U. Johnson and Clarence C. Buel, eds., *Battles and Leaders of the Civil War*, 4 vols. (New York, NY, 1884), 4:535; Henderson, *Petersburg in the Civil War*, 55-56; Greene, *Civil War Petersburg*, 97-98, 104, 108-09, 140, 144, 147.

12 Pryor, *Peace and War*, 257.

13 For operations along the Blackwater River line and in the vicinity of Suffolk, Virginia, in 1862-63, see *The War of the Rebellion: A Compilation of the Official Records of the Union and Confederate Armies*, 128 vols. (Washington, DC, 1880-1891), ser. 1, vol. 18. Hereafter cited as *OR*. All references are to Series 1 unless otherwise noted. See also Brian Steel Wills, *The War Hits Home: The Civil War in Southeastern Virginia* (Charlottesville, VA, 2001), Chapters 3-10.

While not yet directly threatened, Petersburg remained a likely target for a Federal advance because it was an integral part of Richmond's transportation system. With one exception, all of the railroads that linked Richmond with the states south of Virginia converged on Petersburg first. There they merged into a single trunk-line that ran north to the capital. Not only was this thin ribbon of rails the lifeline of the city of Richmond, but the Army of Northern Virginia depended upon it as well. As long as the line remained intact supplies from other states could sustain both the Confederate capital and Robert E. Lee's veterans. If the line were severed, Confederate forces in Virginia would soon be starved into submission unless service was quickly restored. Obviously the most promising place to disrupt this transportation system was either at Petersburg itself or at some point on the single track between that city and Richmond. This simple fact made the possession of Petersburg a Confederate necessity and a potential Federal goal. The importance of the situation had not been lost upon the Confederate government, and Captain Dimmock's defense line was the result of its concern. Yet, until the spring of 1864 Federal commanders were either unwilling or unable to implement a plan of operations that could exploit Petersburg's position astride Richmond's jugular vein.[14]

The appointment of Lt. Gen. Ulysses S. Grant as Federal general in chief on March 12, 1864, was the event that would eventually lead to the destruction of Petersburg's privileged status. Grant had long believed that concerted action in all areas by the numerically superior Federal forces would quickly cause the Confederacy to collapse. Although in March he had no idea that the Army of the Potomac would ever be campaigning in southern Virginia, Grant came to believe that the territory between Richmond and Petersburg would be an ideal place for a smaller Federal army to operate. The advantages of the area were readily apparent: it could be efficiently and safely supplied by water transportation, it was lightly guarded by the Confederates, it afforded the possibility of cooperation with the Army of the Potomac, and, best of all, it provided a matchless opportunity to block the flow of supplies and reinforcements constantly moving north to Lee's army. The strategic

---

14 Black, *Railroads of the Confederacy*, 243; Johnston, *Virginia Railroads*, 189-95; Turner, *Victory Rode the Rails*, 343-46; George A. Bruce, "General Butler's Bermuda Campaign," in *Papers of the Military History Society of Massachusetts*, 14 vols. (Boston, MA, 1912), 9:307. For a survey of previous Federal proposals to operate against Richmond's railroads from the south, see William Glenn Robertson, *Back Door to Richmond: The Bermuda Hundred Campaign, April-June 1864* (Newark, DE, 1987), 14-16.

possibilities were so appealing that Grant ordered the formation of a new army from scattered units in the Department of the South and the Department of Virginia and North Carolina. Named the Army of the James, the new command would operate against Richmond on the south bank of the James River and would act in close cooperation with the Army of the Potomac. In effect, the Army of the James would serve as the detached southern wing of George Meade's army.[15]

Unfortunately, in Grant's estimation, the Department of Virginia and North Carolina in the spring of 1864 was under the command of Maj. Gen. Benjamin F. Butler. A War-Democrat with many valuable connections among the Radical Republicans, the controversial Butler had long since acquired a reputation among his West Point-educated colleagues as a militarily inept political general. Largely based upon his responsibility for the Federal defeat in the insignificant skirmish of Big Bethel six weeks before First Manassas, Butler's military reputation had yet to be established conclusively. Although his prompt action at Annapolis and Baltimore during the first weeks of the war had probably saved Maryland for the Union, this achievement was erased by the fiasco at Big Bethel and the political and diplomatic uproar engendered by his controversial policies during the occupation of New Orleans. Removed from command at New Orleans in December 1862, Butler had languished until November 1863 when he had been given command of the Department of Virginia and North Carolina with headquarters at Fort Monroe. His administration of Norfolk and the surrounding area had been almost as controversial as his actions at New Orleans, although the department had long been a backwater for significant military operations.[16]

Both logic and common practice had previously dictated that a department commander also command the field army operating within that department.

---

15 Ulysses S. Grant, *Personal Memoirs of U. S. Grant*, 2 vols. (New York, NY, 1886), 2:127, 555-56; Alfred P. Rockwell, "The Tenth Army Corps in Virginia, May, 1864," in *Papers of the Military Historical Society of Massachusetts*, 14 vols. (Boston, MA, 1912), 9:267; Robertson, *Back Door to Richmond*, 13-14, 18, 21-22.

16 Richard S. West, Jr., *Lincoln's Scapegoat General: A Life of Benjamin F. Butler, 1818-1893* (Boston, MA, 1965), 45, 82, 138-43, 149-51, 186-204, 212-29, 243, 295-308; Harold B. Raymond, "Ben Butler: A Reappraisal," in *Colby Library Quarterly* (September 1964), 445-50, 478; Ezra J. Warner, *Generals in Blue: Lives of the Union Commanders* (Baton Rouge, LA, 1964), 61. For Butler's activities as the commander of the Department of Virginia and North Carolina prior to May 1864, see Edward G. Longacre, *Army of Amateurs: General Benjamin F. Butler and the Army of the James, 1863-1865* (Mechanicsburg, PA, 1997), 8-30.

Maj. Gen. Benjamin F. Butler

Library of Congress

Initially Grant did not want Butler in charge of such an important component of his campaign plan, but he lacked objective evidence of incompetence that would permit Butler's relief. After all, it was Butler's department, most of the troops to be used came from that department, and the man wielded an inordinate amount of political power in Washington. Besides, Butler was recognized as an excellent administrator even by his enemies, and to base a man's military reputation solely on the outcome of a brief skirmish in 1861 was patently unfair. Nevertheless, Grant harbored serious reservations about Butler which remained strong until after a personal meeting between the two men at Fort Monroe in March. As a result of that meeting, Grant permitted Butler to command the Army of the James in the coming campaign. At the same time, Grant took steps to provide Butler with professional soldiers for his principal subordinates.[17]

Grant envisioned that Butler would lean most heavily upon Maj. Gen. William Farrar Smith, who would organize the XVIII Corps from troops in Butler's department. Known as "Baldy" since his West Point days, Smith was by training an engineer. Normally a capable man, Smith had permitted an unfortunate character flaw to blight his career on several occasions. That flaw was his penchant for being caustically critical of most of the plans produced by his superior officers. Smith's role in a cabal against Ambrose Burnside had cost him his confirmation as a major general by the Senate and he had been banished to the Western Theater in 1863. In a stunning reversal, he had performed brilliantly under Grant's eye at Chattanooga, which led to a major general's stars once again and his return to the Eastern Theater for the spring campaign of 1864. Although he would later change his mind, Grant initially thought highly of Smith, and expected him to guide Butler through the intricacies of military strategy and tactics.[18]

Grant planned a role similar to Smith's for Butler's other corps commander, Maj. Gen. Quincy Adams Gillmore of the X Corps. An engineer like Smith, Gillmore had lately been conducting the siege of Charleston, South Carolina, where he had been relatively unsuccessful. In the words of Bruce

---

17 Adam Badeau, *Military History of Ulysses S. Grant, From April 1861, to April 1865*, 3 vols. (New York, NY, 1885), 2:246-48; Rockwell, "Tenth Army Corps," 297; Bruce Catton, *Grant Takes Command* (Boston, MA, 1969), 146-47; Robertson, *Back Door to Richmond*, 20-22.

18 Mark Mayo Boatner, III, *The Civil War Dictionary* (New York, NY, 1959), 775; Warner, *Generals in Blue*, 462-63; Grant, *Personal Memoirs*, 2:133; Robertson, *Back Door to Richmond*, 26-27.

Maj. Gen. Quincy A. Gillmore
National Archives

Catton, "The experience had left him highly distrustful of any operation that involved attacking entrenched Confederates, but there was no way to know that it had left him very reluctant to make any attack at all."[19] Grant had originally favored retaining Gillmore in the Department of the South, but Gillmore's pleas to accompany the bulk of his troops to Virginia eventually prevailed and Grant relented. Although directing a siege was an entirely different operation from maneuvering a corps in the field, there was no concern that Gillmore could not handle the new task competently. After all, Quincy Gillmore, unlike Butler, was a West Pointer.[20]

As designed by Butler and approved by Grant, the plan of operations for the Army of the James was bold in conception. Butler was to concentrate his forces at Yorktown, feint up the York River, then sail as far as possible up the James River on the night of May 4-5, 1864, a date chosen to coincide with the advance of Meade's Army of the Potomac far to the north. Butler's initial mission was to establish a base in the Bermuda Hundred-City Point area at the confluence of the Appomattox and James Rivers. Bermuda Hundred was a triangular-shaped peninsula of some 30 square miles lying between the two rivers. Its open end was barely three miles wide and lay only two miles east of the trunk-line railroad and turnpike between Richmond and Petersburg. From the mouth of the peninsula, Petersburg was only seven miles away and Richmond 14. City Point, the other half of the initial objective, occupied a small

19 Boatner, *Civil War Dictionary*, 343; Warner, *Generals in Blue*, 176-77; Robertson, *Back Door to Richmond*, 18; Longacre, *Army of Amateurs*, 42; Bruce Catton, *Never Call Retreat* (Garden City, NY, 1965), 346-47.

20 Grant, *Personal Memoirs*, 2:128.

horn-shaped peninsula thrusting out from the south bank of the Appomattox into the roadstead created by the junction of that river with the James. It had to be occupied to prevent the Confederates from dominating the route to Butler's supply base, which lay on the opposite side of the roadstead at Bermuda Hundred Landing.[21]

Realizing that the commander of the Army of the James was a novice in operational matters, Grant tried to be as explicit as possible regarding Butler's movements after the base of operations was secured. After two personal conferences and several letters, Grant's concept of Butler's role became evident. The final objective of the Army of the James was to be the city of Richmond. Butler was to put his troops in motion for that city at once, keeping as close as he could to the south bank of the James. If Butler moved fast enough, he might be able to besiege Richmond from the south. At the very least he could rest a flank on the James either above or below the city with which Grant could connect upon his arrival from the north. The concept of moving toward Richmond and a junction with the Army of the Potomac permeated all of Grant's communications with Butler. The fact that such a move would sever the Richmond and Petersburg Railroad was not mentioned, probably because it was so obvious. In no directive was Butler told to march on Petersburg, although Grant verbally pointed out that city's importance.[22]

Butler's expedition got underway on schedule although Gillmore quickly aroused Butler's displeasure by being tardy in arriving at Fort Monroe and slow in embarking his troops. No resistance was encountered when the leading elements of the Army of the James splashed ashore at Bermuda Hundred Landing on the morning of May 5, 1864. Brigadier General Edward Hinks's division of African American troops from the XVIII Corps occupied City Point unopposed and protected Butler's supply line by securing two other dangerous points several miles down the James. While some units began to unload the mountain of necessary supplies, the remainder of the army pushed inland toward the narrow neck that was to serve as their defense position. Elated by the ease of landing and aware that speed was crucial to subsequent success, Butler proposed to begin the march to Richmond that very night. With some

21 Grant, *Personal Memoirs*, 2:132-33; Rockwell, "Tenth Army Corps," 272-73; Cowles, *Atlas to Accompany the Official Records*, plate 77.

22 For an extended discussion of the mission of Butler's Army of the James, and the sources upon which the discussion was based, see Robertson, *Back Door to Richmond*, 22-25.

difficulty Smith and Gillmore, Butler's corps commanders and professional advisers, managed to persuade him of the folly of a night march into unknown territory. Thus the Army of the James halted several miles short of the vital railroad.[23]

Confederate reaction was immediate, particularly in Petersburg. That city lay within the Confederate Department of North Carolina and Southern Virginia, an administrative division that encompassed the territory stretching from the southern bank of the James River to the northern border of South Carolina. Until April 23, 1864, Maj. Gen. George E. Pickett of "Pickett's Charge" fame had commanded the department, but on that date he had been superseded by Gen. Pierre G. T. Beauregard, the victor of First Manassas and Gillmore's recent antagonist at Charleston. The mercurial Beauregard had been ordered north to counter the Federal buildup at Fort Monroe but he had been slow to arrive. In the meantime Pickett, who had not been himself since the destruction of his division at Gettysburg, had been ordered to report once again to the Army of Northern Virginia as soon as Beauregard appeared. On May 5, 1864, Pickett, though technically relieved of his command, was still exercising district authority in Petersburg while awaiting the arrival of a successor. Consequently the responsibility for repulsing Butler's landings at Bermuda Hundred and City Point fell squarely upon his shoulders. Having only one infantry regiment and a few artillery pieces at his immediate disposal, plus a few other units scattered along the Blackwater River far to the south, Pickett could only mobilize the reserve and militia forces of Petersburg and frantically wire both Beauregard and the Confederate government for reinforcements.[24]

Petersburg's local manpower resources were few in number but more than willing to defend their city. The Petersburg City Battalion, styled the 44th Virginia Battalion and commanded by Maj. Peter V. Batte, mobilized quickly and reported to Pickett five companies strong, as did several independent militia companies in the city. Other male citizens, without army or militia

---

23 Benjamin F. Butler, *Autobiography and Personal Reminiscences of Major General Benjamin F. Butler: Butler's Book* (Boston, MA, 1892), 639, 642, 1061; Rockwell, "Tenth Army Corps," 273; Catton, *Never Call Retreat*, 346-47; Robertson, *Back Door to Richmond*, 57-62, 69-71.

24 Confederate defensive arrangements are detailed in Robertson, *Back Door to Richmond*, 43-52, 65-69. Pickett's only significant infantry force was Thomas Clingman's North Carolina infantry brigade, and all of its regiments were on the Blackwater Line except the 31st Infantry in Petersburg. All of Pickett's cavalry was also on the Blackwater, but the famous Washington Artillery Battalion of New Orleans was in the city, having wintered nearby.

Gen. Pierre G. T. Beauregard
National Archives

affiliation because of age, health, or critical occupational skill, congregated opposite the provost marshal's office on Bank Street and reported themselves willing to fight for their city. This group, which soon numbered several hundred men and boys, was hastily armed with whatever cast-off weapons and equipment were at hand. The guns furnished them were mostly smoothbore muskets which had once been flintlocks but at some time in their long history had been converted to percussion cap ignition. These guns, known as altered percussions, had probably seen service in the War of 1812, but they were all that was available in the emergency and they had to be used. Lacking regular cavalry, Pickett ordered Maj. John Scott to mount 30 of the haphazardly armed civilians and prepare to scout toward the enemy.[25]

Thus organized and equipped, the townspeople were hastily sent to Battery 5 on the Dimmock Line, a commanding position two miles outside Petersburg on the farm of a man named Jordan. Battery 5 seemed to be a good place to make a stand because it guarded the road to City Point, on which a Federal advance was expected at any moment. Taking their position there beside Batte's men the scratch force of defenders presented a curious sight. Counting the City Battalion, there were perhaps 500 armed men at the fortifications, looking for all the world like what they really were, townspeople. No uniforms were in evidence, only clothes appropriate to each man's occupation; no battle flags flapped in the wind; no bayonets sparkled in the sunlight, for there had been none to issue. By any normal standard these men could not be considered soldiers—except for their willingness to risk their lives to defend their homes. Untrained and poorly armed, they waited behind their crumbling breastworks for Butler's legions to approach. In front of the works, on the road leading toward City Point, Major Scott's civilian cavalry established a picket line.[26]

At Bermuda Hundred Benjamin Butler was learning that West Point training did not always guarantee celerity of movement. On May 6, the day after the landing, the Army of the James advanced only as far as the site of the proposed defensive line at the base of the peninsula and began to entrench. In midafternoon Butler ordered both Smith and Gillmore to send brigades forward to the railroad and break Richmond's most important connection with the Confederate hinterland. Gillmore refused to comply with the order, for reasons known only to himself, while the brigade sent by Smith met the first reinforcements Pickett had received from the south (one South Carolina regiment) and was stopped at Port Walthall Junction. Offensively, the Federals had accomplished nothing, although an impressive set of defensive works was

---

25 Walter Harrison, *Pickett's Men: A Fragment of War History* (New York, NY, 1870), 124; William Miller Owen, *In Camp and Battle with the Washington Artillery of New Orleans* (Boston, MA, 1885), 311; Archer, "Defense of Petersburg," 113; John F. Glenn, "Brave Defence of the Cockade City," in *Southern Historical Society Papers* (1907), 35:2; John Scott, "A Ruse of War," in *The Annals of the War Written by Leading Participants North and South* (Philadelphia, PA, 1879), 381-82.

26 Archer, "Defense of Petersburg," 114; Glenn, "Cockade City," 2; Scott, "Ruse of War," 382. The 55 batteries of the Dimmock Line were numbered consecutively from east to west, beginning with Battery 1 on the bank of the Appomattox River northeast of the city.

beginning to take shape to protect the Bermuda Hundred base. That night Butler wrote to his friend Senator Henry Wilson requesting that Gillmore's nomination to major general be rejected by the Senate and that Gillmore be recalled from the field.[27]

The lethargy that plagued Butler's army on May 6 continued unabated for several days. Butler tried once more to reach and destroy the Richmond and Petersburg Railroad on May 7. This time he ordered Gillmore to loan Smith three brigades so that one of Smith's division commanders could lead them and some of his own men toward the railroad. Again the Federals reached the railroad in the vicinity of Port Walthall Junction, but again they found it defended. No longer did a single Confederate regiment bar the way; on May 7 the railroad was defended by two small but vigorous Confederate brigades under Brig. Gen. Bushrod R. Johnson. Although the Federals managed to place part of one brigade on the tracks, little more than 100 feet of rails and ties were destroyed before the expedition withdrew to Bermuda Hundred. Once again a precious day had been lost with nothing to show for it but a minor disruption of the railroad that could be easily repaired. Nor was more accomplished on the following day, May 8. The Army of the James spent that day in relative inactivity, except for work on the fortifications. Even there the strained relations among Butler, Smith, and Gillmore were evident, because the lines constructed independently by the two corps did not meet until Butler forced a junction.[28]

Marking time until he heard that Grant was near Richmond, Butler on May 9 came forward himself and ordered Smith and Gillmore toward the railroad in strength. When Smith found his way contested by a handful of pickets, he called for Gillmore on his right to sweep southward so as to catch the Confederates between the two Federal corps. Although Gillmore complied with the request, the nimble Confederates escaped southward toward Petersburg. The Army of the James followed, but after an advance of two miles halted at Swift Creek, a tributary of the Appomattox that blocked its path. Pickett had entrenched Bushrod Johnson's two brigades behind the creek and their aggressive actions

27 This action, styled the first battle of Port Walthall Junction, is fully described in Robertson, *Back Door to Richmond,* 70-72, 79-82.

28 Bruce, "General Butler's Bermuda Campaign," 318-22; Rockwell, "Tenth Army Corps," 295-96; Butler, *Butler's Book,* 649, 664; Robertson, *Back Door to Richmond,* 83-89, 108-09. The action on May 7 was known as the second battle of Port Walthall Junction.

convinced Butler, Smith, and Gillmore to wait until the following day to attack the Confederate position. On the south side of the Appomattox, the militia, now reinforced by companies from several neighboring counties, waited for 1,800 Federals under Edward Hinks to probe their position at Battery 5. When Hinks fell back without even confronting the Battery 5 defenses, another Federal opportunity to enter Petersburg was lost.[29]

That evening Butler met with his corps commanders and outlined a plan for the next day in which Smith and Gillmore would attack across Swift Creek while Hinks would advance toward Petersburg along the south bank of the Appomattox. After Butler's departure, Smith and Gillmore drew up a counterproposal calling for a return to the Bermuda Hundred base, the building of a bridge over the Appomattox, and an advance by both corps toward Petersburg along Hinks's original route. Angered by the duplicity of his corps commanders, Butler found his situation further complicated by the arrival of several telegrams from the War Department in Washington. These telegrams indicated that Grant had won a great victory in the Wilderness, that Lee was in full retreat, and that the Army of the Potomac was on its way to Richmond. None of these claims was valid, but no one in Washington or at Bermuda Hundred was aware of the fact. In light of Grant's apparent success, Butler reasoned that he could not afford to tarry around Petersburg but would have to march toward Richmond instead. Consequently, Butler peremptorily rejected the Smith-Gillmore proposal, rescinded his own earlier orders for the attack on Petersburg, and prepared to send the Army of the James north toward Richmond and Grant.[30]

In retrospect, Butler's decision was unwise because Grant was nowhere near Richmond and would not be for some time, but in light of the information available to him at the time the decision was understandable. At any rate, as long as the Army of the James remained astride the railroad to Richmond, the capture of Petersburg was unnecessary. Indeed, if captured, Petersburg would

---

29 Butler's demonstration toward Petersburg is described in Robertson, *Back Door to Richmond*, 109-16. The small action that resulted just north of Swift Creek is known as the battle of Arrowfield Church. For the militia contribution, see Archer, "Defense of Petersburg," 114. Counties furnishing companies included Prince George, Dinwiddie, Chesterfield, Amelia, and Nottoway. By May 9 approximately 1,000 militiamen assisted Confederate regular units in defending Petersburg.

30 The relevant messages can be found in *OR* 36, pt. 2, 35-36, 587, 624. For a discussion of the sequence of events and additional sources, see Robertson, *Back Door to Richmond*, 119-21, 128-29.

have been difficult for Butler to hold, lying as it did over seven miles from Butler's base and in the path of increasing numbers of Confederates approaching by rail from the south. Yet neither Butler nor his corps commanders seemed to recognize the critical importance of holding the transportation corridor between Richmond and Petersburg. The Army of the James spent May 10 withdrawing into its Bermuda Hundred camps and the following day preparing for the next forward movement. This Federal lapse permitted Beauregard, who had finally arrived to replace Pickett, to move large numbers of troops past Butler's entrenched lines and into Richmond's outer defenses near Drewry's Bluff. When Butler finally moved against the Drewry's Bluff position, he was soundly defeated by Beauregard on May 16. The Army of the James then withdrew to its fortified base. Beauregard followed the Federals to Bermuda Hundred and soon established a parallel line of works to contain Butler's army and protect the reconstructed railroad. By May 18 the Army of the James had lost its best opportunity to reach Richmond from the south or to destroy the railroad between that city and Petersburg.[31]

In the Cockade City the great excitement of May 5 had begun to subside. During the first few days of the Federal invasion the citizens had stood ready to bury their valuables upon the first notice that Butler's columns were approaching the city. Yet the inactivity of the Federals immediately after their landing served to allay the fears of the city's residents somewhat and they were heartened by the arrival of Beauregard and large numbers of veteran troops from the south. The half-hearted attempt by Smith and Gillmore to force Swift Creek had created some new apprehension but that was soon dissipated by Butler's turn toward Richmond. Beauregard's success at Drewry's Bluff and the subsequent retreat of the Army of the James to its fortified camp greatly reduced the high level of tension. The citizens of Petersburg still felt that certain kind of excitement always generated in a war zone but the urgency imparted by the events of May 5 no longer existed in such an extreme form.[32]

Nowhere was the atmosphere of reduced tension more evident than among the militiamen gathered at Jordan's farm. After the first few days the

31 For postwar analyses by two participants and critics, see Rockwell, "Tenth Army Corps," 283-94, and Bruce, "General Butler's Bermuda Campaign," 324-46. For a modern comprehensive analysis, see Robertson, *Back Door to Richmond*, 121-220, 246-54.

32 Patrick H. Drewry, "The Ninth of June, 1864," *Confederate Veteran* (August 1927), 35:290; Archer, "Defense of Petersburg", 115.

companies from outlying counties had been allowed to return to their homes, thus reducing the number of men immediately available by half. Except for one company from Prince George County, those who remained at Jordan's farm were all from the city of Petersburg. Now that the Federal threat had momentarily abated, there was time to place the conglomerate of independent militiamen and units on a regular footing. Accordingly, the men who did not already belong to a unit were divided into companies and officers were chosen for them. In this way enough companies were formed to create two new battalions under Majs. William H. Hood and Fletcher H. Archer.[33]

While there were similarities between the two new battalions of militia, there were also differences. Hood's battalion consisted of six companies, two of which had been in existence prior to the May emergency. Most of these companies had been formed from employees of particular industrial establishments, with the Southern Foundry, the Ettrick Cotton Works, the Petersburg Railroad, and the South Side Railroad each furnishing a company. Archer's battalion, on the other hand, was not drawn directly from the working classes, but was primarily composed of the professional men and owners of small businesses in Petersburg. Archer's command included six companies from the city as well as the company from Prince George County, which was temporarily attached. The Confederate government designated the men of both battalions as "second-class militia," a classification comprising men between the ages of 45 and 55, and boys between the ages of 16 and 18.[34]

As the end of May approached, the military situation moved toward stability on both sides of the Appomattox. Butler's defenses at Bermuda Hundred were strong enough to keep the Confederates out, but Beauregard's line was strong enough to prevent Butler from risking a frontal attack. As the Army of the James lapsed into inactivity and the bickering among its unhappy senior officers continued, general in chief Grant concluded that Butler's troops probably could be used to greater advantage elsewhere. Seeking confirmation, he sent Gens. John G. Barnard and Montgomery C. Meigs to Bermuda Hundred to investigate the feasibility of further offensive operations south of the James River. Bernard and Meigs eventually reported that while Butler's

---

33 Archer, "Defense of Petersburg," 114; Glenn, "Cockade City," 3; Wallace, *Virginia Military Organizations*, 221, 226.

34 Wallace, *Virginia Military Organizations*, 221, 226, 236; United States Federal Census of 1860, National Archives; Archer, "Defense of Petersburg," 110-11, 114.

original mission below the James remained valid, command changes within Butler's army would be necessary before that mission could be successfully accomplished. Unwilling to wait for this balanced and judicious appraisal, Grant decided on May 25 to transfer up to 20,000 men from the Army of the James to the Army of the Potomac. Butler would be left with only enough troops to secure the defensive enclave around Bermuda Hundred and City Point.[35]

In their report Barnard and Meigs had compared Butler's position at Bermuda Hundred to "a bottle strongly corked," a phrase which appeared so apt to Grant that he later used it in a message to the War Department. The phrase spread, much to Butler's and Grant's chagrin, eventually finding its way into many histories of the war. Nevertheless, the comparison inaccurately described Butler's situation. Although Beauregard's entrenched line prevented Butler from moving directly west toward the railroad, the Army of the James remained free to pass a force through the southern sidewall of the "bottle" toward Petersburg. Edward Hinks had long held a foothold south of the Appomattox at City Point. An additional enclave had recently been seized at Spring Hill, just across the river from the left of the Federal line, and a pontoon bridge had been laid between that point and Bermuda Hundred. Butler was free to cross that bridge at any time and advance toward Petersburg in a manner similar to the abortive plan proposed by Smith and Gillmore on May 9. That plan had been discarded when the Federal objective had been to meet Grant near Richmond. Now, a thrust south of the Appomattox toward Petersburg represented the only remaining opportunity for disrupting Richmond's communications.[36]

Although Petersburg was within reach of the Federals, Grant either did not see the possibilities or was more interested in replacing the tremendous losses he had suffered since the beginning of the campaign. Grant's decision to have Smith's XVIII Corps join him at Cold Harbor rather than make a dash for Petersburg suggests that even in late May Petersburg did not loom large in his thinking. In contrast, Butler hoped that a delay in the arrival of Smith's transports would permit him to use the XVIII Corps against Petersburg before

---

35 Grant, *Personal Memoirs*, 2:150-52, 568-69; Butler, *Butler's Book*, 10-75; Robertson, *Back Door to Richmond*, 224-25, 230-33.

36 Grant, *Personal Memoirs*, 2:152, 568; West, *Lincoln's Scapegoat General*, 244; Butler, *Butler's Book*, 642; Robertson, *Back Door to Richmond*, 246-47.

it had to be shipped to Grant. On the afternoon of May 28 Butler ordered Smith to move against Petersburg, but within a few hours enough vessels had arrived to force adherence to Grant's original plan. When Smith sailed downriver with 16,000 men on May 29, Butler retained only 10,000 infantry to hold the Bermuda Hundred fortifications. Unknown to its handful of defenders, Petersburg had been granted its second reprieve.[37]

As soon as the Confederate War Department discovered the reduction in Butler's army, it reduced Beauregard's strength as well. The departure of numerous veteran units to join the Army of Northern Virginia meant that even greater reliance would have to be placed upon the reserve formations hastily mobilized in May. This fact required, and lessening of the Federal threat permitted, a more efficient organization of the militia units in the Petersburg defenses. According to an act of February 1864, all men between the ages of 45 and 50, and boys between the ages of 17 and 18, would no longer be classed as "second-class militia" but as "reserves." While Petersburg's citizen-soldiers were camped at Jordan's farm, an officer arrived from Richmond to select the companies that could be reclassified in accordance with the law. All of Hood's companies qualified for the new designation, as did five of Archer's, including the attached Prince George Company. The remaining two companies of Archer's command, those of Capts. Owen H. Hobson and James E. Wolff, retained the designation of "second-class militia," but continued to be attached to Archer's battalion of "reserves."[38]

As the shrunken Army of the James remained lethargic, the contribution made by the militiamen to Petersburg's defense was increasingly belittled. Typical of this attitude was the postwar comment of Capt. Walter Harrison of Pickett's staff that "[t]he citizens and militia of every sort and condition were trotted out in the direction of the enemy at least."[39] Such condescending statements angered the men who had risked their lives for their city no matter

37 For a discussion of Grant's motives for reducing Butler's force, as well as a description of Butler's proposed thrust toward Petersburg, see Robertson, *Back Door to Richmond*, 232-35, 243. Butler's plan called for Smith with 11,000 troops to move secretly across the Appomattox River to Spring Hill, where they would be screened by Edward Hinks's cavalry. On May 29 Hinks's men would capture the Confederate sentinels, permitting Smith to fall upon Petersburg's small and unsuspecting garrison with overwhelming force.

38 For the reduction in Beauregard's force, see Robertson, *Back Door to Richmond*, 220-22, 231, 236. For the reorganization of the militia into reserves, see Wallace, *Virginia Military Organizations*, 218, 221, 226, and Archer, "Defense of Petersburg," 114.

39 Harrison, *Pickett's Men*, 124.

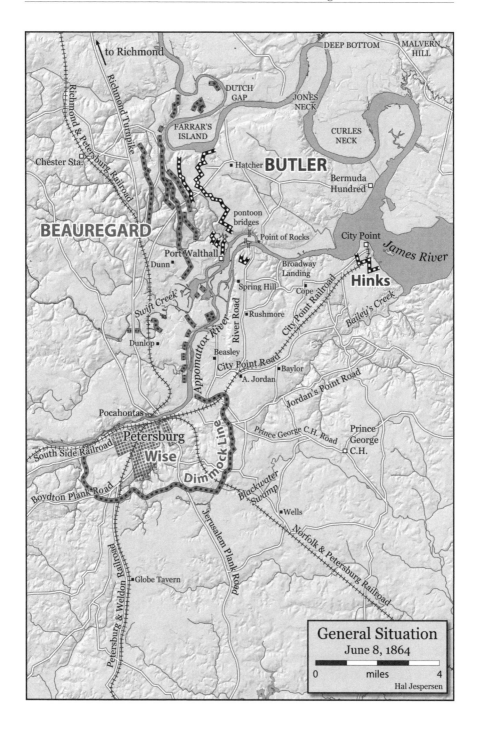

to Richmond

DEEP BOTTOM

MALVERN HILL

DUTCH GAP

JONES NECK

FARRAR'S ISLAND

CURLES NECK

Richmond Turnpike

Richmond & Petersburg Railroad

Chester Sta.

Hatcher • BUTLER

Bermuda Hundred

BEAUREGARD

pontoon bridges

Point of Rocks

City Point

James River

Port Walthall

• Dunn

Broadway Landing

Spring Hill

• Cope

Hinks

Swift Creek

• Rushmore

River Road

City Point Railroad

Bailey's Creek

Appomattox River

• Dunlop

Beasley

City Point Road

• Baylor

• A. Jordan

Jordan's Point Road

Pocahontas

Petersburg

Wise

Dimmock Line

Prince George C.H. Road

Prince George C.H.

South Side Railroad

Boydton Plank Road

Jerusalem Plank Road

Blackwater Swamp

• Wells

Norfolk & Petersburg Railroad

Petersburg & Weldon Railroad

• Globe Tavern

General Situation
June 8, 1864

0   miles   4

Hal Jespersen

how great their inexperience, but there seemed to be little hope of altering the perceptions of the veterans. These perceptions seemed especially strong in regard to Fletcher Archer's newly formed battalion. Gradually, Archer's men were shunted westward from their original position at Battery 5 on Jordan's farm to less critical sectors. Briefly relocated to the vicinity of Battery 12, they soon received orders to continue even farther west to Battery 27, where the Jerusalem Plank Road passed through the fortifications. There at Timothy Rives's farm they established their permanent camp, where they continued to drill and take their turn at guard duty and other tasks incident to routine camp life. Routine soon became monotony, and diversions were few. A member of Wolfe's company remembered years later that quoit throwing was popular but that card games were generally avoided, in his company at least, because of the high proportion of "elderly men, deacons and elders of churches."[40]

Inevitably, the boredom of camp life in a quiet sector caused many militiamen to redirect their thoughts to their private lives. As the danger to Petersburg gradually subsided, a number of Hood's and Archer's men sought and received passes to go into Petersburg to tend to business and family affairs until another emergency recalled them to the entrenchments. When the arrival of June showed no change in the stalemate at Bermuda Hundred, the number of men permitted to leave their companies grew until no more than half of those listed on the rosters answered to their names at morning roll call. Even Major Archer himself was not above making an occasional business trip into Petersburg. During one of those absences Brig. Gen. Henry A. Wise, former governor of Virginia and commander of Petersburg's defenses, paid the militia camp a surprise visit. Upon inquiring for Archer and being told that he was in Petersburg, Wise tartly replied, "Yes, and if the enemy were to come, you would all be there in less time than it would take a cannon ball to reach there." Thus had the heroes of early May become objects of derision by early June.[41]

Henry Wise's caustic comments about the militia revealed not only his opinion of the fighting qualities of Archer's men, but also the frustration he felt in trying to safeguard such an important position with inadequate resources. Without nearly enough men to fill the 10 miles of trenches comprising the

40 Archer, "Defense of Petersburg," 114-15; Glenn, "Cockade City," 4.

41 Glenn, "Cockade City," 76; Scott and Wyatt, *Petersburg's Story*, 178; Archer, "Defense of Petersburg," 114, 116; William N. [B.] Carr, "Battle of the 9th of June," in Hampton Newsome, John Horn, and John G. Selby, eds., *Civil War Talks* (Charlottesville, VA, 2012), 237-38.

Dimmock Line, Wise could only deploy his handful of troops at the most vital positions. The only veteran infantry units available were the 46th Virginia Infantry regiment of Wise's own brigade and Company F of the 23rd South Carolina Infantry regiment. Batte's, Hood's, and Archer's battalions completed the roster of Petersburg's infantry defenders. In addition, Wise had an artillery contingent composed of Capt. Nathaniel A. Sturdivant's Battery of light artillery and a few heavier guns permanently mounted in position. Colonel Valentine H. Taliaferro's Seventh Confederate Cavalry regiment furnished a mounted screen. The 46th Virginia Infantry and the South Carolina company together fielded only a few more than 500 men present for duty and the reserves/militia battalions added another 350, making Wise's infantry total approximately 850 men. The artillery numbered 120 cannoneers and Taliaferro's cavalry had about twice that many troopers, giving Wise an aggregate strength of slightly more than 1,200 men of all ranks.[42]

By the evening of June 8, 1864, Henry Wise had done all he could to protect the Cockade City. The available evidence indicates that his troops were deployed as follows: On Wise's left, in Batteries 2 through 7, were Batte's 44th Virginia Battalion and Hood's battalion of reserves, supported by a few heavy artillery pieces and possibly by two of Sturdivant's light guns. To their right was the 46th Virginia Infantry regiment, distributed from Batteries 8 to 16, protecting the Prince George Court House Road. At Battery 16 there were 30 militiamen supporting four heavy guns in fixed positions, which were sited to protect the Baxter Road. Some distance to their right were the remaining two guns of Sturdivant's Battery, probably in Battery 20. A mile beyond Sturdivant's guns was Archer's battalion of reserves/militia, spread from Batteries 26 to 28, covering the Jerusalem Plank Road. Beyond that point, except for one company of "second-class militia" at Butterworth's Bridge, the remaining five miles of the Dimmock Line were unoccupied. Taliaferro's cavalrymen maintained scattered outposts on most of the threatened roads leading to Petersburg, from

42 OR 36, pt. 2, 316; OR 51, pt. 2, 999. Barton H. Wise, *The Life of Henry A. Wise of Virginia, 1806-1876* (New York, NY, 1899), 342, is in substantial agreement, although his totals are 900 infantry, 125 artillery, and 150 effective cavalry. In Henry A. Wise, "The Career of Wise's Brigade, 1861-5," in *Southern Historical Society Papers* (1897), 25:12, the general claimed he had a total of only 800 men, probably forgetting to include Sturdivant's and Taliaferro's contingents. Some tabulations for June 9, 1864, include Col. Dennis D. Ferebee's 4th North Carolina Cavalry regiment, but this unit did not arrive in Petersburg until the middle of the day, so it cannot be included in the initial deployment.

the River Road on the northeast to the Jerusalem Plank Road on the southeast.[43]

The pitifully small garrison of Petersburg, along with a similar handful guarding railroad bridges far to the south and west, was grandly styled the First Military District of the Department of North Carolina and Southern Virginia. Henry Wise, the district commander, reported directly to Beauregard at Drewry's Bluff, but in case of attack Wise could expect little assistance from that quarter because Beauregard had only 6,500 men of his own to contain Butler. Surveying his little command sadly, Wise could only conclude that Petersburg was ripe for the taking, if the Federals chose to make the effort.[44]

43 Petersburg *Daily Express*, June 13, 1864; Colston, "Repelling the First Assault," 535-36; Archer, "Defense of Petersburg," 114, 118; John A. Cutchins, *A Famous Command: The Richmond Light Infantry Blues* (Richmond, VA, 1934), 139.

44 *OR 36*, pt. 3, 892; *OR 51*, pt. 2, 999.

Chapter 2

"A Quick Decisive Push"

The departure in late May of four of the six infantry divisions in the Army of the James meant that the offensive power of Benjamin Butler's army was drastically curtailed. Butler's mission now appeared to be solely the static defense of a large supply base until such time as Grant and the Army of the Potomac had need of the Bermuda Hundred-City Point facilities. To accomplish this mission Butler had only Brig. Gen. Alfred Terry's division of the X Corps, Brig. Gen. Edward Hinks's African American division of the XVIII Corps, the understrength cavalry division of Brig. Gen. August Kautz, and a few smaller, miscellaneous units under Brig. Gen. John Turner. Baldy Smith's absence did much to reduce the bickering among the army's senior commanders, but it also necessitated changes in the command structure. With Smith out of the way, Quincy Gillmore was given sole command of the Bermuda Hundred fortifications. To hold the line once occupied by six divisions, Gillmore had only Terry's division of three brigades, Kautz's cavalry division of four regiments serving in a dismounted role, and Turner's remnants, reinforced by Col. Samuel Duncan's brigade borrowed from Hinks. Hinks himself remained in command of the City Point defenses, the outpost at Spring Hill, and the James River garrisons at Fort Powhatan and Wilson's Wharf.[1]

The loss of more than half of his troops did not prevent Butler from considering further offensive movements. He remained convinced that his weakness at Bermuda Hundred was matched by Confederate weakness at Petersburg, leaving the Cockade City ripe for capture or at least a destructive

---

1 Butler, *Butler's Book*, 671, 1076; *OR* 36, pt. 2, 275; *OR* 36, pt. 3, 317, 319; According to Andrew A. Humphreys, *The Virginia Campaign of '64 and '65* (New York, NY, 1883), 159, Butler's remaining force consisted of approximately 10,000 infantrymen and 4,600 cavalrymen.

Brig. Gen. Edward W. Hinks
National Archives

raid. On May 31 he summoned August Kautz to his headquarters and broached the idea of breaking the railroad at Petersburg by entering the city and destroying the bridge over the Appomattox River. At the same time he asked Edward Hinks at City Point to determine the number of infantrymen he could contribute to such an operation from his command. Hinks responded on June 1 that by taking some risks and rearranging some defenses he could provide 3,600 troops for the expedition. Upon receiving Hinks's opinion, bolstered by the testimony of a refugee and two escaped slaves that Petersburg was almost defenseless, Butler again sent for Kautz. At that meeting a plan was devised whereby Kautz with 1,200 cavalry, supported by Hinks's command, would attempt to enter Petersburg from the south and destroy the Appomattox bridges and public buildings. That night Kautz wrote in his journal: "I could not agree with him about the feasibility of the plan, but expressed myself perfectly willing to undertake it and made my arrangements accordingly."[2]

Butler scheduled the operation for the next day, June 2, and issued instructions for one of Edward Hinks's subordinates, Brig. Gen. Edward Wild, to gather troops from the river posts and send them to Spring Hill in preparation for the movement. Unfortunately, Hinks was not notified that his troops would be participating so soon and the arrival of 1,200 of Wild's men at City Point around midnight was Hinks's first indication that something was afoot. A hasty message from Butler at 1:00 a.m. clarified the situation momentarily, but events on the Bermuda Hundred lines soon caused Wild's

2   OR 36, pt. 3, 420-21, 475, 521-23; August V. Kautz, "Brigadier General A. V. Kautz in the Great Rebellion," and August V. Kautz, Daily Journal, 31 May, 1 June, and 2 June, 1864, both in August V. Kautz Papers, Library of Congress.

men to receive a change in mission. Unknown to Butler, P. G. T. Beauregard had also planned an operation for June 2. Under pressure from the Confederate government to release more troops to the Army of Northern Virginia, Beauregard on the night of June 1 issued orders for a vigorous reconnaissance to be made of the Federal lines at dawn to determine if the Federals were still present in strength. This reconnaissance, which began at 6:00 a.m., was so vigorously pressed that it captured part of the Federal picket line. In response, Butler indefinitely postponed his thrust toward Petersburg and instead used Wild's troops as a reserve to bolster the Bermuda Hundred defenses. Beauregard's simple reconnaissance had given Petersburg a third reprieve.[3]

Butler's second failure to mount an operation against Petersburg within a week in no way discouraged him from keeping his plan alive. As the first week of June slipped by, additional considerations gave urgency to his desire to attack Petersburg. Grant and the Army of the Potomac were coming nearer every day and Butler knew that their junction with the Army of the James would signal the end of his semi-independent status. Also, some of the Northern newspapers were beginning to raise embarrassing questions about the results of the Bermuda Hundred campaign, and many of their derogatory comments were originating in the camps of the Army of the James. Obviously, the best way to silence all the loose talk would be to achieve a brilliant military success, and with Grant only a few miles away at Cold Harbor it had to be accomplished quickly. Beauregard's fortifications effectively blocked the direct route to Richmond, but in Butler's view Petersburg remained readily accessible, strategically important, and lightly defended. All things considered, the city that had seemed unimportant in May assumed greater significance with every June day that passed, particularly in light of the approach of the Army of the Potomac. In the words of Butler's biographer, Richard S. West, there remained just enough time for "one last throw of the dice," and Benjamin Butler was not a man who feared to gamble.[4]

The more information Butler accumulated about Petersburg's defenses and its garrison, the more he believed an attack upon the city from the south side of

3 Kautz, Daily Journal, 1-2 June, 1864, August V. Kautz Papers, Library of Congress; P. G. T. Beauregard to Bushrod Johnson, 7:30 p.m., June 1, 1864, Letter Book, May-July 1864, P. G. T. Beauregard Papers, Library of Congress; OR 36, pt. 2, 55-56, 63-64, 88, 261-62, 265-66; OR 36, pt. 3, 515-23, 866.

4 West, Lincoln's Scapegoat General, 241-42.

the Appomattox River was feasible. A map taken from Confederate Brig. Gen. William S. Walker, captured on May 20, furnished revealing details of the Dimmock Line, and these details were corroborated by a local resident who was familiar with the fortifications. The size of the garrison was established from interrogation of the trickle of Confederate deserters constantly coming into the Federal lines. Further confirmation came from refugees and escaped slaves arriving at Hinks's headquarters at City Point. From all of these sources Butler learned that there was only one line of works surrounding Petersburg, and he also obtained a reasonably accurate picture of its extent and composition. He estimated that the city's garrison consisted of an infantry regiment, a few field guns, one cavalry regiment, and the local militia, which Butler believed numbered no more than 1,200 men. Though somewhat inaccurate in terms of specific unit designations, Butler's estimate was nevertheless very close to the truth.[5]

The small number of troops available to Butler seriously limited his freedom of action and was the basis of all of his planning. Even if taken, Petersburg could not be held indefinitely because it was too far away from the Federal enclaves and too close to potential Confederate reinforcements. Nevertheless, a quick seizure of the town and destruction of the vital railroad bridge over the Appomattox would serve Federal purposes almost equally as well as permanent occupation. The plan hurriedly created for the abortive June 2 operation served as a starting point as Butler continued to refine his ideas. In its final form Butler's plan envisioned three simultaneous attacks upon Petersburg by two columns of infantry and one of cavalry. Initially all three columns would march together, with the cavalry screened by the infantry. At a designated point the horsemen would diverge from the infantry's route, while the foot soldiers continued to march toward Petersburg. The cavalry would then make a wide detour along the Dimmock Line until the Jerusalem Plank Road was reached, at which point the fortifications would be assaulted and the city entered from the south. Meanwhile the infantry would split into two assaulting columns which would approach the Confederate works on both the

---

5   OR 36, pt. 2, 275, 276, 281; Glenn "Cockade City," 17; Jessie Ames Marshall, ed., *Private and Official Correspondence of Gen. Benjamin F. Butler During the Period of the Civil War*, 5 vols. (Norwood, MA, 1917), 4:324. The map confiscated from Walker is reprinted in Cowles, comp., *OR Atlas*, plate 56, 1. In only one place had a secondary line been constructed. Two lunettes had been built half a mile in rear of the works at Jordan's farm, but these had been abandoned because they were 60 feet lower than the Battery 5 complex and thus were commanded by it. Not only was Butler aware of these details, but he knew the condition of the works as well.

City Point Road and the Jordan's Point Road. Butler envisioned that all three columns would strike at approximately the same time, making it impossible for the Confederates to concentrate against any one of them without allowing the others to capture the city.[6]

Having long believed that African American troops could fight as well as white units, Butler assigned Brig. Gen. Edward Hinks to command the infantry force, while Brig. Gen. August Kautz would lead the cavalry column. Initially Hinks was expected to use only one brigade on the expedition, but Butler soon decided that if one brigade were sufficient, two would make doubly sure of success. Consequently, Col. Samuel Duncan's brigade was to be withdrawn from the Bermuda Hundred lines to join a second brigade Hinks would bring from City Point. Hinks's combined force would thus consist of 3,500 infantrymen, while Kautz would employ 1,400 cavalrymen. Believing that Petersburg's defenders were few in number and low in quality, Butler reasoned that nearly 5,000 soldiers would encounter no difficulty in seizing the city. Scheduling the movement for June 9, 1864, Butler directed Hinks to meet him at Spring Hill on June 8 to make the final arrangements.[7]

On the morning of June 8, Butler's information about Petersburg's weakness was confirmed by the testimony of two deserters from the 46th Virginia Infantry regiment, which occupied part of the Dimmock Line. Cheered by this welcome news, Butler and his chief engineer, Brig. Gen. Godfrey Weitzel, rode across the Appomattox to Spring Hill for the conference with Hinks. Just as the discussion began, Maj. Gen. Quincy Gillmore joined the group. Butler later wrote that Gillmore had been summoned solely to provide information on what troops could be spared from the Bermuda Hundred entrenchments. Whatever the reason for his presence, Gillmore heard the entire discussion of Petersburg's importance and weakness, and the details of the projected expedition, although he said nothing at the time. Upon the adjournment of the conference Butler returned across the river to prepare Colonel Duncan's Bermuda Hundred contingent for the movement.[8]

---

6   Butler's own description of the plan is in OR 36, pt. 2, 275. One of the two infantry attacks was to be a feint, although it could be turned into a real attack if conditions warranted.

7   OR 36, pt. 2, 275; OR 36, pt. 3, 694.

8   Cutchins, *Richmond Light Infantry Blues*, 138n; Glenn, "Cockade City," 17; OR 36, pt. 2, 275; Butler, *Butler's Book*, 672.

Orders for Colonel Duncan to prepare his brigade for the expedition had already been issued when Butler was interrupted by his friend Godfrey Weitzel. The chief engineer reported that after the conference at Spring Hill Gillmore had called him aside and expressed a strong desire to command the proposed expedition. According to Weitzel, Gillmore argued that the importance of the operation to the Union war effort and the necessity for using veteran troops clearly indicated that the X Corps commander should be given the mission. Veteran troops would be especially critical if strong fortifications were to be stormed, or if a disaster required a stalwart rear guard to cover the retreat. To ensure success, Gillmore offered to substitute one of his own brigades for Duncan's men, who were slated to compose one of the infantry columns. Of course, as soon as some of Gillmore's troops were included in the expedition, their commander could make a better case for his own inclusion.[9]

Gillmore's request to assume command of the expedition placed Butler in a difficult position. The army commander had long been dissatisfied with Gillmore's conduct, beginning on May 5 with Gillmore's tardy arrival at Hampton Roads. Several other bruising episodes during the Bermuda Hundred operations had led Butler to request unofficially that Gillmore's promotion to major general be denied and that Gillmore be removed from the Army of the James. Further, Edward Hinks was a competent officer, and Butler was confident that the African American troops would perform well under his leadership. Yet Gillmore had come to Virginia with a generally good reputation and presumably the experience to match, and what he said about the African American soldiers was essentially true. Duncan's men especially had not been tested in serious combat during their nine months in the army. Under such circumstances personal considerations had to be set aside and the decision made upon purely military grounds. On that basis, the veteran troops and the ranking general should be sent on the expedition, and Butler reluctantly agreed to Gillmore's request. Gillmore would command the expedition, although Hinks would also participate as leader of one of the infantry columns.[10]

---

9   *OR* 36, pt. 2, 275-76; *OR* 36, pt. 3, 708.

10 *OR* 36, pt. 2, 35, 276, 392; *OR* 36, pt. 3, 178; Butler, *Butler's Book*, 672-77. For the previous service of Hinks's black regiments, see Frederick H. Dyer, *A Compendium of the War of the Rebellion*, 3 vols. (1908; reprint ed., New York, NY, 1959), 3:1720, 1723-25, 1727, 1730. As for Butler's opinion of Gillmore, the army commander on May 7 wrote: "Gen. Gillmore may be a very good engineer officer, but he is wholly useless in the movement of troops. He has been

Having reached his decision around noon, Butler called Gillmore to his headquarters for consultation. According to Butler, he opened the meeting by reiterating the importance of the Appomattox River bridges, the destruction of which would sever Lee's supply line and isolate much railroad rolling stock. To emphasize his point, Butler remarked that 500 casualties would be a small price to pay for success, and that the loss of 1,000 men would not be excessive for the benefits gained. Using the map captured from Confederate Brigadier General Walker, Butler next outlined the plan. Gillmore was to move an infantry brigade and August Kautz's cavalry across the Appomattox pontoon bridge to Spring Hill by midnight, where he would meet Edward Hinks with a second infantry brigade. The combined force would rest until just before daybreak, then begin its advance toward Petersburg with the infantry in the lead. As soon as the columns uncovered a road leading southwest toward the Jerusalem Plank Road, Kautz would take the cavalry on a wide swing that would bring his horsemen to the fortifications south of the city. Meanwhile, the infantry would approach Petersburg from the east in two columns, the right brigade making the main attack on the City Point Road and the left brigade feinting on the Jordan's Point Road. If conditions were favorable, the left brigade's feint could be turned into a real assault as well.[11]

Although he believed that his expedition would have little difficulty in entering Petersburg, Butler expected the Confederates to react violently, probably with an assault on the weakened garrison of the Bermuda Hundred entrenchments. He therefore expected Gillmore to abandon Petersburg after accomplishing the necessary destruction and return to Bermuda Hundred by dawn of June 10. If by some chance Gillmore could not return within that time, he should send back 1,000 of Hinks's troops to bolster the Bermuda Hundred defenses. Whatever Gillmore did, if the Appomattox River bridges were destroyed successfully, Kautz would lead his cavalry southward along the Petersburg Railroad, destroying it as he went, until halted by a superior force. Thus no permanent occupation of the Cockade City was anticipated by Butler. The operation was to be a brief, destructive raid and nothing more. Believing

behind in every movement. He has lost 24 hours in making his line in a state of defence, but above all he has refused to move when ordered." Marshall, ed., *Butler's Correspondence*, 4:171.

11 OR 36, pt. 2, 276-78, 281, 287; Cowles, comp., *OR Atlas*, plate 56, 1. Apparently only Gillmore and Butler attended this conference, which probably took place at Butler's headquarters at Point of Rocks.

that Gillmore's long experience would permit him to implement such a simple concept with no difficulty, Butler committed none of Gillmore's instructions to writing.[12]

Gillmore spent the afternoon of June 8 immersed in the details of the operation. In addition to a copy of the Walker map, Butler sent the corps commander a refugee from Petersburg named Champlin who was well acquainted with the Dimmock Line. At 3:00 p.m. Butler sent Hinks a similar map and notified him that Gillmore would cross the Appomattox during the night, in preparation for the movement upon Petersburg previously agreed upon. Two hours later Gillmore informed Butler that he proposed to employ four infantry regiments and probably an artillery battery. Responding that only two sections of artillery (four guns) were needed, Butler concluded: "This is not to be artillery work, but a quick, decisive push." Shortly thereafter, Kautz met Gillmore at the latter's headquarters and the two generals together visited Butler to review the details of the plan. Kautz strongly emphasized the fact that his column had much farther to travel than the others and would require extra time to get into position. Gillmore worried that the requirements of picket duty at Bermuda Hundred would prevent him from choosing a brigade for the expedition without warning the Confederates, a problem Butler solved by authorizing the use of a composite brigade. Finally, Butler agreed to create a diversion for Gillmore by bombarding the Confederate positions at Bermuda Hundred as soon as he heard shots from the direction of Petersburg.[13]

Although the conferees parted secure in the belief that all problems had been resolved and that all actions had been coordinated, subsequent events proved that the possibility of serious misunderstanding had not been eliminated. If Quincy Gillmore's post-battle communications with Butler are to be credited, his concept of the operation and his own role in it differed significantly from Butler's. In his report written on June 10, Gillmore stated that he had not been given command of the expedition at the noon meeting but had only been asked to furnish a brigade to serve as the Bermuda Hundred contingent. According to Gillmore, the verbal order placing him in command of the operation had come only on the evening of June 8. In another letter to Butler, dated June 16, Gillmore claimed that he had never received a detailed

12 OR 36, pt. 2, 277.

13 Marshall, ed., *Butler's Correspondence*, 4:324; Cowles, comp., *OR Atlas*, plate 56, 1; OR 36, pt. 2, 276-77, 279-80; OR 36, pt. 3, 705, 707.

statement of the plan of operations, that Kautz's cavalry was to have been the main effort, and that the infantry attacks were to have been simple diversions to facilitate Kautz's entry into Petersburg. Gillmore's own orders to Hinks on the morning of June 9 belie his later statements about the roles of the three columns, and his protestations seem entirely too self-serving in light of his poor performance on June 9, but it remains possible that he left Butler's headquarters without a perfect understanding of the army commander's intent. If so, the lack of written instructions from Butler would have serious consequences on the following day.[14]

While the generals discussed the plan of operations for the last time, the units chosen for the expedition were already beginning their preparations. All three commanders had been forced to make hard decisions on which units would participate and which would remain behind. The choice had been simplest for Edward Hinks, who quickly selected two regiments, the 1st and 6th United States Colored Troops, to meet his 1,200-man quota. August Kautz had also made a rapid selection, although the reasons behind that selection were less straightforward than Hinks's. Kautz's cavalry division consisted of four regiments, organized in two brigades under Cols. Simon Mix and Samuel Spear. Mix, commander of the First Brigade, was the senior of the two, but he had performed poorly during the cavalry's two recent raids, a fact which had not been lost upon Kautz. Because he only needed 1,300 troopers, Kautz elected to leave Colonel Mix and most of his regiment, the 3rd New York Cavalry, behind. Taking part in the expedition would be portions of the 5th Pennsylvania Cavalry, the 11th Pennsylvania Cavalry, the 1st District of Columbia Cavalry, and a section of the 8th New York Battery. As evening approached, the ominous orders that always heralded an offensive movement crackled down the cavalry chain of command: movement at midnight, three days rations for the men, 20 quarts of oats for the horses, and no vehicles allowed except ambulances.[15]

14 Gillmore's version of how he came to take command of the expedition and his understanding of the concept can be found in OR 36, pt. 287-89, 292, 294. For Butler's rejoinder, see OR 36, pt. 2, 280-81. Although ambiguities remain, Butler's testimony appears to be the more credible account, especially when coupled with Gillmore's written orders to Hinks, found in OR 36, pt. 2, 288.

15 Marshall, ed., *Butler's Correspondence*, 4:341-42; August V. Kautz, "The Cavalry Division of the Army of the James," *National Tribune*, September 21, 1899; Rowland Minturn Hall to his

Gillmore's instructions had required him to provide a force of at least 1,800 men. His initial plan was to take three regiments from Brig. Gen. Alfred Terry's division manning the right of the Bermuda Hundred entrenchments and one regiment from Brig. Gen. John Turner's command on the left of the Federal line. During the early evening of June 8, Gillmore ordered Terry to provide a contingent of 1,400 men for the task. Terry complied by choosing his Second Brigade, commanded by Col. Joseph R. Hawley. Hawley's brigade, which by his own estimate numbered 1,540 officers and men, met the numerical requirement only by including all four of its regiments, one of which was on picket duty. Butler had specifically counseled Gillmore not to remove a regiment from the picket line before its normal relief time so as not to attract undue attention, but Terry was simply asked to supply a brigade of 1,400 men and he did so. Thus Terry provided a total of four regiments for the movement, including one from the picket line, a fact which was probably unknown to Gillmore at the time. Meanwhile, Brigadier General Turner identified the 62nd Ohio Infantry regiment, numbering 450 men, as his contribution. Together with Hawley's regiments, the 3rd New Hampshire, 7th New Hampshire, 6th Connecticut, and 7th Connecticut, the Ohio unit brought Gillmore's infantry strength to almost 2,000 men.[16]

Joseph Roswell Hawley, 37, had not been a professional soldier when hostilities began, but his military education had progressed rapidly since that April day in 1861 when he had received a captain's commission in the 1st Connecticut Infantry regiment. Before the war he had been a lawyer and newspaperman by trade, but he had gravitated into politics at an early age. A strong Free-Soil man, Hawley had been one of the founders of the Republican Party in Connecticut and, although his political aspirations were momentarily shelved, he retained many important connections in the Nutmeg State. Among those connections was Gideon Welles, Lincoln's secretary of the navy, with whom Hawley maintained a regular correspondence. Named lieutenant colonel of the 7th Connecticut Infantry regiment in September 1861, Hawley had risen to the rank of colonel and command of the 7th regiment by the following June. Since that time, however, promotion in grade had thus far escaped him,

---

father, June 10, 1864, in Julia Ward Stickley Collection, North Carolina Division of Archives and History; OR 36, pt. 2, 308, 310; OR 36, pt. 3, 708.

16 OR 36, pt. 2, 277, 287, 292, 297, 298; OR 36, pt. 3, 694, 705, 706. Gillmore's message to Terry requiring 1,400 men, with Hawley's appended response, is mistakenly dated June 7 in OR 36, pt. 3, 694.

Col. Joseph R. Hawley
Harpers Weekly

although the responsibilities of brigade command had been his for more than a year. Nor was Hawley lacking in combat experience, having led his troops in numerous small actions in the Department of the South. Coming to the Army of the James with Quincy Gillmore and the X Corps, Hawley and his brigade had been heavily engaged at Drewry's Bluff. Now he was under orders to march on Petersburg.[17]

When he learned of the plan for the expedition, Hawley was incredulous, considering it to be "almost insane." To Hawley it seemed both foolhardy and unnecessary to attempt to enter a heavily fortified city on a raid when the full Army of the Potomac might soon be available for the task. Nevertheless, Hawley momentarily kept his doubts to himself and began to prepare his brigade for the operation. Each regiment was allowed only one wagon for reserve ammunition and forage, and these supplies were hastily loaded at the supply dumps. The three regiments in camp were ordered to prepare cooked rations sufficient for two days, and to be ready to march at 9:00 p.m. Hawley himself, in an effort to learn the way to the pontoon bridge, sent two futile requests to headquarters for guides. This simple act of foresight on Hawley's part demonstrates that many of Gillmore's officers were even at this late date unfamiliar with the left of the Bermuda Hundred position. This was true even though the XVIII Corps, which had formerly occupied it, had been gone for more than a week.[18]

While Hawley hurriedly tried to familiarize himself with the roads in rear of the Federal fortifications, Alfred Terry at division headquarters was making

17 Boatner, *Civil War Dictionary*, 387-88; Warner, *Generals in Blue*, 219-20; Joseph R. Hawley to Gideon Welles, June 19, 1864, in Joseph R. Hawley Papers, Library of Congress.

18 OR 36, pt. 2, 298; OR 36, pt. 3, 694. As mentioned earlier, Hawley's instructions are misdated by one day.

arrangements to support the operation. The first task was to fill Hawley's place in the entrenchments. Terry accomplished that by shifting one of the regiments of Col. Harris Plaisted's Third Brigade into the gap, and Hawley was notified that this action would be taken. Other orders from Terry insured that a diversion would be created to prevent the Confederates facing the Army of the James from reinforcing the Petersburg garrison. Colonel Alvin Voris, Officer of the Day, was directed to demonstrate vigorously on the Federal picket line as soon as firing was heard in the direction of Petersburg, but he was cautioned not to assault the Confederate lines. Similar orders went to the commander of the Federal heavy artillery, who was told to bombard the Confederates vigorously if firing were heard to the south. Beyond those simple precautions, Terry could only wait and hope for the best.[19]

Three of Hawley's regiments, Lt. Col. Lorenzo Meeker's 6th Connecticut, Capt. Theodore Bacon's 7th Connecticut, and Lt. Col. Josiah Plimpton's 3rd New Hampshire, had no trouble forming on their color lines by the 9:00 p.m. deadline, but Col. Joseph Abbott's 7th New Hampshire was late in arriving because it had to be relieved from picket duty. All of the regiments were combat-tested, having served with honor in hard fights throughout the Department of the South, including the assault on Fort Wagner at Charleston, South Carolina. In that attack the 7th New Hampshire had lost 11 officers killed, the largest number of officers killed in one regiment in one battle during the war. During the Bermuda Hundred campaign in May, Hawley's four regiments had suffered a total of 631 men killed, wounded, and missing. Since that time the brigade had been employed in a necessary, but far more prosaic, task. As a member of the 7th Connecticut expressed it, "From the 1st to the 8th of June our only occupation was the tedious, dangerous and never ending labor of strengthening our lines."[20]

Although Hawley's men were ready to move shortly after 9:00 p.m., they did not receive further orders for some time. Quincy Gillmore did not send Hawley's movement orders to division commander Alfred Terry until an hour later, and Terry's staff did not draft a copy for Hawley until 10:20 p.m. When Hawley finally received the orders around 10:30, he found that he was to march

19 OR 36, pt. 3, 706, 707; Daniel Eldredge, *The Third New Hampshire and All About It* (Boston, MA, 1893), 492.

20 OR 36, pt. 2, 13, 298, 301; Dyer, *Compendium*, 3:1009, 1348, 1350; William F. Fox, *Regimental Losses in the American Civil War, 1861-1865* (1889, reprint ed., Dayton, OH, 1974), 138, 141, 179; Stephen Walkley, *History of the Seventh Connecticut Volunteer Infantry* (Southington, CT, 1905), 144.

through the darkness to Butler's headquarters at Point of Rocks, where he would pick up a guide and then cross the Appomattox River on the pontoon bridge. After reaching the south bank of the Appomattox, Hawley would assume command of a fifth regiment, the 62nd Ohio, and an artillery unit. The entire command was then to halt and await further orders. Hawley was specifically cautioned to be silent in his movements. If he needed a guide to show the way to Butler's headquarters, he was permitted to utilize the services of Terry's messenger.[21]

By the time Hawley received the order to move, his brigade had been formed in line for at least 90 minutes, and the men in the ranks no doubt were quietly commenting about the old army game of "hurry up and wait." At last, when an orderly brought the long awaited command to advance, Hawley got his four regiments into motion somewhere between 10:30 and 11:00 p.m. The direction of the march was eastward toward a road junction known as Hatcher's where Quincy Gillmore maintained his headquarters. Leaving his men under the personal direction of two of his aides, Hawley rode ahead of the column to the intersection, where he found Brig. Gen. Robert S. Foster, Gillmore's chief of staff. Ignorant of the way to the pontoon bridge and apparently unsure of the qualifications of the courier-guide who had brought his orders, Hawley asked Foster if he could furnish the necessary directions. In turn Foster detailed to Hawley a cavalryman who claimed that he had been to Butler's headquarters and the bridge many times. While this individual was being attached to Hawley's staff, the leading elements of the brigade began to arrive at Hatcher's. After a brief halt of five minutes duration, the troops were put in motion eastward on the road to Bermuda Hundred Landing, with Hawley, his staff, and his guides riding at the head of the column. Following somewhere behind the last infantry regiment was Col. Samuel P. Spear's Second Cavalry Brigade, which had also been camped near Hatcher's.[22]

If Quincy Gillmore's original idea had been adopted, Hawley's brigade would not have marched eastward at all. Gillmore's first thought had been to send the troops southward toward the Appomattox River pontoon bridge by

---

21 *OR* 36, pt. 2, 298; *OR* 36, pt. 3, 706, 707.

22 *OR* 36, pt. 2, 278, 298, 299, 302, 303, 310-11; Eldredge, *Third New Hampshire*, 492; *OR* 51, pt. 1, 1269. Colonel Abbott's report, *OR* 36, pt. 2, 305, echoed by Walkley, *Seventh Connecticut*, 264, places the time of departure at 10:00 p.m., but Abbott certainly did not move before his orders arrived.

way of the entrenchments. This was the most direct route, but the unavoidable noise generated by 1,500 marching men quite probably would have been audible to Confederate pickets and raised Beauregard's suspicions. The possibility of inadvertently warning the Confederates apparently did not occur to Gillmore, but it was all too obvious to Alfred Terry, who tactfully recommended a more circuitous but quieter route some distance behind the Federal lines. It was this route that Hawley and his guides adopted when they left Hatcher's. Even though the road was initially good, the night was dark and the march was difficult. There was a halting, uneven motion to the column as the soldiers felt their way along in the blackness, trying to avoid mudholes and other obstacles. Yet Hawley's men were veterans of numerous similar night marches, and many of them consoled themselves with pleasant thoughts of the sutler's delicacies they had brought along.[23]

As long as the troops marched toward Bermuda Hundred Landing the road conditions were generally favorable. Unfortunately, about two miles east of Hatcher's the cavalryman serving as the lead guide led the column to the right into a path that followed a telegraph line. Soon the path virtually disappeared into an almost trackless swamp. The infantrymen cursed as they struggled through mud and water which reached a depth of two feet in places. As the soldiers waded ever deeper into the morass, the ammunition wagons accompanying each regiment mired deeply in the muck and stalled, forcing the men to file around them and attenuating the column. Although many of the soldiers doubted they were on a road of any sort, Hawley's guides repeatedly assured him that the command was indeed on the correct road to Point of Rocks. Leaving his hapless men floundering in the swamp, "like sheep without a shepherd" in Butler's expressive phrase, Hawley rode ahead with one of the guides in an attempt to find a way out of the morass. Speed was essential because the night was passing rapidly.[24]

After traveling some distance, Hawley and his guide reached the large field near Point of Rocks where Butler's headquarters was located. Still unable to find the road to the pontoon bridge, Hawley sent his companion forward to elicit directions from Butler or his staff. No doubt Hawley was uncomfortable in having to admit that his brigade was lost behind its own lines, but he was

23 OR 36, pt. 2, 297; Eldredge, *Third New Hampshire*, 492.

24 OR 36, pt. 2, 278, 299; Eldredge, *Third New Hampshire*, 492. The column probably was crossing Johnson's Creek, swollen by recent rains.

secure in the knowledge that he had done his best to alleviate the situation. While waiting for the guide to return, he commiserated with Colonel Spear, who was similarly seeking directions for his Second Cavalry Brigade. Soon the guide returned with the simple instructions that solved the problem. Before Hawley could return to his command, the brigade approached out of the darkness, led by two of Butler's aides who had already been dispatched by the army commander. Since Hawley had last seen them, his regiments had somehow wandered through a burned-over woods and the men had become covered with soot and ashes as well as mud. Because of its wanderings, the column had straggled badly, causing the loss of more time in gathering its components. Therefore it was a little after 2:00 a.m. when Hawley's weary men finally reached the approaches to the bridge over the Appomattox River.[25]

Brigade commanders were not the only officers behind schedule that evening. At Hatcher's, final preparations for the expedition had taken longer than anticipated, but Quincy Gillmore did not appear unduly concerned about the delay. When at last everything was ready, Gillmore mounted and rode toward Point of Rocks with his staff and his escort, a detachment of the 4th Massachusetts Cavalry. At some point along the way, Gillmore paused long enough to dictate a message to Col. Henry Abbott, Butler's artillery chief, requesting that the heavy guns at Spring Hill open fire upon the railroad as soon as the action began at Petersburg. Upon reaching the vicinity of Butler's headquarters, Gillmore found himself confronting the same problem that had troubled Hawley and Spear: Where was the bridge? Riding to Butler's quarters, Brigadier General Foster, Gillmore's chief of staff, sheepishly awakened the army commander and asked for the necessary directions. Astounded that neither the commander of the entrenched line, his chief of staff, nor two of his brigade commanders knew their way around their own lines in the darkness, Butler provided the information in unequivocal terms. Returning to his chief, Foster related what he had learned, and the expedition commander made his way to the bridge at last.[26]

While Gillmore, Hawley, and Spear were all stumbling through the darkness, other components of the expedition calmly made their own preparations. At the cavalry camp near Point of Rocks Lt. Col. Everton J. Conger of the 1st District of Columbia Cavalry, leading Kautz's First Brigade,

25 OR 36, pt. 2, 299; Eldredge, *Third New Hampshire*, 492.

26 OR 36, pt. 2, 278, 299; OR 36, pt. 3, 720.

mustered his men on the ground in front of division headquarters around midnight. As soon as the artillery contingent, Lt. Peter Morton's right section (two guns) of the 8th Independent New York Battery, and a handful of men from the 3rd New York Cavalry joined the 1st D.C. in formation, the First Brigade crossed the pontoon bridge, climbed the hill on the opposite bank, and went into bivouac. Already on the south side of the Appomattox were Lt. Col. Samuel Taylor's 62nd Ohio Infantry regiment and Lt. Joseph Sanger's four guns of Battery D, 1st United States Light Artillery. Taylor's and Sanger's commands were to be attached to Hawley's brigade for the duration of the expedition, so they waited patiently for Hawley and his men to appear.[27]

Not far from Spring Hill Edward Hinks's troops also waited for the Bermuda Hundred contingent to arrive. Hinks himself was no stranger to desperate enterprises. Born in Maine in 1830, he had moved to Massachusetts and became a state legislator by 1855. Entering the Union Army in April 1861, he had been appointed colonel of the 19th Massachusetts Infantry four months later. Hinks and his regiment had fought at the Ball's Bluff debacle, on the Peninsula, and in the Maryland campaign. He had been wounded at Glendale in June 1862 and more seriously at Antietam in September of the same year. While convalescing, he had been promoted to brigadier general of volunteers. Miscellaneous assignments on court martial, recruiting, and prison camp duty had occupied his time until the spring of 1864, when he took command of the Third Division of the XVIII Corps. His division had served as guard for the Army of the James's line of communication during the Bermuda Hundred campaign and therefore had seen little action. Nevertheless, Hinks was an enthusiastic proponent of African American troops and had great confidence in his command. Although physically weakened by his wounds, Edward Winslow Hinks, 34, was ready to move on Petersburg.[28]

Determined not to be the cause of delay, Hinks had departed the City Point fortifications as soon as night fell with two regiments, the 1st and 6th United States Colored Troops, and Battery B, 2nd Colored Light Artillery. One of the regiments he left at a road junction midway between City Point and Spring Hill known as Cope's; the other was halted nearer Spring Hill not far from

27 OR 36, pt. 2, 298, 309, 320; OR 51, pt. 1, 1271. At least one man from the 3rd New York Cavalry went along on the expedition, because he became a casualty.

28 Boatner, *Civil War Dictionary*, 402-03; Warner, *Generals in Blue*, 229-30. For variations in the spelling of Hinks's name, see Warner, *Generals in Blue*, 630, and John H. Eicher and David J. Eicher, *Civil War High Commands* (Stanford, CA, 2001), 298.

Broadway Landing. Leaving his troops resting beside the road, Hinks rode forward to Spring Hill and the pontoon bridge, reaching there about 9:00 p.m., June 8. He waited there until 11:00 p.m. when a courier delivered a message from Butler. The message informed Hinks that Gillmore would arrive by midnight and that the two officers should confer regarding the expedition. Hinks was also instructed to have a guide ready to direct Gillmore's troops to an assembly area within the Federal picket line. Acknowledging receipt of the message, Hinks made the required preparations and waited for Gillmore to arrive. Midnight came and went, but neither Gillmore nor his troops were to be seen. Like the other troops gathered in the darkness at Spring Hill, Hinks could only speculate on the reason for the delay and hope that the lost time would not be critical to the success of the operation.[29]

Shortly after 2:00 a.m., June 9, Hawley's leading elements began to cross the pontoon bridge. As the bedraggled infantrymen stepped onto the span, they encountered a pleasant surprise. Butler's engineers had spread 10 bales of hay on top of the wooden bridge planking in order to muffle the hooves of the cavalry and artillery horses when they passed. Most of the cavalry was still behind Hawley's column and would need the hay, but the foot soldiers saw it only as an excellent device for cleaning their shoes and trousers. Without a word from anyone, the hay vanished quickly as the men from Connecticut and New Hampshire marched across the bridge. As the head of the column reached the far shore and toiled up the slope, Hawley again rode ahead. Locating the 62nd Ohio and Sanger's Battery D, he ordered them to fall in behind his command and then went in search of Quincy Gillmore. It would be almost 3:00 a.m. before the last of Hawley's brigade cleared the pontoon bridge.[30]

The commander of the expedition finally crossed the Appomattox River sometime after 2:30 a.m. and met with Hinks a little before 3:00 a.m. in a house on top of the hill overlooking the river. Soon after, Hawley arrived. Upon learning the position his brigade would occupy in the order of march, Hawley returned to his troops. Although it was almost time for the final advance to begin, Hawley allowed his men to fall out of formation and eat a quick

29 Marshall, ed., *Butler's Correspondence*, 4:341-42; Dyer, *Compendium*, 3:1722; OR 36, pt. 2, 299, 306; OR 36, pt. 3, 707. Cope's can be found in Cowles, comp., *OR Atlas*, plates 56, 1, and 65, 1. In the Federal reports it was initially spelled Copsa's. The owner of the house which gave the junction its name was W. D. Cope, a ship captain originally from England. United States Federal Census of 1860, Prince George County, Virginia, National Archives.

30 OR 36, pt. 2, 278-79, 299.

breakfast. Considering the events of the evening's march, the veterans were in a jovial mood. As they sat chewing their rations, they noticed their muddy and blackened condition and commented vigorously upon each other's appearance. Daniel Eldredge, an officer of the 3rd New Hampshire, the last regiment in Hawley's column, remembered vividly some of the comments years later: "As we lay there—mud, muddy, muddier, muddiest—one said he would like to swap his nest for a place in his father's pigsty. Another declared, 'pon honor, he'd sleep in his father's barn from preference, if he could only get there.'"[31]

While Hawley's men enjoyed their leisure, Gillmore and Hinks stood watching Spear's Second Cavalry Brigade move across the unmuffled pontoon bridge. To Gillmore, the noise made by the animals' hooves upon the wooden planks was deafening, and there was no doubt in his mind that the Confederates in Petersburg could hear the commotion as well. After Spear's men had gained the heights above the river and Hinks had ridden off to arouse his two regiments, Gillmore penned a brief note to Butler, timed 3:40 a.m.: "My command has just crossed the river; some of it has been delayed by losing the road. I have no doubt that the enemy are fully apprised of our movements by the noise of the bridge. It is not muffled at all, and the crossing of the cavalry can be heard for miles." Upon receiving Gillmore's gloomy progress report, Butler's expectations sank: "From the hour of receiving that dispatch, heartsick I doubted the result of the expedition."[32]

Having informed Butler of the operation's progress, Gillmore and his staff mounted and watched Hawley's and Kautz's men depart on the road to Cope's, where Hinks would join with his units. Kautz's troopers were in the lead, Gillmore having reversed the original order of march after consulting with the cavalry commander. Before starting, Kautz and Gillmore had agreed that the horsemen would need at least four hours to reach the Confederate lines from Cope's, and the change in plan was designed to recover some of the time already lost. Hawley's brigade followed Kautz, the infantry's order of march being: 7th New Hampshire, 7th Connecticut, 6th Connecticut, 3rd New Hampshire, 62nd Ohio. Distant objects were already becoming visible in the morning twilight when the 7th New Hampshire began to move, and by the time the last of Hawley's men got on the road around 4:00 a.m., it was only half an hour before sunrise. Butler had originally planned that the infantry from Bermuda Hundred

31 OR 36, pt. 2, 278, 299, 306; Eldredge, *Third New Hampshire*, 492-93.

32 OR 36, pt. 2, 306; OR 36, pt. 3, 718; Butler, *Butler's Book*, 677.

View from Butler's Signal Tower at Point of Rocks.
Library of Congress

would rest between the hours of midnight and 3:00 a.m., but the long detour through the swamps had rendered that prudent step impossible. Most of Hawley's men had had less than an hour to relax when the company officers called them into formation. Even so, they departed Spring Hill at least 40 minutes behind schedule.[33]

Compared with the earlier portion of the journey, the march to Cope's was uneventful. A short distance from his starting point Hawley saw a column of troops approaching on a road that converged with his line of march. The column proved to be one of Hinks's regiments and, after its commander conferred with Hawley, the regiment fell in behind the 62nd Ohio and the march continued. Upon arriving at Cope's, Hinks's reunited command took the lead from Hawley's brigade, although Kautz's cavalrymen preceded them both. According to Hinks, his brigade left Cope's at 5:00 a.m., following closely upon the heels of the cavalry. At the same time, somewhere to the rear, the commander of the expedition drafted his final written orders for Hinks and sent them forward by a staff officer. At 5:30 a.m., one hour after sunrise, Gillmore dispatched another message from Cope's to an anxious Butler. The note simply reviewed the plan and recommended that the Spring Hill garrison demonstrate near the river.[34]

33 *OR* 36, pt. 2, 278, 293, 296-97, 299, 302, 303, 305. According to a member of Gillmore's staff, the column left Spring Hill at 3:40 a.m. A table in Boatner, *Civil War Dictionary*, 820, establishes the time of morning twilight on June 9, 1864, at approximately 3:30 a.m.

34 *OR* 36, pt. 2, 288, 299, 306; *OR* 36, pt. 3, 719; Marshall, ed., *Butler's Correspondence*, 4:327-28.

While Gillmore was writing messages at Cope's, August Kautz's van was moving rapidly through the morning stillness. Samuel Spear's Second Brigade had the advance and Lt. Col. George Stetzel's 11th Pennsylvania was the leading regiment. Approaching the City Point Road, Stetzel's troopers suddenly came upon an outlying Confederate picket station and overwhelmed it so quickly that four of the Confederates were captured. As word of the encounter filtered back through the column, the cavalrymen became more wary and gripped their weapons more tightly. Picket posts meant that the main body of the enemy could not be far away. Arriving at the City Point Road, Kautz's men turned to the right, in the direction of Petersburg. They advanced for nearly a mile, until at last the road upon which they were to make their long flank march diverged to the left. At this junction, known as Baylor's, Kautz quickly turned the column into the new road and headed southward.[35]

Shortly after the last cavalryman cleared the intersection at Baylor's, the leading regiment of Hinks's brigade reached the junction. There Gillmore's 5:00 a.m. message caught up with Hinks, who scrutinized it carefully. The order read, in part: "Unless the attack is made promptly and vigorously there will be danger of failure, as the enemy will re-enforce Petersburg from their lines in front of General Terry. Should you penetrate the town before General Kautz, who is to attack on the Jerusalem Road, the public buildings, public stores, bridges across the Appomattox, depots, and cars, are all to be destroyed." Apparently Gillmore arrived at Baylor's soon after his written order, and Hinks asked if he was to hold any Confederate works taken. According to Hinks, Gillmore responded, "No; unless we take them within an hour it will be useless to attempt it, and you must use your discretion in the attack." Because Hawley's brigade, with which Gillmore was traveling, would separate from Hinks at Baylor's, Gillmore attached one of his aides, Lt. James Barnard, Jr., to Hinks's column. Barnard's instructions were to follow Hinks until he met the enemy, then return by the shortest route and open communication with Gillmore. With Hinks and Barnard in the lead, the African American regiments followed Kautz's men to the left and marched about a mile until they struck the Jordan's Point Road.

---

35 OR 36, pt. 2, 308, 311; OR 51, pt. 1, 1269-70. Baylor's was known to the Federals at this time as Bailey's. It was the residence of farmer Thomas G. Baylor. United States Federal Census for 1860, Prince George County, Virginia, National Archives.

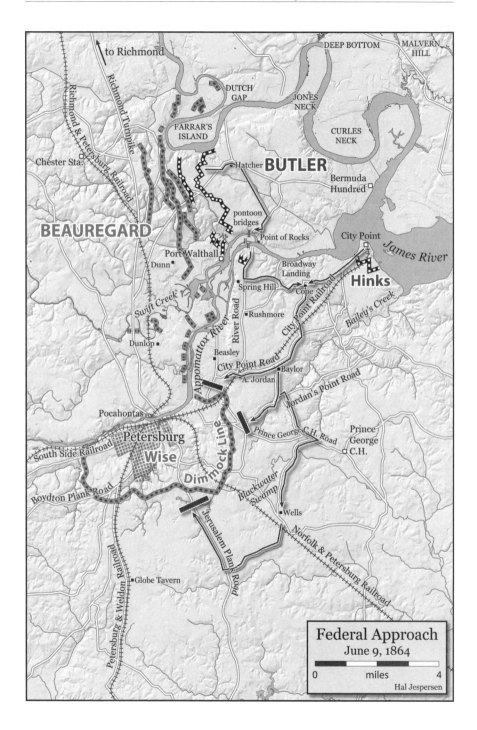

to Richmond

DEEP BOTTOM

MALVERN HILL

DUTCH GAP

JONES NECK

FARRAR'S ISLAND

CURLES NECK

Richmond & Petersburg Railroad

Richmond Turnpike

Chester Sta.

Hatcher

BUTLER

Bermuda Hundred

pontoon bridges

BEAUREGARD

Port Walthall

Dunn

Point of Rocks

City Point

James River

Broadway Landing

Spring Hill

Cope

Hinks

Swift Creek

Rushmore

City Point Railroad

Bailey's Creek

Dunlop

Beasley

City Point Road

Baylor

A. Jordan

River Road

Appomattox River

Jordan's Point Road

Pocahontas

Prince George C.H. Road

Prince George C.H.

Petersburg

Wise

Dimmock Line

South Side Railroad

Blackwater Swamp

Boydton Plank Road

Wells

Jerusalem Plank Road

Norfolk & Petersburg Railroad

Globe Tavern

Petersburg & Weldon Railroad

Federal Approach
June 9, 1864

0   miles   4

Hal Jespersen

There they parted company with the cavalry which continued southward, and turned west for the final advance toward Petersburg.[36]

Joseph Hawley's brigade, which remained on the City Point Road, was now alone, although it was screened by Gillmore's escort, a detachment of the 4th Massachusetts Cavalry. As Hawley cautiously advanced, Confederate scouts could be glimpsed in the distance, but no firm opposition was met for more than a mile. Suddenly the Confederate resistance stiffened, and a sharp skirmish began to develop. One of the Massachusetts cavalrymen was killed in a rash attempt to push the Confederates aside, and it soon became evident that cavalry alone could not clear the way. Riding to the head of the column, Hawley quickly surveyed the situation. The Confederates had taken position and were resolutely standing their ground at the edge of a large field, beyond which ran the City Point Railroad. Correctly concluding that infantry was required, Hawley threw his leading regiment, the 7th New Hampshire, into line of battle and called for a company from his second regiment, the 7th Connecticut, to advance as skirmishers. The time was approximately 7:00 a.m.[37]

Nearly half an hour was consumed in forming line of battle and in shaking out a skirmish line. Hawley could not afford to delay his advance much longer, and when the Confederates did not immediately retreat, he sent another company of the 7th Connecticut to join the first. Thus reinforced, the skirmish line finally began to move forward. Having successfully delayed the Federals, the Confederate skirmishers, dismounted troopers of Col. Valentine H. Taliaferro's 7th Confederate Cavalry, continued to resist tenaciously but began to give ground slowly. Pushed out of the field by weight of numbers, Taliaferro's men retreated across the City Point Railroad to another strong defensive position behind it. Once again the Federal advance slowed to a crawl. Just behind the railroad the City Point Road dropped down a steep, wooded slope to a narrow ravine through which flowed a small stream. It was perfect

---

36 OR 36, pt. 2, 288, 295, 306; Marshall, ed., *Butler's Correspondence*, 4:327-28.

37 OR 36, pt. 2, 299. Colonel Abbott of the 7th New Hampshire, in OR 36, pt. 2, 305, placed the time at "not far from 7 a.m.," and this is indirectly corroborated by the distance of the march from Cope's, and comparable times and locations given by Hinks. Captain Bacon of the 7th Connecticut, however, in OR 36, pt. 2, 303, set the time of the initial contact at "about 8 o'clock," while Gillmore, in OR 36, pt. 2, 288, said it was as early as 6 o'clock.

country for delaying tactics and the Confederate skirmishers took advantage of every physical feature.[38]

As the action flared ahead of them the units toward the rear of the Federal column waited for orders to advance. With the firing growing in intensity, the veterans of the 3rd New Hampshire reasoned that no better opportunity to eat their lunch would present itself. Consequently, the men passed the time by calmly opening their haversacks and gulping down their cold rations. Lieutenant Daniel Eldredge even made a little lemonade, sharing it with his fellow officers, but expecting every moment to be called into action. Eventually the Confederates were driven out of the defile into more level ground, and the 3rd New Hampshire's impromptu picnic was interrupted as the Federal column resumed its forward motion. With Taliaferro's skirmishers now in full retreat, it appeared at first that the Federal advance could continue at a more rapid pace. As Hawley's men pressed ahead, they began to catch glimpses through the trees of a strong earthwork atop the continuation of the ridge they had just descended. Soon the boom of a cannon and the rush of a projectile overhead furnished incontrovertible evidence that the fortification was manned. Taliaferro's men had done their work well—it was now 8:30 a.m. and the Federals were still over two miles from Petersburg.[39]

38 OR 36, pt. 2, 229, 303; Petersburg *Daily Express*, June 13, 1864.

39 Eldredge, *Third New Hampshire*, 493; OR 36, pt. 2, 279, 297, 299-300, 302-03; OR 36, pt. 3, 884. Gillmore, in his report, in OR 36, pt. 2, 288, stated that "Hawley drove in the enemy's pickets on the City Point road shortly after 6 a.m., and about 7 was before the enemy's works." He was either misinformed or under great pressure to make a favorable case for himself, because all other evidence, direct and indirect, indicates that his times are at least an hour too early.

Chapter 3

"Lions in the Way"

Years later everyone would agree that Thursday, June 9, 1864, had been a beautiful late spring day. The previous few days had been somewhat showery but Thursday morning dawned bright and fair, with the promise of some heat around midday. By the calendar it was still spring but on that morning in Petersburg an observer would have believed that summer had long since arrived. Flowers bloomed everywhere, the sun's rays had begun to warm the still air, and except for the absence of so many young men and the presence of the military hospitals in the city, it was easy to forget that armies were locked in combat somewhere to the northeast. On Thursday morning, June 9, 1864, the situation in Petersburg was "business as usual."[1]

By 9:00 a.m. nearly all of the town's residents had begun their normal routine. Breakfast had been finished, the men had departed for their jobs, their wives were beginning their domestic chores, and many of their children were in school. Downtown the merchants were opening their stores to receive the handful of customers that would appear during an average business day. Volume was low because money was scarce and goods were difficult to acquire, and the army did most of what little purchasing was done. Even so, men like Erasmus O. Hinton, 33, and George B. Jones, 42, both druggists, opened their doors as usual. Down at the Exchange Bank, William C. Banister, 55 years old and the father of six children, settled into his work as a bank officer. In another part of town Anthony Keiley, a 31-year-old lawyer who had recently been

1 Anne A. Banister, "Incidents in the Life of a Civil War Child," typescript, Petersburg National Battlefield; Archer, "Defense of Petersburg," 115, 143; Pryor, *Peace and War*, 274; S. Millet Thompson, *Thirteenth Regiment of New Hampshire Volunteer Infantry in the War of the Rebellion, 1861-1865* (Boston, MA, 1888), 370.

elected to the state legislature, leaned back in his office chair in anticipation of spending the morning immersed in the latest Richmond papers. At the Petersburg Female College on Sycamore Street, professor of mathematics William B. Carr, 43, was distributing the day's assignment in algebra and geometry. Over on Washington Street Professor Charles Campbell, 57, principal of Anderson Seminary, and Branch T. Archer, 19, his young assistant, also were just getting classes started.[2]

Some of Petersburg's women were already at the military hospitals tending the wounded, but many were still at home around 9:00 that morning. William Banister's wife and children were there after watching the head of the household leave for his office. Bessie Callender was at home too, but she had not seen her husband off to work because he was still in bed. David Callender, 33, was a manager at a cotton mill in town but he was also a militiaman. He and a neighbor, William Weddell, 47, had been on duty all night at Uriah Wells's foundry on Old Street guarding prisoners and had returned only a short time earlier. While he slept, his wife, her sister Lottie, and their mother busied themselves with housework in their home on Jefferson Street. Not far away three members of the Petersburg Common Council, Robert A. Martin, 39, Charles F. Collier, 37, and James Boisseau, 45, were all heading out to the militia camp on the Jerusalem Plank Road at Timothy Rives's farm. They too were members of the militia but had been in town for a council meeting the previous day. Reaching the heights above Lieutenant Run they passed near William Cameron's palatial residence on Adams Street. Like Callender, tobacco manufacturer Cameron, 34, was at home in bed. Returning from a business trip to North Carolina, he had been forced to walk the last 14 miles into town because of recent damage to the railroad.[3]

At the militia camp near the fortifications, the day also began normally. Reveille had sounded at its usual early hour, breakfast had been cooked and eaten, and the morning guard had been established. With nothing else to do, the citizen-soldiers lolled around the camp amusing themselves as best they could until time for daily drill. Their commander, Maj. Fletcher H. Archer, had been

2 Drewry, "Ninth of June," 291; Archer, "Defense of Petersburg," 135, 140, 148n; Glenn, "Cockade City," 7; Anthony M. Keiley, *In Vinculis; or, The Prisoner of War* (New York, NY, 1866), 14; Carr, "Battle of the 9th of June," 236.

3 "Historical Stories About Petersburg," bound collection of local material, Petersburg National Battlefield; Archer, "Defense of Petersburg," 136, 139, 142, 148n; Callender, "Personal Recollections," 13-14.

Maj. Fletcher H. Archer (postwar)
War Talks of Confederate Veterans

an officer in both the Mexican War and in Confederate service, and he knew how to keep soldiers busy, but he also knew that his present command was not composed of regular soldiers. Archer's men were either too young or too old for active military service and included boys like teenager Wayles Hurt and the young Crowder brothers from Matoaca across the Appomattox, as well as graybeards like William C. Banister, and the three returning councilmen. Such a diverse group shared only one thing, military inexperience, yet they were charged with the defense of their city. Strangely enough, a man with a great deal of experience was also in Petersburg that day, but he had no responsibility for defending anything. Brigadier General Raleigh E. Colston, 38, had been relieved from his last command and had not yet received orders posting him to a new one. On June 9, 1864, his only task was to wait, and like all the other inhabitants of Petersburg at 9:00 a.m. on that bright Thursday morning, he was pursuing his task.[4]

The alarm came first to the militiamen sitting around their camp at Rives's farm waiting for drill to begin. While thus passing the time several of the men noticed the hurried approach of a courier mounted on a black horse. The horseman appeared to be on urgent business and when he reined in his mount in front of Major Archer, all eyes were upon their commander. Leaning down,

---

4 Archer, "Defense of Petersburg," 115; Colston, "First Assault," 535. Greene, in *Civil War Petersburg*, 176, asserts that Colston was the ranking Confederate general officer in Petersburg on the morning of June 9, 1864. He was not. Brigadier General Henry A. Wise, who outranked Colston by six months, commanded the First Military District from an office in Petersburg. Beauregard had briefly and informally placed Colston in charge of the district during a portion of the May emergency, but by May 31, 1864, the Confederate War Department had disapproved that arrangement. Thus Colston was without either a command or orders on the morning of June 9 when the Federals advanced upon the city. See Raleigh E. Colston to Samuel Cooper, May 31, 1864, Raleigh E. Colston Compiled Service Record, National Archives, Washington, DC.

the courier presented Archer with a note from Col. Randolph Harrison of the 46th Virginia Infantry regiment, which was manning a section of the Dimmock Line some distance to the east. Harrison's message warned Archer that the 46th Virginia was under attack from one Federal force and that another large body of Federals had passed across its front and was moving in Archer's direction. Quickly comprehending the danger, Archer ordered Adj. Guy Johnson to have the long roll sounded and to form the men by companies. As the call to arms resounded through the camp, men raced to their quarters, gathered up their arms and accouterments, and hastened to join the ragged company formations beginning to appear. As John F. Glenn, 26, of Capt. James E. Wolff's company rushed outside, Wolff gave him a list of the company's absent members and ordered him to go into Petersburg and summon them to duty. Neither Glenn nor any of his comrades knew the reason for the alarm. The demeanor of the courier seemed to portend something momentous but no one could be sure, because there had been similar scares before.[5]

The town received its warning only a few minutes after the militia camp. No one could remember later who had brought the first news, but around 9:00 a.m. all of the bells in the city began to peal incessantly. Sometime earlier when the city had appeared to be endangered it had been announced that the signal for community warning and preparation would be the tolling of the bells at the courthouse and fire stations. The bells galvanized almost every citizen into immediate action. A few believed the commotion to be simply another false alarm, but most of Petersburg's inhabitants responded promptly. People poured into the streets to see if there was anything visible that might have caused the alarm. Some ran to the courthouse on Sycamore Street to discover what had happened, while others milled around seeking information from their neighbors. Gradually the word spread around the city that a large Federal force was moving toward Petersburg on the Jerusalem Plank Road and that everyone who could possibly go was needed to join the militiamen in stopping them. Hearing the news, Raleigh Colston, the general without a command, knew that he could not remain idle at a time of such great peril for the city. Saddling his fine black mare, he mounted and rode off to tender his professional services to Henry Wise.[6]

5   Archer, "Defense of Petersburg," 115-16; Glenn, "Cockade City," 7.

6   Keiley, *In Vinculis*, 15; Archer, "Defense of Petersburg," 139, 142; Glenn, "Cockade City," 7; Banister, "Civil War Child," 1; Colston, "First Assault," 536. A brief item in "Historical

Anthony Keiley, the young lawyer, was lost in his newspapers when the sudden clanging of the bells brought him up with a start. Dashing into the street, the Richmond papers forgotten, he halted the first person he saw and tried to get some news. Thoroughly rattled, Keiley's informant blurted out that 20,000 enemy troopers were menacing Petersburg and at that very instant were less than two miles away. Discounting somewhat the number of approaching Federals, Keiley nevertheless realized that a crisis existed and he determined to do what he could to help defend the city. A former lieutenant in the 12th Virginia Infantry regiment, Keiley had been elected to the state legislature and was therefore exempt from further military service. Not a member of the militia, he was technically not obligated to respond to the tolling bells, yet he impulsively decided to answer the call anyway. He locked the door of his office, gathered up a little food at his home, then headed toward the Jerusalem Plank Road. Unknown to Keiley, he would see neither his home nor his office again for a long time.[7]

Others took no longer to make up their minds than had Anthony Keiley. At their home in the South Ward of the city, members of the Banister family hoped desperately that William C. Banister, at his office in the Exchange Bank, would not hear the alarm bells. Banister was doubly exempt because he was a bank officer and suffered from deafness, yet his infirmity was not so great as to prevent him from hearing the alarm and rushing home to get his gun. Upon his arrival his family begged him not to go to the fortifications, arguing that he could not hear the officers' orders. Such an appeal was their only hope to dissuade him from going to the front, though it fell on truly deaf ears because William Banister had already decided where his duty lay. Explaining that he was not too deaf to fire his gun, he admonished his worried family, "This is no time for any one to stand back. Every one that can shoulder a musket must fight. The

Stories About Petersburg" gives the credit for sounding the alarm to Tom Jones, who supposedly met the Federals while picking raspberries. It is more likely that one of Taliaferro's cavalrymen provided the critical information. According to the Petersburg *Daily Express* of June 10, 1864, the alarm was sounded at 8:00 a.m. While possible, this time appears to have been too early, because stores, offices, and banks were open and children were in school when the bells rang. General Colston, in "First Assault," 536, stated in 1884 that the alarm came around 9:00 a.m. Although not a contemporary account, Colston's statement appears to agree more closely with supporting information. Hawley's movements, and Butler's statement in OR 36, pt. 2, 279, also give credence to Colston's recollection. Hawley's appearance before the Dimmock Line in force around 8:30 a.m. probably caused the dispatch of a messenger two miles into Petersburg to inform Wise, who around 9:00 a.m. ordered the bells to be tolled.

7   Keiley, *In Vinculis*, 15-16; Archer, "Defense of Petersburg," 128.

enemy are now right upon us." With that firm declaration, William Banister said his goodbyes to his family, shouldered his antique musket, and stepped out of the house.[8]

For Bessie Callender the crisis did not yet seem to be a question of civic duty. She felt herself bound by a different obligation, that of allowing her husband David to get the rest he so desperately needed after guarding prisoners all night. She also at first believed that the entire affair would prove to be another false alarm, which would hardly necessitate awakening her husband. When militiaman James Kerr, 50, burst into the house looking for her husband, Mrs. Callender forced him to explain himself. As Kerr did so, he was suddenly interrupted by the appearance of David Callender in the room. Callender had been awakened by Kerr's voice and, perceiving the seriousness of the situation, had made his decision quickly, like most of the other men. Telling Kerr to go ahead, he promised to follow after eating a quick breakfast. Callender soon joined his neighbor William Weddell, and together they started south on Jefferson Street toward the Jerusalem Plank Road. Bessie Callender watched them go but refrained from saying anything that would frighten the other residents of the household. After all, she reasoned, it was still possible that nothing would come of the affair.[9]

Bessie Callender was virtually alone in her optimistic views that morning. Elsewhere, the tolling of the alarm bells seemed to galvanize the most unlikely combatants into vigorous action. About the same time that James Kerr was disrupting the Callender household with his loud talking, a heated discussion broke out at the drugstore of George B. Jones. When a messenger arrived at the store to summon Jones to the fortifications, he excitedly informed his father-in-law and business partner, Francis Major, 59, of certain dispositions to be made in case of Jones's death. Major, who was not about to be left behind, suddenly interrupted Jones with the caustic remark that the druggist had better tell someone else, because he himself would be at the front as soon as any other man. The result was the hasty closing of the drugstore as both men departed for their homes to get their weapons before heading for the fortifications.[10]

---

8 Archer, "Defense of Petersburg," 148n.

9 Callender, "Personal Recollections," 13-14.

10 Archer, "Defense of Petersburg," 140.

Well before 10:00 a.m. almost every able-bodied man in Petersburg had decided whether or not he would join Archer's command at the Dimmock Line. The women said their farewells to their fathers, husbands, brothers, and sons, then stood in yards or at front windows watching the defenders of the city go forth, either singly or in little groups of twos and threes. At one point a handful of young boys on their way out to the lines saw some women watching fearfully as they passed and one of the boys called out, "Do not weep ladies; do not fear; we will fight for you as long as we have a cartridge left." Bessie Callender finally realized the seriousness of the situation when she saw George Jones, the druggist, moving down Jefferson Street past her house in the direction of the Jerusalem Plank Road. Knowing that he was exempt from service, like so many others she had seen take the same route, she called out that she was sorry to see him go. "From all I hear, every man is needed to defend our town," he replied and hurried on down the street.[11]

John Glenn met the pitiful stream of reinforcements as he hastened into the city to summon those absent from Wolff's militia company. He first met the three councilmen—Martin, Collier, and Boisseau—who were unaware of the trouble, and quickly told them of the enemy threat. In later years Robert Martin would remember that Collier then stated his willingness to "have a scrimmage with the enemy," but that one of his companions took a more cautious view, wisely preferring to leave that business with General Lee. Wasting no time, Glenn left the three and continued toward Petersburg. Nearing the bluff that in better times had been called the Delectable Heights, he met William Banister and George Jones, now in company, moving toward the militia camp. Banister especially caught Glenn's eye as he advanced in such a determined manner, his gun at the ready and a blanket slung over his back. Up the hill in town people were still talking about how Banister had buttonholed every man he had met, urging him in the strongest terms to go out to the lines.[12]

Finally Glenn entered the city. By now many of the men on his list could not be found, having already gone toward the camp at Rives's farm by different routes. Nevertheless, Glenn continued his search in obedience to orders. Coming to the Anderson Seminary on Washington Street, he found that class was still in session amid all the uproar. Entering, he had the attention of every student in the room as he stood there, gun in hand, relating the circumstances of

11 Archer, "Defense of Petersburg," 142, 144; Callender, "Personal Recollections," 14.

12 Glenn, "Cockade City," 7-8; Archer, "Defense of Petersburg," 139, 148n.

the emergency. The principal, Charles Campbell, was the author of a well-known history of Virginia and exempt because of age and occupation. He had volunteered to serve for 30 days during the May emergency, but this time he believed he should remain with his young charges. His assistant, Branch T. Archer, however, chose a different course of action and hastened to answer Glenn's call. Leaving the Anderson Seminary, Glenn continued to look for absent militiamen. After summoning a few others of his company he discovered that his work was done. Because the day was already becoming uncomfortably warm, John Glenn tarried a while in town to get some refreshments before returning to Rives's farm two miles away.[13]

Petersburg now presented a strange picture. The frenetic activity that had so recently filled the streets had at last subsided, as had the clanging of the bells. An unnatural calm accompanied by a strong undercurrent of anxiety had descended upon the town. Few people were now seen outdoors. Except for John Glenn "refreshing" himself, all of the men who were going to fight the Federals had left for the probable scene of action. Having watched their men depart, the town's women had begun to congregate in each other's homes, hoping to bolster their courage by staying together. At Erasmus Hinton's drugstore at the corner of Sycamore and Lombard Streets, a group of non-fighters had collected. There, men like Judge William T. Joynes, 46, Leroy Roper, 56, Z. W. Pickrell, 30, and President Thomas H. Campbell of the South Side Railroad, 41, wealthy conversationalists all, warmed to the topic of the morning—the possibility of an attack against the city by the menacing Federal force.[14]

At his home, "Mount Erin," between Adams and Sycamore Streets near the city waterworks, William Cameron also wondered about the possibility of a battle. His 14 mile walk of the previous night had so exhausted him that he had not felt able to participate when his brother George brought him the news shortly after 9:00 a.m. George Cameron, 25, had gone to the front, but William hoped to resume his badly needed rest. Unfortunately, Cameron's house lay on the direct path from Petersburg to Rives's farm and that morning it seemed as if the whole town was passing that way. Unable to sleep, Cameron watched the procession flow past his gate, descend the slope to Lieutenant Run, and finally disappear through the trees toward the Jerusalem Plank Road. Situated as he

---

13 Glenn, "Cockade City," 7-8.

14 Banister, "Civil War Child," 1; Archer, "Defense of Petersburg," 135.

was, Cameron expected to be one of the first to know the results if the militia had to fight for the city. Like everyone else in Petersburg, William Cameron waited to see what would happen.[15]

Seven miles to the northeast, the commander of the Army of the James was also awaiting the unfolding of events. Benjamin Butler had expected to hear Quincy Gillmore's opening guns for some time, but no gunfire broke the morning stillness. As the early morning hours passed uneventfully, with no sign that the expedition had made contact with the Confederates, Butler had become increasingly pessimistic of the chances for success. He passed part of the time by writing a brief note to his wife, saying among other things that "I have ordered an attack on Petersburg this morning. I had to put it under the command of Gillmore. I think it will fail from that cause. . . . All well except the dilatory movements of Gillmore." Not content to remain out of sight of the action, Butler then had himself hoisted to the top of the signal tower on the bluff overlooking the Appomattox River valley. The tower was 125 feet high; perhaps some sign of Gillmore's progress could be detected from such a great height.[16]

From Butler's vantage point the Virginia countryside was revealed in a sparkling panorama of varying shades of green and brown. As Butler faced southward the Appomattox River flowed lazily in a great bend directly below him. Slightly off to his left the fragile thread of the pontoon bridge crossed two islands and three river channels before gaining the south shore. To the left, far beyond the bridge, the site of City Point could barely be discerned; a similar distance to the right were the spires of Petersburg. In the center of Butler's view were the fortifications of Edward Hinks's outpost at Spring Hill. The scene of Gillmore's departure only a few hours before, the works now seemed almost deserted in the bright morning sunlight. Behind Spring Hill a wide vista of alternating woods and fields reached to the far horizon. Although Gillmore was out there somewhere with nearly 5,000 men, even with the aid of a telescope Butler could find no trace of him. Finally, after what seemed to be an interminable delay, the distant rumble of artillery fire began to roll down the valley of the Appomattox toward the signal tower. The sound appeared to be emanating from just east of Petersburg and apparently signified the opening of

15 Archer, "Defense of Petersburg," 136.

16 Marshall, *Butler's Correspondence*, 4:328; OR 36, pt. 2, 33, 279; OR 40, pt. 1, 676.

Gillmore's attack. With disgust, Butler looked at his watch; it was almost 9:00 a.m.[17]

The cannon shots that reached Butler's perch in the form of a faint echo sounded somewhat louder to Brig. Gen. Henry A. Wise at his headquarters in Petersburg, nearly three miles from the scene of action. After what seemed like an eternity, a breathless courier reined in his mount before the commander of the First Military District of the Department of North Carolina and Southern Virginia and blurted out the news of the Federal approach. Details were lacking, but Wise realized that his tiny defense force would need all the assistance it could get. Accordingly, he ordered the alarm bells to be sounded in Petersburg. One of the first to respond was Brig. Gen. Raleigh Colston, who arrived just as Wise prepared to ride to Bermuda Hundred to seek reinforcements from Beauregard. When Colston offered his services, Wise thanked him graciously and placed him in temporary command of the city's garrison until the district commander's return. Wise instructed Colston to use his own judgment in defending Petersburg, except for one specific directive: Battery 16, covering the Baxter or Sussex Road, was to be held at all costs. With no time for more prolonged conversation, Wise headed for the Appomattox River bridge, calling out as he galloped away, "For God's sake, General, hold out till I come back, or all is lost!"[18]

Fortunately for Wise, P. G. T. Beauregard was nearby. On the morning of June 9 his headquarters was temporarily at Dunlop's, a station on the Richmond and Petersburg Railroad just two miles north of Petersburg. Finding Beauregard at Dunlop's, Wise excitedly reported that Petersburg's outer defenses were under attack. Beauregard had few reinforcements to give Wise, and none that were immediately available, but he promised to dispatch some kind of aid. For the present, however, Wise would have to conduct Petersburg's defense with the pitifully small force already at hand. As Wise rode away, Beauregard drafted orders for Col. Dennis D. Ferebee's 4th North Carolina Cavalry regiment to saddle up and head for Petersburg. He also ordered his cavalry commander, Brig. Gen. James Dearing, to join Ferebee's men and report to Wise. In addition, he instructed Brig. Gen. Bushrod Johnson to bombard the Federal positions at Bermuda Hundred as a demonstration. Until

17 OR 36, pt. 2, 279. Butler's signal tower is pictured in Butler, *Butler's Book*, 680, and Cowles, comp., OR *Atlas*, plate 124, 9.

18 Colston, "First Assault," 536.

Brig. Gen. Henry A. Wise (prewar)
Library of Congress

the situation at Petersburg was clarified, Beauregard was unwilling to risk a further diminution of the Bermuda Hundred garrison. Notifying Gen. Braxton Bragg, President Davis's military adviser, of what he had done, Beauregard explained that the Federal movement was probably no more than "a reconnaissance connected with Grant's future operations." Nevertheless, he used the occasion to argue for the return of the units he had loaned to the Army of Northern Virginia.[19]

The target of the cannon fire that galvanized both Butler and Wise was the leading element of Joseph Hawley's brigade, Colonel Abbott's 7th New Hampshire regiment. After Taliaferro's Confederate skirmishers had been driven down the slope and across the brook at its foot, Gillmore ordered Hawley to continue his advance. Abbott's regiment returned to the road and began to move onto what Hawley described as "a broad plain diversified with woods, and with roads skirted by hedges, and crossed in various directions by ditches lined with bushes." The terrain over which Hawley was moving was new to him, and he was equally ignorant of Petersburg's defenses. He had heard a report that both the fortifications and garrison were weak, but this report had also described Petersburg as "a point vital to the daily existence of the rebellion, and within a few hours' reach of 100,000 rebels." With only that sketchy

19 OR 36, pt. 3, 884; P. G. T. Beauregard to Henry A. Wise, 9:20 a.m., June 9, 1864, Official Telegrams, April 22-June 9, 1864, P. G. T. Beauregard Papers, Library of Congress; P. G. T. Beauregard to James Dearing, June 9, 1864, Letter Book, May-July 1864, P. G. T. Beauregard Papers, Library of Congress.

information and his own observations to guide him, Hawley led his regiments down to the plain.[20]

Unsure of the wisdom of leaving the high ground, Hawley advanced with great caution. The two companies of skirmishers from the 7th Connecticut remained in the lead, but they were followed closely by the 7th New Hampshire. On Hawley's left was a mixture of woods and fields and on his right was a large open meadow. In the meadow near the road stood the home and outbuildings of the R. R. Beasley family, which now sheltered the Confederate skirmishers. Determined to evict the Confederates from the Beasley farm, Hawley called upon Capt. Lucius Richmond's detachment of the 4th Massachusetts Cavalry for assistance. Once again, the Confederate skirmishers gave ground slowly, and the Federal column inched forward down the road. As the advance continued, Hawley became increasingly concerned about the high, wooded ridge across the railroad on his left flank. Riding back to the 6th Connecticut regiment, Hawley ordered Company D to advance along the railroad and adjacent ridge as a flank guard for the main body moving on the plain. The company immediately headed down the track toward Petersburg. Some of its men moving on the slope could see the tall spires of the city only two miles ahead.[21]

Shortly after 9:00 a.m. the Federals on the side of the ridge saw the Confederate skirmishers on the plain retreat from a tree line into a wheat field, indicating that Hawley's column was again making progress. Soon a line of Federal skirmishers appeared, followed by Colonel Abbott's 7th New Hampshire regiment in column on the road. At this point the City Point Road made a sharp turn to the south, and both Hawley's skirmishers and the regiments behind them conformed to the new direction. After pushing forward another 500 yards, Hawley halted his men. Approximately half a mile ahead of the 7th New Hampshire a long low line of fortifications could be seen crossing the road at a right angle along a slight elevation. Far more significant, however, was a heavy earthwork on the high ridge to Hawley's left. This work, Battery 5 of the Dimmock Line, had been engaging the Federal column with artillery for some time, but with little success. The battery attracted Hawley's attention because of its commanding position atop an extension of the ridge which the

20 OR 36, pt. 2, 299, 305.

21 OR 36, pt. 2, 299-300, 302-03, 305. The best contemporary map of the terrain is the Confederate map printed in Cowles, comp., OR *Atlas*, plate 40, 1.

Federals had descended in order to reach the plain. Between Hawley's men and Battery 5 the ground was as level as a table and completely bare of cover except for scattered bushes and trees along ditch lines. Any movement toward the works in front of Abbott would be enfiladed by Battery 5.[22]

The situation in which Hawley found himself could be likened to a rough quadrilateral: the north side, along which the Federal regiments lay, was formed by the City Point Road; the west side was also bounded by the City Point Road, which at that point turned sharply to the south; the south side was delineated by Batteries 2 and 3 of the Dimmock Line, which were connected by an infantry parapet; and the east side was determined by the City Point Railroad. Just beyond the railroad and running along its entire length was the high ridge, which was crowned near the southeastern point of the quadrilateral by Batteries 4 and 5. This ridge abruptly rose 60 feet above the plain and the Confederate works stood even higher than that. Hawley carefully noted the lay of the land and the Confederate defenses. He also discussed the situation with Gillmore's chief of staff, Brig. Gen. Robert Foster, who had come forward. Although Gillmore was apparently informed of the conditions at the front, he did not make an appearance on the plain.[23]

By 10:00 a.m. the Federal advance on the plain had come to a standstill. The two companies of skirmishers from the 7th Connecticut, eventually augmented by 20 men from a third company, were far out on the plain, still engaging the Confederates with sporadic firing. Five or six hundred yards behind them the 62nd Ohio regiment was drawn up in line of battle in the field as a support, but the other regiments were standing or lying idly in the road. The 7th New Hampshire occupied the most advanced position on the road, at the northwest corner of the quadrilateral, followed by the remainder of the 7th Connecticut, then the 6th Connecticut. Hawley's last regiment, the 3rd New Hampshire, had just moved out on the plain when it was ordered to retrace its steps to the high ground and advance along the crest of the ridge toward Battery 5. To secure the connection between the 3rd New Hampshire and the troops on the plain,

22 OR 36, pt. 2, 296, 300, 305; Cowles, comp., *OR Atlas*, plate 40, 1. Battery 5 was the only fortification mentioned by Colonel Abbott in his report, although Batteries 2, 3, and 4 were certainly visible.

23 Cowles, comp., *OR Atlas*, plate 40, 1; OR 36, pt. 2, 296, 300.

The plain at Hawley's position.
Library of Congress

Hawley reinforced the company from the 6th Connecticut moving along the railroad with a second drawn from the same source.[24]

While the 3rd New Hampshire climbed the ridge and headed through the woods toward Battery 5, action on the plain was confined to a brisk fire among the skirmishers and intermittent shots from Confederate artillery pieces on the ridge. The handful of gunners in Battery 5 divided their attention between the Federal skirmish line, at which they fired canister, and the massed regiments in the road, which were the recipients of fused shell. All of the Federals on the plain were more or less exposed to the view of the artillerymen, but the 6th and 7th Connecticut regiments somehow believed they received undue attention from the whistling shells. The shelling was never heavy and came from long range, but it was nevertheless galling to men drawn up in the road because they were powerless to reply. Ominously, as the hours passed, the bombardment became increasingly more accurate.[25]

Throughout the morning, Hawley maintained close contact with Brig. Gen.. Robert Foster, Gillmore's chief of staff. Because Gillmore remained at the A. Jordan house, in the field on the ridge where the first contact had been made hours earlier, Foster came to direct much of the action by default. Indeed, it was Foster who had ordered Hawley to return the 3rd New Hampshire to the top of the ridge. As soon as Lieutenant Colonel Plimpton's men regained the

24 *OR* 36, pt. 2, 298, 300, 301, 303, 304; Eldredge, *Third New Hampshire*, 493. None of the Federal regiments on the plain moved forward after 10:00 a.m.

25 *OR* 36, pt. 2, 300, 303; Charles K. Cadwell, *The Old Sixth Regiment, its War Record, 1861-5* (New Haven, CT, 1875), 94.

heights, it became apparent that Hawley could not control their movements from his position on the plain. Realizing the potentially dangerous position in which his scattered command lay, Hawley asked Foster to supervise the movements of the 3rd New Hampshire and the two companies of the 6th Connecticut on the ridge and the railroad.[26]

Foster readily agreed to assume direction of the units on the ridge. He at once deployed eight companies of the 3rd New Hampshire in a heavy skirmish line and connected their right flank with the two companies of the 6th Connecticut near the railroad. While this combined force prepared to begin a cautious advance toward Battery 5, he sent the remaining two New Hampshire companies to support the four guns of Lieutenant Sanger's Battery D as they took position on the left of the skirmish line. Concerned about the safety of his guns, young Sanger had requested an entire regiment to support the battery, but he was forced to be content with only two companies. When all was ready, the long line lurched forward through the underbrush, passing over the still smoldering ashes of the campfires of the Confederate pickets.[27]

Unlike their comrades on the open plain, the Federals on the ridge found themselves impeded by the terrain. The top of the ridge was intermittently gashed by steep-sided ravines which made the footing difficult, but Lieutenant Colonel Plimpton's skirmishers pressed forward through the woods until they reached a cleared area only 200 yards from the battery. In order to get a closer look at the objective, Lt. Edwin N. Bowen lay down in the tall grass and crawled forward as far as he dared. Peering through the weeds, Bowen counted several artillery pieces in the battery before scurrying back to the relative safety of the skirmish line. Upon receiving Bowen's report, Foster decided that no farther advance could be made on the ridge and he simply attempted to maintain contact with Hawley's men on the plain. As the firing momentarily abated, both

---

26 *OR* 36, pt. 2, 300; *OR* 36, pt. 3, 719. In a 12:30 p.m. message to Butler, Gillmore located his headquarters at Elick Jordan's. According to Butler's later account in *Butler's Book*, 678, Gillmore at 10:00 a.m. "halted his troops and went to a 'secesh' lady's house to get his dinner. While there, as he afterward averred, he was informed by her that Petersburg was full of troops." Presumably the "secesh" lady was a resident of the same Jordan dwelling.

27 Eldredge, *Third New Hampshire*, 493. A. Jordan's house does not appear on plates 40.1 and 56.1 in Cowles, *OR Atlas*, but does appear on plate 65.1 in the same source. It also can be found on the "Map of Prince George County, 1863," in the Jeremy Francis Gilmer Collection, Virginia Historical Society, Richmond, Virginia.

Foster on the ridge and Hawley on the plain could hear sharp firing to the southeast, where Edward Hinks's regiments were supposed to be.[28]

While Hawley and Foster had impaled themselves on the horns of the plain versus ridge dilemma, Hinks had also been approaching the Confederate works. Shortly after beginning their advance westward on the Jordan's Point Road, Hinks's men found their forward progress hindered by Confederate skirmishers. For some reason the Confederates facing Hinks did not resist as strongly as Hawley's opponents and were rapidly driven toward their works. When his column reached the vicinity of the John Ruffin house, approximately 1,300 yards from Battery 9 astride the Jordan's Point Road and hidden from it by a low intervening ridge, Hinks deployed his command in line of battle on both sides of the road. He then moved the entire command forward to the crest of the ridge and halted it in full view of the Confederate defenders in the Dimmock Line. Almost instantly Hinks's men came under a flanking fire from an artillery piece located in Battery 7, the right emplacement of the projecting salient that culminated in Battery 5. The cannon completely enfiladed Hinks's entire line and could, when joined by the fire from the works in Hinks's front, make an assault an extremely costly affair.[29]

To neutralize the threat to his right flank, Hinks ordered forward his own artillery. While the guns of Battery B, 2nd Colored Light Artillery, moved to the front, Hinks called for the aide from Gillmore's staff who had accompanied the column. The aide, Lt. James Barnard, was told to inform Gillmore that Hinks was in position, that his right flank was exposed to an enfilading fire, and that he would advance as soon as he could bring his own artillery into position. As Barnard galloped off, Hinks's artillery battery arrived and began to search for a site from which it could shell the Confederate fortifications. The search proved to be fruitless, because no position could be located that would not leave the

28 OR 36, pt. 2, 296, 300, 304; Eldredge, *Third New Hampshire*, 493, 495, 869. Lieutenant Bowen was then only 21 years old.

29 OR 36, pt. 2, 306; Thomas L. Livermore, *Days and Events, 1860-1866* (Boston, MA, 1920), 353. Batteries 4 through 7 of the Dimmock Line were all located in the great salient around the Jordan house plateau, with Battery 5, the largest work, at the apex. On June 9, 1864, Hawley and Hinks inadvertently positioned their brigades so that this salient protruded between their forces and divided them. Consequently, Federal lateral communications were hampered while the Confederates had fine enfilading positions no matter which way the Federals chose to attack. Strangely, Brig. Gen. Henry Wise, in "Career of Wise's Brigade," 13, considered the Battery 5 section of the Dimmock Line "the worst constructed line of the war . . . leaving the most commanding ground outside of our line in front."

battery without support and exposed to enfilading fire. Accordingly, Hinks ordered his gunners back to the safety of the Ruffin house while he pushed the two infantry regiments another 50 yards toward the Confederate works. Unless Gillmore could do something about the offending Battery 7, Hinks believed any farther advance on his front would be extremely costly. Meanwhile, his men continued to dodge shells from Battery 7 and suffer occasional casualties.[30]

Because the Battery 5 salient protruded between the two Federal forces, Lieutenant Barnard had to retrace Hinks's approach route as far as Baylor's and then follow the City Point Road eastward in order to reach Quincy Gillmore's headquarters. This circuitous route was approximately three miles long and its use meant that there would be a substantial delay in communication between Gillmore and Hinks. Reaching Gillmore's headquarters a little after 9:00 a.m., Barnard reported that Hinks had said he could not advance until Battery 7 was taken. Gillmore responded by ordering Barnard back to Hinks with still another message. Barnard was to tell Hinks that Hawley would soon advance and drive the Confederates facing him into their works. Hinks was to do the same, and if an opportunity came to assault the works successfully, he was free to do so. Hinks's actions were to be left totally to his own discretion, and he was not to construe Gillmore's message as a direct order to make an assault. Carrying these timid and not very helpful instructions, Barnard set out for Hinks's position using a slightly more direct route across country.[31]

While he waited for Barnard to return with new instructions or for some kind of cooperative action by Hawley's column, Hinks observed the Confederate fortifications closely. It appeared that there was a considerable force of Confederates within the works in his front and that they were adequately supplied with artillery. Even as Hinks watched, two Confederate units of possibly regimental size appeared to arrive as reinforcements. Although the presence of additional defenders would make a Federal assault all the more difficult, the Confederates did not seem to present an offensive threat to Hinks and showed no sign of advancing from their works. Therefore the only immediate danger to Hinks's command was the fire of the Confederate artillery

---

30 *OR* 36, pt. 2, 295, 306-07; Marshall, ed., *Butler's Correspondence*, 4:339-42.

31 *OR* 36, pt. 2, 295. Gillmore's reference to an advance by Hawley apparently referred to the movement beyond the Beasley house. This advance was brief, covering only 500 yards, and was essentially complete by 10:00 a.m.

Dimmock Line near Hinks's position.
Library of Congress

on his right flank. To shield his men from the shelling as much as possible, Hinks withdrew his right companies slightly and placed them under cover.[32]

Around 10:00 a.m. Lieutenant Barnard again joined Edward Hinks on the Jordan's Point Road. After receiving Gillmore's promise that Hawley would advance, Hinks informed the aide that his own troops could go no farther until something was done about the enfilade fire from Battery 7 on his right. On the other hand, Hinks also emphatically stated that he could easily maintain his own position facing the Confederates and would remain in front of the works a while longer in hopes that Hawley's advance would provide an opportunity for his own men to charge. Barnard was then sent back to Gillmore with that information, as well as an account of what Hinks had seen taking place within the Confederate lines. The aide rode away, leaving Hinks anxiously awaiting the results of Hawley's advance. Unknown to Hinks, that advance had been of brief duration and had stalled before the commanding presence of Battery 5. Hinks would get no relief from Hawley's actions. Thus by 10:00 a.m. two of Benjamin Butler's three assaulting columns had ponderously ground to a halt. Elements of seven infantry regiments and two batteries, approximately 3,300 men, lapsed

32 OR 36, pt. 2, 295, 307; Marshall, ed., *Butler's Correspondence*, 4:340-41.

into the role of passive spectators watching the minor drama enacted by the skirmishers of both sides.[33]

On the plain Joseph Hawley was unhappy with his enforced inactivity but, try as he might, he could find no really practical alternative. Gillmore's orders were simply to "simulate an attack." Hawley was to keep his troops under cover as much as possible, but if the enemy showed signs of flight, he was to press them vigorously. Therefore Lieutenant Colonel Plimpton would maintain his advanced position on the ridge and the Connecticut skirmishers on the plain would continue their deadly target practice, but no assault would be attempted. Such a cautious policy was favored by many of Hawley's officers, as he discovered when he canvassed his regimental commanders for their opinions. Visiting Colonel Abbott of the 7th New Hampshire, Hawley was told that an advance would probably lead to "disastrous results." Next, Captain Bacon of the 7th Connecticut declared that an assault would be "in the highest degree unwise" and would have "only the most desperate chances of success." Unable to visit the 3rd New Hampshire on the ridge, Hawley sent for Lieutenant Colonel Plimpton's opinion, which was that the Federal force was "entirely too small to attempt to enter the town." Echoing these views was Brigadier General Foster, who believed nothing could be "accomplished without serious loss of life." Clearly, the consensus in Hawley's command was that a menacing inactivity was the best and only sane course of action.[34]

Although he tended to agree that the Confederate works were impregnable, Hawley expected to be ordered forward. He stood for some time at Abbott's position staring at the Confederate line, thinking about the alternatives. He concluded that Battery 5 was too powerful to assault successfully and too dangerously situated to leave on his flank. Hawley had been told that Petersburg's garrison was weak, but he did not believe it and feared that the Confederates manned the works all the way to the Appomattox River on his right. The plain was large and flat, too large for Hawley's brigade to cover

---

33 *OR* 36, pt. 2, 280, 295; Marshall, ed., *Butler's Correspondence*, 4:340-41. According to Butler, in explaining to Barnard that he could hold his ground, Hinks said that he "could do so until doomsday."

34 *OR* 36, pt. 2, 296, 300, 301, 304, 306. Colonel Abbott noted later that his opinion had been "formed without any further information in regard to the strength of the work, its armament, and the force within it, than was apparent to any one from the point which I occupied." Only Quincy Gillmore had better information, and he apparently had not shared it with subordinate commanders.

without unacceptably dissipating its strength, and any concentrated assaulting column would have no reserve. Even if the works were successfully carried at some point, Hawley would still be two miles from Petersburg and the railroad bridge. There might be more defenses to encounter, there certainly would be additional Confederate units to defeat, and simply negotiating the intervening ravines, streams, and suburbs would consume much precious time. Hawley also knew that he could expect no reinforcements and that he would have to evacuate Petersburg by nightfall. If he were ordered to attack, Hawley concluded that he would have to withdraw most of his regiments from the plain and assault Battery 5 along the crest of the ridge. Mentally he reviewed the necessary movements while he waited for further orders from Gillmore.[35]

At his headquarters at the A. Jordan house, out of sight of either Battery 5 or the plain, Quincy Gillmore had apparently decided that no attack was feasible. Although he seems not to have visited Hawley's front in person, he had received reports from Foster, his chief of staff, and their negative tone no doubt affected his deliberations. He may have also been influenced by the testimony of Lieutenant Barnard, who arrived from Hinks's command shortly before 11:00 a.m. Barnard brought news of conditions on the Jordan's Point Road, but the conditions he described were not exactly those Hinks had seen. The aide reported that there was a "full field battery of brass pieces in each of the batteries" facing Hinks, that two Confederate regiments had entered the works from Petersburg, that Hinks thought "it would be slaughter to attempt an assault," and that Hinks had seen the works in Hawley's front and "considered them formidable." On seeing Barnard's report two days later, Hinks denied some of the aide's statements and characterized others as half-truths, but Barnard's version of Hinks's situation fitted neatly in Gillmore's mind with what Foster was reporting from Hawley's position. At any rate, Gillmore

---

35 OR 36, pt. 2, 300, 302. Ten days later Hawley wrote to a friend: "I knew little of the plan but expected to assault & repeat the story of Wagner. Though I had been told that the forces were small, I could not believe them so very light as to be unable by the help of their several lines of works & the creeks as to be unable to keep us from the centre of the city at least, and I knew that before the day was over Beauregard's forces could get over from the vicinity of Walthall Junction & either help drive us out or capture our disconnected columns." Joseph R. Hawley to Gideon Welles, June 19, 1864, Joseph R. Hawley Papers, Library of Congress. If ordered to assault, Hawley anticipated leaving one regiment on the plain as a flank guard, while the others retraced their steps up the ridge and deployed behind the 3rd New Hampshire.

needed little urging to dismiss any idea of an offensive movement on either front.[36]

The defensive cast of Gillmore's mind was evident in the message he gave Lieutenant Barnard to carry to Hinks around 11:00 a.m. This message informed Hinks that the Confederates facing Hawley were advancing a strong skirmish line and that defensive arrangements were being made to receive it; in case Hawley was forced to retreat, Hinks was to adjust his movements to the sound of the firing. Taking the now familiar route back to the Jordan's Point Road, Barnard could not find Hinks. Locating one of the general's staff officers, Barnard discovered that Hinks was in the process of withdrawing his line of battle half a mile to the rear because of the enfilading artillery fire, but that his skirmishers would remain in their advanced positions. Unable to locate Hinks, Barnard returned to Gillmore and reported what he had seen. The aide's latest report further convinced Gillmore that no assault was possible.[37]

As the minutes passed, Gillmore gradually convinced himself that not only was an attack impossible, it was also unnecessary. Reviewing his instructions, he concluded that "[i]t was no part of the plan to assault the enemy's works on the right, where it was known they have an interior line of redoubts, unless there was a strong probability of success, or until General Kautz's attack should divert them." The only available course of action, then, was to hold the enemy in position and wait for Kautz. Yet Kautz had promised to be in position by 9:00 a.m. and it was now approaching noon. As he waited, Gillmore's fears began to overcome his judgment. Considering his command to be in an extremely hazardous position, he believed he could not remain in front of the Confederate works much longer. Even the sound of distant firing in Kautz's direction after 11:00 a.m. was not a sign of Federal success; to Gillmore it meant only that Kautz was meeting resistance. By 12:30 p.m. he could stand it no

36 OR 36, pt. 2, 289, 295, 296. It is possible that Gillmore may have also been influenced by statements of a resident of the Jordan house. Butler, *Butler's Book*, 678. As for Barnard's testimony, Hinks on June 11, 1864, penned a rejoinder to Butler. According to Hinks, he had stated only that "the enemy's works in my front were mounted with brass field guns," not a full battery in each of the works as Barnard had reported; that the two units which had entered the works after Hinks's arrival came from an unknown point, not from Petersburg as Barnard had stated; that the flanking fire from Battery 7 was what he considered "formidable," not the works in his front; and finally, that he knew nothing of the fortifications facing Hawley and therefore could not characterize them. If Hinks's testimony is correct, Barnard's report to Gillmore significantly misrepresented conditions in Hinks's front and may have influenced Gillmore's decision not to attack at all.

37 OR 36, pt. 2, 295.

longer. Ordering Hawley to begin a withdrawal, Gillmore explained his decision in a message to Butler at Bermuda Hundred. Citing the report of a prisoner, Foster's and Hawley's doubts, and Barnard's misleading statements about Hinks, Gillmore explained that he was withdrawing in order to reunite the command and communicate with Kautz.[38]

Hawley later stated that he received the orders to begin the retrograde movement around 1:00 p.m., but three of his regimental commanders placed the time of their withdrawal nearer to noon. Whenever it began, the movement was conducted professionally. First, the 62nd Ohio retired approximately 500 yards for the purpose of drawing in the skirmishers, then ascended the ridge and took up a rear-guard position near the A. Jordan house. There the regiment was joined by Lieutenant Sanger's battery, which unlimbered nearby. While the three regiments on the plain toiled up the slope and filed past the 62nd Ohio, Lieutenant Colonel Plimpton covered their retreat with his own 3rd New Hampshire and the two attached companies of the 6th Connecticut. When all Federal infantry had left the plain, Plimpton signaled his men to fall back and they too passed through the position occupied by the 62nd Ohio. At last, Sanger's gunners limbered their pieces and joined the retreat, followed closely by the Ohio regiment. None of the Federal units was molested in its departure by the watching Confederates. As Hawley's men marched away from Petersburg, distant firing was heard somewhere off to the south, though no particular notice was taken of it. When the column reached the road junction at Baylor's, Gillmore permitted the men to file out of the road, stack arms, and eat dinner.[39]

Not long after noon Edward Hinks learned that Gillmore was withdrawing Hawley's brigade, but he received no immediate instructions to do the same. Unwilling to be left to face the Confederates alone, Hinks began a partial withdrawal of his own by sending his artillery and an infantry reserve half a mile to the rear at the Henry T. Bryant house. At 1:00 p.m., on receiving instructions to commence his retrograde movement, he complied by moving the remainder of his command to Bryant's. Finally, 30 minutes later, the ubiquitous Lieutenant Barnard appeared with orders for Hinks to join Gillmore's column at Baylor's. Reaching the intersection where Hawley's men sprawled in a clover field, Hinks

38 OR 36, pt. 2, 289; OR 36, pt. 3, 719; Marshall, Butler's Correspondence, 4:329-30.

39 OR 36, pt. 2, 289, 298, 300-01, 303, 305, 307; Joseph R. Hawley to Gideon Welles, June 19, 1864, Joseph R. Hawley Papers, Library of Congress.

met Gillmore, who asked about news from Kautz. When Hinks could provide no information, Gillmore concluded that Kautz had probably ridden south to raid the railroad. Therefore no purpose would be served by waiting at Baylor's for Kautz to appear. Already out of contact with the Confederates and believing that further delay would be both futile and dangerous, Gillmore ordered Hawley and Hinks to begin their return march to Bermuda Hundred and City Point. As the long lines of tired men tramped past, Gillmore drafted a final message to Butler, then joined the column. Whatever Kautz's fate was to be, Quincy Gillmore seemed willing to leave him to it.[40]

As the brigades of Joseph Hawley and Edward Hinks marched away from Petersburg, the men in the ranks began wondering what had been accomplished. Soldiers in at least one regiment, the 7th New Hampshire, were told that the operation was a success, but without knowing the purpose of the expedition, the troops had no way to judge the merits of the claim. Had they known Butler's plan and the weakness of their enemy, Hawley's and Hinks's men would hardly have considered themselves successful. Leaving the absent cavalry out of the equation, Gillmore had brought more than 3,300 mostly veteran troops and eight cannon against the Dimmock Line, which had been held by no more than 1,000 Confederates of all descriptions. Hawley, with 2,000 infantrymen and four pieces of artillery, had been facing approximately 250 reserves under Majors Hood and Batte, no more than 150 dismounted troopers of Taliaferro's 7th Confederate Cavalry, and a handful of artillerymen with fewer than a half dozen cannon. The odds against Hinks had been somewhat different, but even so, Hinks had deployed 1,300 men and at least four field pieces against some 500 men of the 46th Virginia Infantry regiment and a few field pieces.[41]

Of course Petersburg's defenders had been fighting from behind entrenchments, while both Hawley's and Hinks's men had maneuvered in the open. On Hinks's front, the combination of 500 entrenched veterans and enfilading artillery was unbeatable; Hinks could hardly have been expected to do more than he did. Such was not the case on Hawley's front. Hawley had a

40 OR 36, pt. 2, 295, 307; OR 36, pt. 3, 719-20; Marshall, *Butler's Correspondence*, 4:331.

41 Henry F. W. Little, *The Seventh Regiment New Hampshire Volunteers in the War of the Rebellion* (Concord, NH, 1896), 264; Eldredge, *Third New Hampshire*, 493; OR 36, pt. 2, 298, 306; OR 36, pt. 3, 694. The reinforcements which Hinks saw arriving during the course of the action probably were companies of the 46th Virginia Infantry regiment which had originally been stationed farther to the south. Cutchins, *Richmond Light Infantry Blues*, 139.

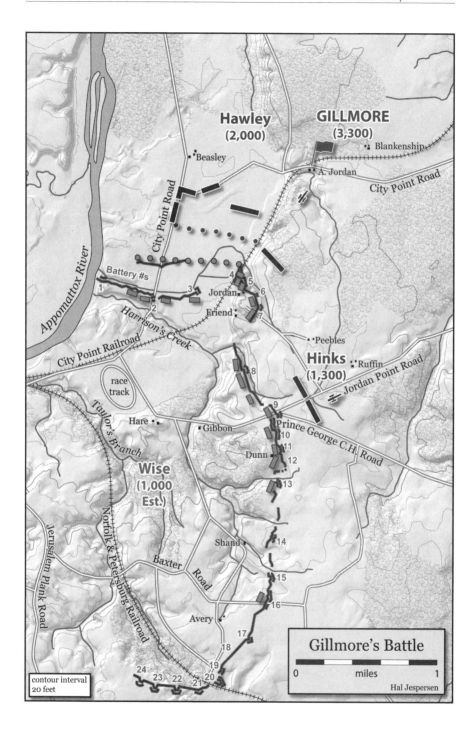

Gillmore's Battle

0   miles   1

Hal Jespersen

contour interval
20 feet

strength advantage approaching five to one, and his troops were experienced and well-armed. By comparison, the battalions of Hood and Batte were poorly equipped, out of condition, and almost totally lacking in training, much less combat experience. Yet Joseph Hawley was as good a soldier as Edward Hinks, and he did not believe he could have accomplished any more than he did on the morning of June 9, 1864. In addition, Brigadier General Foster and the regimental commanders seconded Hawley's opinion that a further advance would have been extremely hazardous. The strength of the Confederate fortifications certainly played a role, but the explanation for Hawley's failure lay beyond the walls of Battery 5.

Although the aggressiveness of the Confederate defenders, particularly Taliaferro's dismounted cavalry skirmishers, also contributed to Hawley's timidity, the key to Hawley's failure lay in the position he finally came to occupy in front of the Confederate works. Hawley had begun his final approach totally unfamiliar with the terrain around Battery 5 and he had unwittingly allowed the Confederate skirmishers to draw his column off the ridge and onto the plain, following the City Point Road. This movement put most of Hawley's brigade into the worst possible position from which to launch an assault against the massive Battery 5. To attack Battery 5 from the plain, Hawley's men would have to cross a wide expanse of open ground under the plunging fire of Batteries 4 and 5, and the enfilading fire of Batteries 2 and 3. Even if the plain were traversed successfully, the attackers would then have to surmount the steep incline of the ridge itself and force their way over the parapet in the face of the defenders' opposition. From the perspective of the plain, it is hardly surprising that the prevailing military opinion favored a course of threatening inactivity.[42]

Yet Hawley probably could have succeeded if he had made the dash across the plain and up the ridge. The handful of Confederate defenders were too few and too poorly armed and trained to have prevented a successful assault, even though their strong position would have allowed them to inflict some casualties upon Hawley's force. Although he had been told that Petersburg's garrison was weak, Hawley did not credit the information, and his exposed position on the plain did not permit him to get close enough to ascertain the truth for himself.

---

42 *OR* 36, pt. 2, 300. In a letter written long after the war, Maj. William H. Hood ascribed the Federal retreat solely to a flanking movement by a handful of cavalrymen maneuvering near the Appomattox, but far more was at play in Federal minds than this feeble ruse. W. H. Hood, "The Defense of Petersburg," in Hampton Newsome, John Horn, and John G. Selby, eds., *Civil War Talks* (Charlottesville, VA, 2012), 242.

Butler's excellent information on the size of Petersburg's garrison and the weakness of the fortifications had apparently not been communicated to Hawley in any meaningful way. Joseph Hawley was a conscientious officer, but the validity of the decisions he could make was directly related to the quality of the information he had at the time. Neither what he had been told nor what he could see gave Hawley an accurate picture of the reality before him.[43]

Even with all his difficulties, Hawley had been able to devise an alternative to attacking Battery 5 from the plain. He had eventually concluded that Battery 5 might be more easily approached by returning most of his troops to the ridge and assaulting through the position held by the 3rd New Hampshire. Such a movement would not have been free of casualties, but the loss could hardly have been overwhelming. In fact Plimpton's regiment had been able to get within 200 yards of the Confederate works with the loss of only one man killed and none wounded. Indeed, when Battery 5 was captured six days later by troops from William F. Smith's XVIII Corps, the attack came from the position Plimpton had occupied and was accomplished by no more than a heavy skirmish line. The only detrimental factor in Hawley's alternate plan was the additional time needed to redeploy the regiments from the plain to the ridge. Still, had the time been taken, Battery 5 would have fallen.[44]

Clearly, greater success could have been attained by the infantry columns on June 9 than was actually the case. If Hawley and Hinks were not responsible for the failure of their columns, then the fault was Quincy Gillmore's. Supposedly an officer competent to hold the rank of major general and command an army corps, Gillmore had from the beginning of the Bermuda Hundred campaign shown that he was not capable of forcefully leading troops in the field. His performance on June 9, 1864, did nothing to redeem his earlier blunders and indeed confirmed him as an incompetent field commander. Butler had made Gillmore aware of the nature of the terrain surrounding the Dimmock Line through the use of both maps and guides, but Gillmore had failed to fully share this information with Hawley, the officer who needed it most, and did not act upon it himself. Consequently, Hawley was allowed to descend to the plain where he would be in the worst possible position to make

43 OR 36, pt. 2, 299; Joseph R. Hawley to Gideon Welles, June 19, 1864, Joseph R. Hawley Papers, Library of Congress.

44 OR 36, pt. 2, 300; Eldredge, *Third New Hampshire*, 493; Thompson, *Thirteenth New Hampshire*, 382-403.

the most effective use of his men. Once Hawley had become involved on the plain, Gillmore neither ordered an attack from there nor directed a deployment to Plimpton's more favorable position on the ridge. Plainly stated, Gillmore abdicated control of the largest portion of his force at the most critical time.

Given the Confederate weakness, an assault from either the plain or the ridge would have succeeded, and Butler had taken great pains to inform Gillmore of the true strength of Petersburg's garrison. Disregarding this information and refusing to survey the scene for himself, Gillmore instead chose to rely upon the reports of his chief of staff, who of course could not see behind the Confederate fortifications. Robert Foster's fragmentary messages were decidedly unfavorable to an assault from either the plain or the ridge, and Gillmore accepted that judgment without question. Therefore Hawley's mistake was allowed to stand, Lieutenant Colonel Plimpton's advantageous location was not exploited, and Hinks's line remained enfiladed. Gillmore's performance amounted to a failure to exercise decisive leadership at a time when such leadership was essential to success. His failure to seize control of the situation meant that two of the three prongs of Butler's attack plan were doomed to accomplish nothing.[45]

As might be expected from the nature of the action, Gillmore's casualties were extremely light. Hawley lost only 10 men killed and wounded out of the 2,000 he brought to the field, while Hinks's casualties amounted to two killed and three wounded out of 1,300. Counting the lone casualty from his escort, Gillmore had lost a total of 16 men, far from the 500 to 1,000 casualties Butler had considered an acceptable price for success. Confederate casualties are unknown, but the loss must have been very small because of the defenders' protected position. Weak in numbers, the troops who manned Petersburg's eastern defenses had been strong in courage and lucky in their choice of enemy. Perhaps one of Kautz's cavalrymen characterized Gillmore's movement best when he wrote years later of the infantry's role on June 9: "When General

---

45 Neither Foster, Hawley, nor any of the regimental commanders mentions Gillmore's presence on the battlefield. Perhaps Gillmore's absence from Hawley's front can be justified by the fact that he was responsible not only for Hawley's brigade but also for Hinks's troops and, to a lesser degree, Kautz's cavalry. Nevertheless, Hawley's brigade represented two-thirds of the expedition's infantry strength and the decisions made in reference to its employment would be crucial ones, particularly after Hinks's column was blocked by enfilading fire which Hawley alone could silence.

Gillmore came within sight of the enemy's lines, he saw lions in the way, not going far enough to see if they were chained."[46]

North of the Appomattox at Dunlop's, only three miles from the scene of Gillmore's action, P. G. T. Beauregard was unable to get a clear picture of what was happening around Petersburg. By the time he received any report from Henry Wise, it was so outdated that it did not reflect the actual state of affairs on the Dimmock Line. Nevertheless, Beauregard attempted to keep the Confederate War Department in Richmond abreast of the situation. At 10:15 a.m., shortly after Hawley's farthest advance, Beauregard wired Braxton Bragg that Wise was being threatened by only two regiments. Thirty minutes later, the news from Wise was grim and Beauregard transmitted a far different message to Richmond. Written at a time when the troops of both Hawley and Hinks were quiescent, the message was ominous in tone. After explaining that Wise was being pressed on three fronts and that no more reinforcements were available, Beauregard stated: "Without the troops sent to General Lee I will have to elect between abandoning lines on Bermuda Neck and those of Petersburg. Please give me the views of the Government on the subject." At the same time Beauregard informed Wise that no more reinforcements would come from north of the Appomattox until the Federal intentions became clear.[47]

Beauregard must have known that it would take a great deal of time to transfer troops from Robert E. Lee's army at Cold Harbor to Petersburg, and it was almost a certainty that they could not affect the outcome of the battle, even if sent. His motivations therefore are unclear. Perhaps he believed that the crisis at Petersburg presented a good argument for the return of the troops that had been taken from him in late May, and that such an argument would gain greater acceptance if coupled with expressions of the desperate nature of the situation. Certainly, posing the dilemma of retaining either Petersburg or the Bermuda Hundred fortifications would gain the attention of the War Department. On the other hand, Beauregard may have truly thought that the situation was desperate and required extreme measures. Either way, Gen. Braxton Bragg and Secretary of War James A. Seddon were unwilling to take the responsibility for

46 OR 36, pt. 2, 299, 301; Marshall, *Butler's Correspondence*, 4:341-42; *History of the Eleventh Pennsylvania Volunteer Cavalry, Together with a Complete Roster of the Regiment and Regimental Officers* (Philadelphia, PA, 1902), 121.

47 OR 36, pt. 3, 884; P. G. T. Beauregard to J. H. Pearce, June 9, 1864, Official Telegrams, April 22-June 9, 1864, P. G. T. Beauregard Papers, Library of Congress.

determining which positions Beauregard should relinquish. In their view, Beauregard alone would have to decide how to deploy the forces available in his department, and he was notified to that effect. With no assistance forthcoming from Richmond, Beauregard could only hope that the cavalry regiment he had ordered to Petersburg earlier would be enough to sustain Wise.[48]

According to an account in a Petersburg newspaper, as Henry Wise directed the defense of the Dimmock Line against the troops of Hawley and Hinks, "a smile played on his face as the enemy were driven back." Given Quincy Gillmore's ineptitude, this may well have been an accurate description of Wise's reaction. Unknown to Wise, however, the third element of Benjamin Butler's plan had not yet been heard from. Before the long day was to end, August Kautz's 1,300 cavalrymen would temporarily banish the smile from Wise's face, and they would not be long about it.[49]

---

48 OR 51, pt. 2, 999-1000; Alfred Roman, *The Military Operations of General Beauregard in the War between the States, 1861 to 1865*, 2 vols (New York, NY, 1883), 2:566. The War Department also forwarded Beauregard's telegrams to Robert E. Lee for comment, but it would be midafternoon before they were received. OR 51, pt. 2, 996; Clifford Dowdey and Louis H. Manarin, eds., *The Wartime Papers of R. E. Lee* (Boston, MA, 1961), 770.

49 Petersburg *Daily Express*, June 13, 1864.

Chapter 4

"A Question of Minutes Only"

Born in the German state of Baden in 1828, August Valentine Kautz had spent all of his adult life in the military service of the United States. Immigrating to Ohio as a child, Kautz volunteered for duty in the war with Mexico. He then attended the United States Military Academy at West Point, receiving his commission in 1852. He spent the next nine years on the frontier, being wounded twice in encounters with Indians. Originally an infantry officer, Kautz was promoted to the rank of captain in the 3rd United States Cavalry shortly after the Civil War broke out in 1861. Quickly transferring to the 6th U.S. Cavalry, he served with that regiment during the Peninsula campaign. Soon realizing that promotion was more rapid in the volunteer service, Kautz accepted a commission as colonel of the 2nd Ohio Cavalry in the fall of 1862. As such, he participated in numerous operations in Kentucky and Ohio, including the capture of John Hunt Morgan and his raiders. By the time he left the Army of the Ohio, Kautz was the Chief of Cavalry of the XXIII Corps. Returning to the Eastern Theater in 1864, he served in the Cavalry Bureau in Washington before coming to the Army of the James in April as its Chief of Cavalry. A man of "swarthy complexion, a square massive German Head," and close-cropped hair and beard, August V. Kautz nevertheless had the "breeding of a gentleman," according to one of his Confederate opponents.[1]

On June 9, 1864, Kautz's cavalry division of two brigades was badly understrength. For the expedition to Petersburg Lt. Col. Everton J. Conger's First

---

1 Boatner, *Civil War Dictionary*, 448-49; Warner, *Generals in Blue*, 257-58; Keiley, *In Vinculis*, 32. For a detailed recital of the facts of August V. Kautz's life prior to June 9, 1864, see Lawrence G. Kautz, *August Valentine Kautz, USA: Biography of a Civil War General* (Jefferson, NC, 2008), 3-125.

Brig. Gen. August V. Kautz
National Archives

Brigade was especially weak, consisting of only six companies of Conger's own 1st District of Columbia Cavalry, plus a few men temporarily attached from the 3rd New York Cavalry. Few in number, the men of the 1st D.C. were armed with the 15-shot Henry repeating rifle, which greatly enhanced their firepower. Much larger than Conger's command, Col. Samuel P. Spear's Second Brigade consisted of two relatively large regiments, the 5th Pennsylvania Cavalry with 450 men and the 11th Pennsylvania Cavalry with 640 more. In addition, each of Spear's regiments carried two light mountain howitzers for extra firepower. Still heavier support was furnished by Lt. Peter Morton's section (two guns) of the 8th New York Independent Light Artillery, which also accompanied the column. All told, the cavalry division August Kautz took to Petersburg numbered no more than 1,300 effective troopers.[2]

After leaving Edward Hinks's infantrymen on the Jordan's Point Road, Kautz's column continued southward on the long flanking march that Kautz hoped would bring them to the Confederate works on the Jerusalem Plank Road by 9:00 a.m. As the hours passed, Kautz discovered that he had been overly optimistic about both the distance and the time of arrival. Not long after they crossed the Prince George Court House Road, troopers of the 11th Pennsylvania Cavalry, in the advance, came under fire from the woods in their front. The entire column halted while the men of the 11th Pennsylvania dismounted and deployed as skirmishers. Close behind them came two mounted squadrons of the 5th Pennsylvania, which had been called forward by Spear to add weight to the Federal

---

2 August V. Kautz, "First Attempts to Capture Petersburg," in Robert U. Johnson and Clarence C. Buel, eds., *Battles and Leaders of the Civil War*, 4 vols. (New York, NY, 1884), 4:534; OR 36, pt. 2, 308-11; OR 51, pt. 1, 1269, 1271; Samuel H. Merrill, *The Campaigns of the First Maine and First District of Columbia Cavalry* (Portland, ME, 1866), 256-57; John D. McAulay, *Civil War Breech Loading Rifles* (Lincoln, RI, 1987), 45.

thrust. East of the road Capt. George Ker's squadron advanced rapidly, driving the troopers of the 7th Confederate Cavalry across a ravine. There the Confederates attempted to make another stand, supported by light howitzers, but before more than a few shots could be exchanged, Capt. Bardele Galisath's squadron west of the road outflanked the Confederates and sent them into precipitate retreat. Galisath then charged once again and routed the last Confederates from their camp.[3]

Brief in duration, Spear's encounter with Taliaferro's Confederate cavalry nevertheless consumed valuable time. Leaving part of the 5th Pennsylvania behind to destroy the arms, harness, and clothing in the abandoned Confederate camp, Kautz's division resumed its march toward the Jerusalem Plank Road. As the column moved, Kautz interrogated several prisoners, who confirmed Benjamin Butler's estimate of Petersburg's garrison. Upon reaching the Norfolk and Petersburg Railroad, the 11th Pennsylvania encountered and quickly charged more Confederate pickets. One of the Confederate cavalrymen was mortally wounded in the ensuing fight, but the remainder escaped into the underbrush. As the Federals again resumed their march through the heavily wooded countryside, it was apparent that the fall of each picket post clearly indicated their progress to Petersburg's defenders. Two miles beyond the railroad, the Federals finally reached the Jerusalem Plank Road and at last turned northward toward Petersburg. As the sun climbed toward the meridian, Kautz's promise to be in position at 9:00 a.m. appeared to be more and more unrealistic. In fact, it was not until 11:30 a.m. that the troopers of the advance guard saw the fortifications of the Dimmock Line in the distance.[4]

Among those aware of the approach of Kautz's column was Brig. Gen. Raleigh Edward Colston, the general without a command. Earlier that morning Colston had eagerly accepted Wise's offer of a role in the city's defense, perhaps in hopes of rejuvenating his tarnished reputation. Born in France in 1825, Colston had been adopted by a Virginian and sent to the Virginia Military Institute for his education. There he compiled a distinguished record, first as a student and later as an instructor of French. Commissioned brigadier general in 1861, Colston saw service as an infantry brigade commander at Williamsburg and Seven Pines before falling victim to illness. His prewar association with Stonewall Jackson assisted his return to the Army of Northern Virginia upon his recovery in 1863, and he commanded Jackson's old division during the famous flank attack at Chancellorsville. Yet

3   OR 36, pt. 2, 308, 311, 313-15; *Eleventh Pennsylvania Cavalry*, 121.

4   OR 36, pt. 2, 308, 311, 313-15; OR 51, pt. 1, 1269-70; August V. Kautz, "The Siege of Petersburg," *National Tribune*, May 18, 1899.

Brig. Gen. Raleigh E. Colston
Centre Hill Museum

Colston's performance in that battle had not pleased his superiors, and he had been relieved from duty with Lee's army. Although no specific reason for the banishment was ever given, Colston left the Army of Northern Virginia with his reputation sullied, and he had held nothing but minor administrative posts ever since. Nevertheless, his zeal for the Confederate cause had not flagged, as shown by his willingness to volunteer in Petersburg's hour of need.[5]

Sent by Wise to Battery 16 southeast of the city, Colston spent the morning supervising a handful of artillerymen and waiting anxiously for signs of the approaching enemy columns. Nothing served to break the stillness of the morning until around 11:00 a.m., when a mounted courier appeared with a message from Henry Wise. The note informed Colston that Federal horsemen were advancing toward the position held by Fletcher Archer's battalion on the Jerusalem Plank Road, a mile and a half to Colston's right, but that Confederate reinforcements were on the way. Colston had not seen the Federals, who had passed across his front at a distance of two and a half miles, but the message instantly galvanized him into action. Realizing that he could be of more service at Battery 27 than where he was, Colston placed his aide, Lt. James T. Tosh, in charge of Battery 16, then rode toward Archer's camp at Rives's farm.[6]

---

5   Boatner, *Civil War Dictionary*, 166-67; Ezra J. Warner, *Generals in Gray: Lives of the Confederate Commanders* (Baton Rouge, LA, 1959), 58-59; Douglas Southall Freeman, *Lee's Lieutenants: A Study in Command*, 3 vols. (New York, NY, 1943), 2:505-06, 660-61. After Chancellorsville, Colston spent a brief time in Southside Virginia, then was transferred to Savannah, Georgia, from the fall of 1863 until April, 1864. Returning to Virginia, he was placed in command at Petersburg in late May by Beauregard, but was removed by War Department fiat at the end of the month. On June 9, 1864, therefore, he was technically between assignments. *OR* 27, pt. 3, 874; *OR* 28, pt. 2, 434; *OR* 35, pt. 2, 434; *OR* 36, pt. 3, 850; Colston, "First Assault," 535; Raleigh E. Colston to Samuel Cooper, May 31, 1864, Raleigh E. Colston Compiled Service Record, National Archives, Washington, DC. For a scathing account of Colston's Civil War performance, see Robert K. Krick, "Raleigh Edward Colston," in William C. Davis and Julie Hoffman, eds., *The Confederate General*, 6 vols. (Harrisburg, PA, 1991), 2:12-15.

6   Colston, "First Assault," 536; *OR* 36, pt. 2, 317.

By the time Raleigh Colston headed in its direction, Fletcher Archer's command was already on the alert, having been warned around 9:00 a.m. by the message from Colonel Harrison of the 46th Virginia Infantry in Battery 9. That warning had turned the camp into pandemonium, which was compounded by the gradual arrival of missing militiamen and volunteers from Petersburg throughout the morning. Among the new arrivals was lawyer Anthony Keiley, who was given the gun of an absent militiaman after refusing to accept one of the ancient specimens proffered by Archer's ordnance officer. When everyone had fallen into line, Major Archer stepped forward and surveyed his command. The sight was not reassuring. Many of the men in line were gray-haired with advancing years, while others were downy-cheeked youths. There was not a uniform in sight, not a bayonet, not a weapon of recent manufacture. It was inconceivable that the motley rabble facing Archer had any chance at all of repelling an attack by veteran Federal cavalrymen armed with the latest repeating carbines—yet there were no other troops available to do the job.[7]

Resigning himself to what seemed to be a certain fate, Archer began to address the assembled battalion. He spoke first about the magnitude of the task confronting them, then closed with "a word of cheer and counsel." However eloquent they may have been, Archer's words meant less to the men standing in formation than the occasional glances they cast toward the rooftops and church spires of Petersburg only a short distance away. While Archer spoke, the thought of family members waiting anxiously in the city came to many of the assembled citizens and underlined the gravity of the situation. Archer's last words to his men were an admonition "never to yield, but to stand up to the end in defense of their homes and firesides," and the citizen-soldiers responded with an air of quiet determination but no more. Archer then assigned each company to a particular position behind the fortifications and the men marched away to make their stand.[8]

The position defended by Archer's battalion was not particularly advantageous. Unlike the terrain at Battery 5, the ground along the Jerusalem Plank Road was generally level. Battery 27 was located where the road passed through the fortifications. The work was pierced for seven guns, but on June 9, 1864, it was, in Anthony Keiley's phrase, "all innocent of ordnance." On either side of the battery were the low breastworks which connected Battery 27 with Battery 25 on the east and Battery 28 on the west. Approximately 250 yards to the rear of Battery 27, east

---

7 Keiley, *In Vinculis*, 17-18; Archer, "Defense of Petersburg," 116; Colston, "First Assault," 536.

8 Archer, "Defense of Petersburg," 117; Keiley, *In Vinculis*, 21.

of the road, was Battery 26, while 175 yards to the right and front of Battery 28 was Battery 29, detached from the main line of fortifications. All of the works showed the scars of nature's ravages and none were insurmountable, although they did offer some protection from small-arms fire. Several houses complicated the natural aspects of the position, notably the Timothy Rives house to the rear of Battery 25, and the William A. Gregory house and outbuildings located west of the road some 250 yards in front of Batteries 27 and 28. Directly behind the entrenchments were the tents of the militia camp.[9]

Archer deployed his handful of men behind the fortifications as judiciously as he could. On the left of his position he placed Capt. James E. Wolff's company of second-class militia in Battery 27 and part of the trench stretching toward Battery 25. On Wolff's right flank, where the road split the earthworks, he ordered the men to overturn a wagon and construct a barricade of fence rails around it. Immediately on the right of the road he placed Capt. Richard F. Jarvis's company of Junior Reserves. Beyond Jarvis's men, Archer extended the line in the direction of Battery 28 with the reserve companies of Capt. Peter D. Hare (the Prince George Reserves, under Lt. Berthier Bott), Capt. Peyton Alfriend, Capt. Joseph A. Rogers, and Capt. William H. Jarvis. On the left a mile-wide gap existed between Wolff and some artillerymen in Battery 20, and on the right there was only Capt. Owen H. Hobson's second-class militia company between Jarvis and the river; Archer's battalion was effectively isolated. While a few men advanced a short distance beyond the works as skirmishers, the remainder of the command stood behind the waist-high breastworks and waited for the enemy to appear.[10]

If Archer's six companies had been at full strength, they would have numbered more than 400 men, but the long weeks of inactivity and false alarms had reduced the battalion to only a fraction of its normal complement. Archer estimated his total force on June 9, 1864, to be no more than 125 effectives, including those who returned from the city to rejoin their units. Henry Wise believed Archer had only 113 men, a participant claimed 122, and another participant was confident that no more than 96 defenders were present. Raleigh Colston, on the other hand, placed the total at slightly under 150. No matter which total is credited, the defenders of Battery 27 and the Jerusalem Plank Road were woefully few in numbers. According to Professor William B. Carr, a militiaman, Archer ordered the men to stand six feet apart, so as to give the appearance of a much larger force to the enemy. Archer also

9   Keiley, *In Vinculis*, 20-21; Cowles, OR *Atlas*, plate 40, 1; Archer, "Defense of Petersburg," 117; Glenn, "Cockade City," 9.

10 Archer, "Defense of Petersburg," 117-18; Colston, "First Assault," 536; Glenn, "Cockade City," 10; Petersburg *Daily Express*, June 13, 1864.

detailed three men to stand atop the works at wide intervals to serve as lookouts, a necessary but exceedingly dangerous task.[11]

The citizens who manned the breastworks were a diverse lot. From the available names of those who participated at Rives's farm, it appears that Archer's battalion was composed primarily of business and professional men. Of 57 whose occupations have been identified, 15 were merchants, eight were farmers, six were professors or teachers, four were clerks, three were tobacconists, two were lawyers, two were druggists, and two were ministers. Other occupations with one or more representatives included: contractor, dentist, saddle maker, cabinet maker, shoe maker, carpenter, town official, accountant, master painter, tailor, "gentleman," overseer, printer, and laborer. Many of the men were too young to have established a work history by 1864. Among the wealthiest men present were merchant and city councilman Robert A. Martin, 39, whose total worth in 1860 was nearly $43,000; lumber dealer Joseph H. Cooper, 51, with $37,500 in 1860; dry goods merchant E. A. Broadnax, 42, with $23,500 in 1860; "gentleman" Robert R. Hill, with $21,500; and Francis Major, a druggist, 59, with $21,000. At the other end of the income scale were saddle maker Peyton Alfriend, 50, whose total worth in 1860 was $150; farm worker James H. Cain, 44, and painter Thomas Chalkley, each with $100; Methodist minister John A. Jefferson, 36, with $75; and laborer Simon Crowder, 43, with $25. The poorest was undoubtedly overseer George R. Conway, who in 1860 had been able to claim no real or personal property whatsoever.[12]

Most of Archer's men were married and had large families. Grocer Thomas W. Clements, 46, had a wife and eight children. Farmer Robert H. Daniel, 52, had a wife and seven children, as did farmer John L. Emory, 42, and carpenter, James R. McCann, 48. Bank officer William C. Banister, 55, had a wife and six children, the same number as china and glass dealer James Kerr, 50, tailor Henry A. Blanks, 52, druggist George B. Jones, 42, tobacconist Norborne T. Page, 51, tailor John N. Roper, 49, and shoe maker Warren Russell, 42. City councilman and grocer James Boisseau, 45, teacher Thomas D. Davidson, 37, carriage dealer A. C. Harrison, 47, and city chamberlain John B. Stevens, 44, each had a wife and five children, and most of the others had from two to five dependents. Some men stood in line beside their older sons: Oscar F. Vaughan, 53, with his son Alexander, 16; James Kerr, 50,

11 Archer, "Defense of Petersburg," 118; Keiley, *In Vinculis*, 21; Wise, "Wise's Brigade," 12; Carr, "Battle of the 9th of June," 238; Scott and Wyatt, *Petersburg's Story*, 178; OR 36, pt. 2, 317. Years later, in Colston, "First Assault," 536, Raleigh Colston accepted the total of 125 defenders.

12 Archer, "Defense of Petersburg," 121, 135, 139; Keiley, *In Vinculis*, 25; United States Federal Census of 1860 (Virginia), National Archives.

with his son Johnny, 14; Joseph H. Cooper, 51, with his son Joseph D., 16; William Lecture, Sr., 45, with his son William, Jr., 18; and Simon Crowder, 47, with his two sons, John and William, both 21. These family groupings accent the fact that the defenders were generally either middle-aged or extremely youthful. Major Archer, the battalion commander, was 47, as were Simon Crowder, William Weddell, John E. Smith, and Robert R. Hill. Peyton Alfriend, William H. Hardee, and James Kerr were 50; James E. Wolff and Norborne T. Page were 51; Henry Blanks, Sr., Robert H. Daniel, William T. McCandlish, and George V. Scott were 52; A. S. Shafer was 53; Charles L. Bartlett and William C. Banister were 55; G. Guy Johnson and Francis Major were 59. At the other end of the scale, Johnny Kerr was 14; Joseph D. Cooper, Wayles Hurt, Joseph L. Peebles, Nathan B. Prichard, and Alexander Vaughan were 16; Samuel H. Cuykendall and William Harwood were 17; William B. Daniel and William W. Lecture were 18; and Branch T. Archer was 19.[13]

Many of the men in Archer's command need not have been behind the breastworks that morning. Several of the older men had infirmities of varying degrees such as deafness and poor eyesight. At least one of the citizen-soldiers had to carry a pocket knife to cut open his cartridges, because he did not have enough teeth left to bite them open. Such conditions could have been the basis for exemption from active participation, as could certain critical occupations such as druggist, but the presence of men in each category testifies to their patriotism. In addition, several young boys, unaffiliated with the Junior Reserves, joined the militiamen as well. Old or young, rich or poor, infirm or in sound health, all of the individuals gathered at Rives's farm were resolved to give the best possible account of themselves as they crouched behind the breastworks of the Dimmock Line.[14]

In 1861 Petersburg initially had been opposed to secession because its citizens foresaw the possibility of dire consequences. After the separation had occurred and the Confederacy created, doubts had been washed away as the bands played "Dixie," the young men marched off to war in their bright uniforms, and the news of great victories splashed across the pages of the *Daily Express*. As the months and years passed and the war dragged on with no end in sight, a gradual souring of the glittering promises of 1861 had taken place, but the full price had not yet been exacted for the choice Petersburg's citizens had made after the firing on Fort

13 United States Federal Census of 1860 (Virginia), National Archives; Archer, "Defense of Petersburg," 140-41; Petersburg *Daily Express*, June 13, 1864; Robert Alonzo Brock, *Virginia and Virginians*, 2 vols. (Richmond, VA, 1888), 2:654-55. Four years have been added to the ages found in the Census of 1860. Whatever their ages were on June 9, 1864, Archer's men invariably described themselves as "the boys."

14 Archer, "Defense of Petersburg," 139-41; Drewry, "Ninth of June," 292.

Sumter. Secession had always been a kind of dream, but until 1864 the dream had remained intact, although somewhat tarnished. Now on the morning of June 9, 1864, the dream was to be shattered for the citizens of Petersburg. Instead of bands and uniforms and victories, secession had suddenly come to mean 125 ill-equipped old men and young boys huddled behind a decaying earthwork awaiting the approach of 1,300 Federal soldiers armed with the most modern repeating weapons.

Around 11:30 a.m. two mounted pickets from Taliaferro's 7th Confederate Cavalry dashed up the Jerusalem Plank Road and into the works, shouting that the Federals were right behind them. Almost instantly the head of the blue column appeared in the distance. In the lead was Col. Samuel P. Spear's Second Brigade. Spear was an experienced soldier, but like many cavalrymen he tended to be impetuous in action. He had molded his old unit, the 11th Pennsylvania Cavalry, now under Lt. Col. George Stetzel, in the same pattern. The 11th Pennsylvania was especially noted for its ability to capture enemy pickets with a single mad rush. These tactics had usually served Spear well in the past, and when he came upon the Dimmock Line with its handful of defenders, another ideal situation for their employment seemed to be at hand. William Gregory's house and outbuildings, along with a belt of woods some distance to the rear, partially screened Spear's brief preparations from the watching militiamen, but they could see enough to know that the action would soon be joined.[15]

Spear quickly ordered Lieutenant Colonel Stetzel to send his leading squadron of four companies in a wild charge straight down the road toward Archer's men in Battery 27. Shortly after 11:30 a.m. the charge began, with the cavalrymen brandishing drawn sabers in the best European style. Heralded by a billowing cloud of dust and the thunder of hundreds of hooves, the sight was so indescribably grand that the officers of Archer's companies had difficulty keeping their men under cover of the breastworks. The men wanted to open fire immediately, but Archer called for restraint. Thus the cavalrymen were allowed to approach the works until the chevrons could be seen on the arm of the non-commissioned officer in the lead. At that point a ragged volley crashed out from the antique weapons of Archer's battalion. The Federals recoiled from the shock as the leading horse and rider went down in a heap. Suddenly the ground in the immediate front of Battery 27 was filled with rearing, plunging horses and shouting men. Some of the Federals lost control of their mounts and were carried into the Confederate lines or off at a tangent along the works. These unfortunate souls were quickly

15 Keiley, *In Vinculis*, 20, 22; OR 36, pt. 2, 309; Archer, "Defense of Petersburg," 139.

Col. Samuel P. Spear
Miller's Photographic History of the Civil War

disarmed and led to the rear, while their comrades retreated in confusion toward the Federal position. Spear's impetuous charge had cost his old regiment one killed, several wounded, and four or five captured.[16]

The Federal repulse caused a great deal of excitement and elation among Archer's men as they watched the Pennsylvanians withdraw. Unable to restrain himself, one man jumped on top of the breastworks, waved his blanket, and yelled at the Federals to "try it again." The less demonstrative contented themselves with joking about the ease of the repulse and making predictions that the enemy would be seen no more. Only a few looked upon the brief action with more insight, knowing that the affair had served to disclose beyond doubt the weakness of the Confederate position. They believed that the Federals would come again in strength, and soon.[17]

Undaunted by his lack of success, Spear was about to send a second squadron of the 11th Pennsylvania toward the Confederate works when August Kautz reached the scene with his staff. Kautz had been riding far back in the column when he heard the shooting from Spear's initial effort, and he had hastened to the front.

---

16 OR 36, pt. 2, 309, 311; OR 51, pt. 1, 1270; Eleventh Pennsylvania Cavalry, 121; Archer, "Defense of Petersburg," 118, 137, 139; Keiley, *In Vinculis*, 22. Several times earlier in his career Spear had sent the 11th Pennsylvania Cavalry regiment against manned earthworks with results similar to those of June 9, 1864. On March 17, 1863, he had ordered two charges against a redoubt at Franklin, Virginia, both of which were repulsed at a cost of up to 28 men. OR 18, 200n; Eleventh Pennsylvania Cavalry, 62. In regard to that incident, the regimental historian speculated that Spear might "not have been in proper mental condition when he ordered these charges." Apparently Spear was still afflicted with this malady 15 months later. As for the prisoners, Lieutenant Colonel Stetzel reported that four of his men were captured, one of whom soon escaped. Yet the Petersburg *Daily Express* of June 10, 1864, lists the names of four 11th Pennsylvania captives excluding the escapee, Philip Andrews. A check of the names listed in the newspaper against the regimental roster, found in Eleventh Pennsylvania Cavalry, 190-285, shows that the man called John Logan of Company D in the *Daily Express* was really John Rogan of the same company. According to the roster, Rogan deserted on June 9, 1864, but it now appears that he was one of those captured in Spear's first charge. Rogan probably died, perhaps in a Confederate prison, without ever clearing his name.

17 Archer, "Defense of Petersburg," 118, 137, 139, 140; Colston, "First Assault," 536.

Realizing that the defenders were few and that charging straight down the road gave them what little advantage they had, Kautz halted Spear's second charge and ordered that the enemy position be developed more fully by reconnaissance and skirmishing. Kautz further ordered that the entire command be deployed in front of the works. He dismounted one squadron of the 11th Pennsylvania and placed it on the right of the road, matching on the left with the entire 5th Pennsylvania, also dismounted. To balance the line, Kautz then ordered forward two dismounted squadrons of the 1st District of Columbia on the right of the 11th Pennsylvania. One squadron of the 1st D.C. was held in reserve, while the remaining two squadrons of the 11th Pennsylvania were deployed, on the extreme left and right flanks. About an hour's time was required to perfect the Federal dispositions.[18]

While Kautz paused to rearrange his forces, considerable activity was taking place within the Confederate lines. At the militia camp behind the works, the two ordnance guards, wealthy tobacco manufacturer Edmund H. Osborne, 54, and "gentleman" Robert R. Hill, 47, had watched the first charge and repulse with great interest. In the moment of comparative quiet that ensued, the guards were approached by an elderly slave named Thomas Jordan, 52. Jordan was the servant of a Confederate cavalry officer, who happened to be home on furlough on June 9. A relative of Jordan's master was in the militia and the slave had come out to the camp at Rives's farm for a visit. Seeing the Federal repulse and realizing its significance, Jordan sought Osborne, whom he had known for many years, and warned him to leave: "Marse Edmund, if you want to save your things you had better load them up and move off, for them Yankees just made that charge to find out your force, and having found that out, it will not be long before they will be here." Osborne took the advice to heart, decided to "save his things," and departed from the front. Unwilling to be left alone and unarmed, Robert Hill moved forward, found a gun, and took position behind the earthworks with the others.[19]

Hill was not alone in joining the defenders. Francis Major arrived from Petersburg about the same time, as did Brig. Gen. Raleigh Colston from Battery 16. Colston had been halfway to Archer's position when he heard the action begin at Battery 27. Seeing a section of Sturdivant's battery nearby, probably in Battery 20,

18 *OR* 36, pt. 2, 308, 310, 311, 315; Eleventh Pennsylvania Cavalry, 121; "Kautz in the Great Rebellion," August V. Kautz Papers, Library of Congress; Kautz, "Siege of Petersburg," *National Tribune*, May 18, 1899. Kautz was incensed by Spear's disastrous attack, which, as he wrote in a postwar letter to militiaman William B. Carr, "met the fate of his stupidity." Carr, "Battle of the 9th of June," 240.

19 Archer, "Defense of Petersburg," 140-41; United States Federal Census of 1870 (Virginia), National Archives.

Colston ordered the sergeant in command to limber one of his guns and follow him to the Jerusalem Plank Road. Riding ahead at a gallop, Colston arrived at Archer's position only minutes after the first charge, and in time to see the Federals deploying in a long line which overlapped the Confederates on both flanks. By virtue of his rank, Colston immediately assumed command of the defense, a situation which Archer accepted but which did not please him. Surveying Archer's dispositions, Colston found them basically sound, and simply ordered the men to extend their line left and right to counter the coming Federal envelopment. The militiamen dutifully obeyed, even though the effort seemed futile in the face of such overwhelming force. At the same time, young Branch T. Archer led a detail of men in front of the works to gather more fence rails to strengthen the barricade in the road.[20]

The interlude following the first repulse was all too brief, for Samuel Spear was impatient to have his troopers advance again. As soon as the Federal deployment was completed, they moved to the attack and sharp firing broke out all along the front. While his men answered the Federal carbines with their own smoothbore muskets, Major Archer paced up and down the line warning his men not to expose themselves recklessly. His admonitions had some effect, although several of the novice soldiers, like city councilman Charles F. Collier, continued to jump up after every shot to see whether or not their targets had fallen. As the action grew in intensity, such exposure became increasingly dangerous, especially after several Federals occupied the nearby Gregory house. Entering the house, the troopers climbed to the attic, knocked holes in the roof, and utilized the slight elevation thus attained to good advantage. Nevertheless, Archer's men continued to load and fire without flinching. Godfrey Staubly, erstwhile professor of French at the Petersburg Female College, even kept up a personal duel of sorts with one of the Federal sharpshooters.[21]

20 Archer, "Defense of Petersburg," 140-41; *OR* 36, pt. 2, 317; Colston, "First Assault," 536; Glenn, "Cockade City," 10. Archer's displeasure at being superseded is inferred from several references in Archer's account of the action, and is found in Archer, "Defense of Petersburg," 118-20. Archer was proud of his military record, which included service in two wars, and he considered himself capable of defending the position without instructions from superiors. Colston's arrival without troops of his own meant that Colston would, in effect, take Archer's command, leaving that officer in a distinctly subordinate position. In addition, because Colston had been in Petersburg for some time, Archer was probably aware of the gossip concerning Colston's hasty departure from the Army of Northern Virginia in 1863 after the Battle of Chancellorsville..

21 Archer, "Defense of Petersburg," 119, 140; Colston, "First Assault," 536; Glenn, "Cockade City," 10.

Initially, Federal progress was slow. The most immediate gains occurred on the Federal left where the 5th Pennsylvania advanced to and seized Battery 29, a detached work in front of the main line of fortifications. Lieutenant Colonel Kleinz's men could advance no farther, however, and they settled down to wait for their comrades in the 11th Pennsylvania and 1st District of Columbia to flank Archer's men out of their position east of the road. Both Colston and Archer could see the developing threat to their left and Lt. George V. Scott was ordered to take part of Wolff's company eastward to Battery 25. Realizing that Scott's force was too small to be more than a temporary expedient, Colston and Archer conferred on what to do next. It was obvious that the position could not be held without reinforcements. Colston then called for a volunteer to take a message to Henry Wise requesting aid. Lieutenant Wayles Hurt of the Junior Reserves immediately volunteered for the task. Mounted on Colston's own horse, he galloped toward Petersburg with Federal bullets kicking up dust at his heels.[22]

Somewhere on his way into town, Hurt met John Glenn hurrying to the battlefield after dallying in town getting "refreshments." Glenn was already aware that one charge had been repulsed, having gained his information from two Confederate soldiers who had been spectators and were leaving the field. Nevertheless, he asked the youthful courier for more details. Hurt was leading one of the heavy Federal cavalry horses that had been captured in the first moments of the battle, and the observant Glenn noted the strong contrast between that mount and Colston's well-bred mare. Detaining Hurt no longer, Glenn doubled his pace and soon approached the fortifications. Passing through the deserted camp, he inquired of the lone guard, Pvt. W. W. Grigg, as to the location of his company. Told that Wolff's company of second-class militia was holding the extreme left of the line, Glenn hastened to join his comrades.[23]

Not too long after John Glenn arrived at Battery 27, the rumble of wheels and the creak of harness announced the arrival of the 12-pounder howitzer Colston had ordered forward some time earlier. As the weapon and its caisson approached, Archer's men cheered loudly. Colston ordered the howitzer emplaced in Battery 28 on his right and Archer directed Capt. William H. Jarvis to extend the right flank of his company toward the gun as a support. Before the wheels stopped rolling, the gun crew leaped to the piece, unlimbered it, and prepared to go into action. The howitzer had arrived none too soon, for the Federals were also bringing up artillery

22 OR 36, pt. 2, 308, 315; Archer, "Defense of Petersburg," 119; Colston, "First Assault," 536-37. Archer reported that Hurt was sent after a consultation between the two officers, implying that he had a hand in the decision.

23 Glenn, "Cockade City," 8-9.

support. Across the way Lt. Peter Morton was emplacing his two rifled guns approximately 600 yards from the Confederate lines. He was joined by the cavalrymen manning the two small mountain howitzers belonging to the 5th Pennsylvania.[24]

The first target of the Confederate gun was the advancing line of Federal skirmishers from the 5th Pennsylvania directly in its front. Archer's men watched with pride and relief as a few quick rounds drove the Federals back to the relative safety of Battery 29. Colston next ordered the gun crew to fire upon the Federal mounted reserve beyond the Gregory house with canister. To Colston's "intense vexation," the artillery sergeant reported that he had brought no canister with him. Shell was then substituted, but the first few rounds passed over the Federals before exploding because of the extremely short range. Colston ordered the next fuse to be cut at the shortest point and stepped forward to point the piece himself. Aiming very low, Colston pulled the lanyard. The gun recoiled violently, and the shell exploded in the proper place, a little above and ahead of the mounted troopers. Colston next turned his attention to the sharpshooters in the Gregory house. In hopes of setting the house ablaze with explosive shell, he aimed several shots at the building, but the range was so short that the projectiles passed completely through the dwelling before exploding. Disgusted, Colston turned his attention to other matters. Later, Archer visited the gun position in hopes of setting the house afire, but by that time the gun's stock of explosive shells was exhausted, leaving only solid shot in the ammunition chest.[25]

While the lone Confederate howitzer ineffectually flailed away at the Gregory house, the Federal artillery was beginning to find the range. Lieutenant Peter Morton was firing both shell and case shot as rapidly as possible, and his ammunition expenditure was approaching 100 rounds. As near as he could judge, Morton's crews were firing "with great accuracy and with good execution." After a short time, however, one of his guns became disabled when the iron axle bands on the carriage broke under the shock of the discharges. With the carriage in danger of falling apart, Morton was forced to lash the axle to the carriage with rope over the tube. His many difficulties notwithstanding, Morton was making his fire felt within the Confederate lines. The bombardment was so troublesome that Major Archer began to speculate about making a charge in order to capture one of the offending pieces. When asked how he would like to make such a attack, Capt. James Wolff, no

24 Glenn, "Cockade City," 10; Keiley, *In Vinculis*, 23; Archer, "Defense of Petersburg," 118-19; Colston, "First Assault," 536; *OR* 36, pt. 2, 311, 317; *OR* 51, pt. 1, 1271.

25 Colston, "First Assault," 536; Glenn, "Cockade City," 10; Archer, "Defense of Petersburg," 119.

doubt perceiving the utter futility of the suggestion, could only reply that his men had no bayonets. Snapped out of his reverie by Colston, Archer retorted, "I do not intend to order the charge, but my order is that you increase Lieutenant Scott's force at [Battery 25]." Relieved that he was not being ordered to assume the offensive and advance to almost certain death, Wolff complied readily with the substitute directive.[26]

The uneven struggle was not destined to last much longer. While Morton's guns and the mountain howitzers of the 5th Pennsylvania pounded the Confederate position, the skirmishers of the 11th Pennsylvania and 1st District of Columbia were slowly but surely creeping around Archer's left flank. Powerless to prevent the Federal envelopment, Capt. James Wolff's company of second-class militia watched helplessly as the dismounted cavalrymen reached and took position in the house of Timothy Rives, just a few yards from Lieutenant Scott's detachment in Battery 25. Other Federals circled even farther behind the left flank until they neared the unoccupied Battery 26, almost directly in rear of the main position at Battery 27. From those two locations the Federal skirmishers began to pour a deadly hail of bullets into the rear of the Confederate defenders. Assailed from both front and rear, Archer's men began to fall in increasing numbers. Wealthy contractor John E. Friend, 33, husband and father of one, was among the first to be killed, shot by a trooper stationed behind a tree in Rives's yard. Ship chandler Lt. George V. Scott, 52, commanding the detachment in Battery 25, fell to the earth, painfully wounded through both cheeks and leg. At age 41, professor of French Godfrey Staubly lost his duel with the Federal sharpshooter as a fatal bullet found him.[27]

Seeing what was happening, Colston and Archer both realized the end was near. Colston faced a hard decision. He knew that to delay the order to retreat would cause the annihilation of Archer's men, but he also knew that every minute the position was held would enable Confederate reinforcements to come that much nearer. Colston was confident that reinforcements were indeed on the way, so he decided to withhold the order to retreat for a while longer. To buy a little more time, he desperately tried to withdraw Capt. Peyton Alfriend's company from its position in the center of his line in order to present a new front to the encircling Federals. When Alfriend's movement collapsed in failure, Colston realized that further delay would be fatal to the entire command. Reluctantly, Colston told Archer to look to

26 *OR* 51, pt. 1, 1271; Archer, "Defense of Petersburg," 120; Colston, "First Assault," 536.

27 *OR* 36, pt. 2, 310, 318; Archer, "Defense of Petersburg," 120; Colston, "First Assault," 537; Glenn, "Cockade City," 10-11.

the safety of his men and the battalion commander issued the order to fall back by the left flank.[28]

It was now every man for himself in Archer's command, especially in Captain Wolff's company of second-class militia. Most of Wolff's men began to retreat, but William C. Banister failed to hear the order to withdraw and continued to hold his ground. Called upon to surrender, he either did not hear the command or attempted to resist, for he was shot through the head and killed instantly. Near him, James Kerr dropped to one knee to give the approaching Federals one last shot and received a painful wound for his trouble. John Glenn also was wounded as he attempted to retreat. Shot in the wrist, he feared to brave the bullet-swept open ground behind the works and took refuge in a little ditch until the fighting abated. Thinking of escape a few minutes later, he arose, only to be confronted by two Federal troopers who unceremoniously took him prisoner. True to their trust, Colston and Archer remained in the thick of the fight, trying desperately to prevent the retreat from becoming a rout. In a last gesture of defiance, Colston began to pick up discarded muskets and discharge them at the advancing Federals. Near Archer, the battalion adjutant, G. Guy Johnson, was shot down. As Johnson fell mortally wounded, Archer caught the eye of city councilman Charles F. Collier and promoted him to adjutant on the spot.[29]

As Wolff's company disintegrated, the triumphant Federals overran the abandoned Confederate camp and drove westward, pushing Archer's command away from the entrenchments all along the line. Leaving the works, lawyer Anthony Keiley was falling back alongside Dr. William Bellingham when the dentist was struck by a shot that would prove to be mortal. Keiley stopped to do what he could to help his friend in his dying moments, but encouraged the city gas works superintendent, William Baxter, who had also halted, to continue his retreat. Baxter, 34, took the advice while Keiley remained behind to shift Bellingham to a more comfortable position. Having done all that he could for the dentist, Keiley rose to leave. As he did so, his path was blocked by a trooper of the 1st District of

28 OR 36, pt. 2, 318; Colston, "First Assault," 537; Archer, "Defense of Petersburg," 120. Whether intentionally or not, Archer cast aspersions on Colston's conduct when he wrote: "General Colston, seeing the desperate condition of affairs, then suggested to the commandant [Archer] that he had better take care of his men, and left the lines." Henry Wise, on the other hand, had nothing but praise for Colston's performance and thanked him personally. OR 36, pt. 2, 318-19. Throughout the remainder of his life, Colston was bitter about the way Petersburg's citizens omitted references to his role in the battle. Hampton Newsome, John Horn, and John G. Selby, *Civil War Talks* (Charlottesville, VA, 2012), 234-235n.

29 Glenn, "Cockade City," 11; OR 36, pt. 2, 319; Colston, "First Assault," 537; Archer, "Defense of Petersburg," 138.

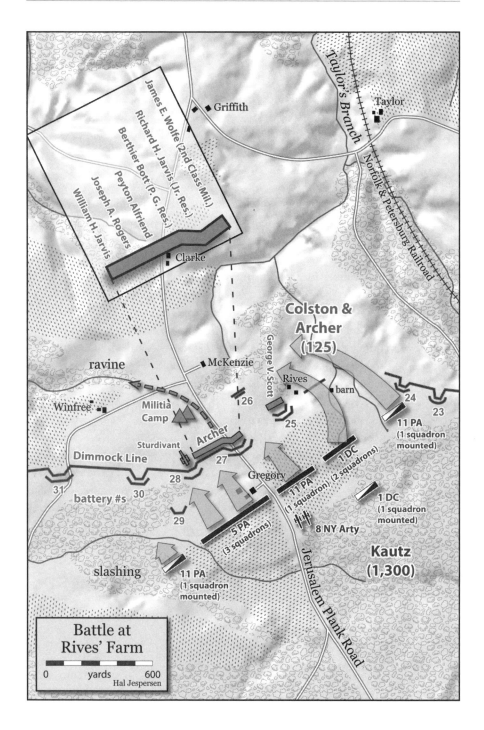

James E. Wolfe (2nd Class Mill.)
Richard H. Jarvis (Jr. Res.)
Berthier Bott (P. G. Res.)
Peyton Alfriend
Joseph A. Rogers
William H. Jarvis

Griffith

Taylor's Branch

Taylor

Norfolk & Petersburg Railroad

Clarke

Colston & Archer
(125)

ravine

McKenzie

George V. Scott

Rives

barn

24

23

Winfree

Militia Camp

Archer

Sturdivant

Dimmock Line

27

26

25

11 PA
(1 squadron mounted)

1 DC

Gregory

28

31

battery #s

30

29

5 PA
(3 squadrons)

11 PA
(1 squadron)

1 DC
(2 squadrons)

8 NY Arty

1 DC
(1 squadron mounted)

Kautz
(1,300)

slashing

11 PA
(1 squadron mounted)

Jerusalem Plank Road

Battle at
Rives' Farm

0   yards   600
Hal Jespersen

Columbia Cavalry, who jumped over the breastworks and violently demanded the lawyer's surrender.[30]

As Keiley was led away, resistance had ceased in the Confederate position except within Battery 28. There a desperate struggle continued around the lone howitzer. The cannoneers loaded and fired to the last, showing a heroism that Archer claimed he had never seen surpassed. As the Federals closed in from three sides, the sergeant commanding the piece called for the team and limber, but he was too late to save the gun. The gunners struggled valiantly to move the weapon, but a withering blast of fire at point blank range cut down the horses in their traces. One of the cannoneers also fell dead beside the howitzer and the piece was lost. The driver of the caisson tried to escape with a three-horse team, but the Federals soon caught up with him, shot him, and returned the caisson to the fortifications.[31]

The few militiamen who were able to escape ran westward through a low ravine leading back toward the heights. Before departing, Robert A. Martin fired his musket one more time, the last shot of the action. At the other end of the position, Lt. J. Frank Cummings, a member of Samuel Spear's staff, looked at his watch. It was 1:15 p.m. With the action over, most of the Federals halted within the fortifications and waited for the horse-holders to come forward with their mounts. The mounted squadron of the 11th Pennsylvania which had guarded Kautz's right flank throughout the battle now trotted up the Jerusalem Plank Road in search of more Confederates. Blocked by obstructions, the left flank squadron was unable to cut off the remnants of Archer's battalion, who made their disorganized way toward the city through fields, yards, and footpaths.[32]

The position where Archer's battalion had made its stand presented a pitiful sight to the victors. The ground in all directions was strewn with dead, dying, and wounded men—old men and boys—as well as weapons, blankets, and accoutrements of all descriptions. In Battery 28 the howitzer of Sturdivant's Battery stood mute, its blackened muzzle testifying to the number of rounds it had fired in defense of its position. Nearby stood the captured caisson, drawn up beside the gun, and by the wheel of the piece lay the dead cannoneer who had given his life in the finest traditions of the artillery service. Yet the tragic scene was not without activity. Hundreds of Federal troopers wandered around the position, gathering weapons and equipment, looking for souvenirs in the deserted camp, and herding

30 Keiley, *In Vinculis*, 24; "Historical Stories About Petersburg," Petersburg National Battlefield, Petersburg, Virginia.

31 Archer, "Defense of Petersburg," 119-20; Colston, "First Assault," 537; OR 36, pt. 2, 315.

32 Colston, "First Assault," 537; Callender, "Personal Recollections," 16; Archer, "Defense of Petersburg," 141, 141n; OR 36, pt. 2, 312, 314-15.

prisoners together into a single group. When John Glenn's captor brought him to the assembly point, the militiaman, thinking himself alone in his misfortune, was startled to find so many of his comrades already in custody. Meanwhile, other Federals peered purposefully at the nearby bushes, demanding that those hiding inside come out or be shot. Believing that they had been seen, some of those concealed by the foliage sheepishly gave themselves up. At least one, printer Richard E. Taliaferro, 30, saw through the ruse, refused to show himself, and eventually escaped.[33]

Around the captured Confederate cannon an argument broke out among the victors. All three of Kautz's regiments vigorously claimed the honor of being first in Battery 28 and laying hands on the captured howitzer. No doubt the first men to reach the gun had been too busy with more pressing matters, such as chasing Confederates, to remain by the piece and press their claim. As each successive unit reached the howitzer, it claimed the honor of the gun's capture as its own. When the original captors returned and reasserted their claim, the latecomers refused to yield. According to members of the 11th Pennsylvania, Sergeant Augustus H. Malcolm of Company A had been the first to reach the gun, but the Pennsylvanian's claim was vigorously disputed by Lieutenant Colonel Conger of the 1st District of Columbia. According to Kautz, Conger physically embraced the weapon "as if he feared someone contemplated depriving him of it." Conger was so overwrought that Kautz had to order him peremptorily to leave the gun and reform his command. Although repelled by Conger's outburst, Kautz nevertheless accepted the 1st District of Columbia Cavalry as the true captors of Sturdivant's piece.[34]

Their internal disputes notwithstanding, the Federals did not neglect the Confederate wounded who were scattered about the position. Those casualties who could be moved were carried to the Gregory house where they were treated with great kindness and humanity. Whether wounded or not, the prisoners were interrogated by Maj. James Wetherill, provost marshal of Kautz's division. A wounded man named William H. Griffith was the most talkative, although other prisoners also gave considerable information, as did slaves living in the vicinity. From these sources the Federals heard that several regiments had defended the works at Rives's farm and that Henry Wise's brigade was nearby. Anthony Keiley,

33 OR 36, pt. 2, 310, 315; Keiley, *In Vinculis*, 24-25; Glenn, "Cockade City," 11; Archer, "Defense of Petersburg," 141. According to Lieutenant Colonel Conger of the 1st District of Columbia Cavalry, "By actual count of officers, from 30 to 40 of the enemy were killed." Archer's losses were indeed grievous, but the number of killed was not nearly so high.

34 OR 36, pt. 2, 309, 310, 315; OR 51, pt. 1, 1270; *Eleventh Pennsylvania Cavalry*, 121; Kautz, "Siege of Petersburg," *National Tribune*, May 18, 1899.

who provided his captors nothing but a fictitious company designation, watched the interrogations with barely concealed amusement. As the questioning neared its end, a carriage containing elderly Timothy Rives, 57, owner of the battle site, came into the captured position. Rives, who had originally opposed secession in 1861, somehow was unaware of what had just transpired in his fields and yard. Stumbling into the hands of the Federals, he was immediately taken into custody as a Confederate. Cursing the Yankees roundly, Rives was placed under guard with the captive militiamen.[35]

The last task remaining was the destruction of Confederate military property. All of the ancient weapons, which had served Archer's battalion better than anyone could have expected, were collected and broken into useless fragments by strong-armed troopers. During the process one of the guns accidentally discharged, giving its assailant a nasty wound. All blankets and accoutrements that could be found were destroyed, as was the battalion's camp, which was burned to the ground. Ammunition and artillery supplies having been discovered in Timothy Rives's house, the torch was also applied to it, and the building was soon consumed. Their work of destruction accomplished, the troopers stood idly chatting while waiting for further orders. Their chief topic of conversation was the gallant defense made by their elderly and youthful opponents, whose tenacity was evident to all.[36]

Within Petersburg the sounds of the battle at Rives's farm were clearly audible. Fanny Waddell heard it from her sickbed. Bessie Callender heard it while working in her garden. William Cameron heard it from his vantage point on the heights at the southern edge of the city. Others heard it too and winced as the crackle of musketry rose and fell, fearing that some relative or friend had been struck with each volley. Still, there was no panic, only a growing apprehension about the outcome. Certainly there was no panic among the men gathered downtown in Erasmus O. Hinton's drugstore. There the conversation tended toward boastful hyperbole. Thomas Campbell, president of the South Side Railroad, remarked that it was impossible to imagine a serious Federal threat to the city. Scornfully rejecting the report that the attackers numbered in the thousands, Campbell boasted:

---

35 Petersburg *Daily Express*, June 10, 1864, and June 13, 1864; Keiley, *In Vinculis*, 24-27; OR 36, pt. 2, 314; Glenn, "Cockade City," 14-15. Griffith, a Prince George County farmer, apparently had seen brief early war service in a cavalry unit, but does not appear on the rolls of Archer's command. As a native of Pennsylvania, he would most likely have felt free to converse with his Pennsylvania captors. He was wounded in both legs. United States Federal Census of 1860 (Virginia), National Archives; Compiled Service Records of Virginia Troops, National Archives.

36 OR 36, pt. 2, 310, 312; Keiley, *In Vinculis*, 25; Petersburg *Daily Express*, June 10, 1864; Eleventh Pennsylvania Cavalry, 122.

"Gentlemen, give me a brigade of twenty-five hundred men, and I will obligate myself to drive every Yankee this side of City Point into James River before sunset this evening." This absurd pledge struck one of Campbell's listeners as ludicrous, and he jokingly responded: "If Mr. Campbell will do this, he must have the brigade. Can't we get him the 2500 men? He must have them. It will not do to lose the opportunity to drive those Yankees into James River." In like fashion the banter continued.[37]

Standing in his hilltop yard, William Cameron saw no humor in the situation whatsoever. He had been listening to the firing for some time but had been unable to see anything because of the intervening woods. Suddenly he saw a few men emerge from the tree line in the distance and retreat toward the ravine gouged by Lieutenant Run as it flowed to the Appomattox. As Cameron watched, the number of people streaming toward him increased, and it was apparent from their disorganization and haste that they had not been victorious. Behind them came a column of mounted men in blue uniforms. Cameron continued to watch as the Federals turned from the Jerusalem Plank Road into New Road, which bisected the ravine, and began to descend to the stream.[38]

Not far away, Bessie Callender saw them too. From her upstairs window she could clearly see that they were Yankees from the style of their uniforms. Going downstairs into her yard, Mrs. Callender noticed several slaves hurrying past laden with clothing, bedding, and other personal possessions. Recognizing them as residents of a farm near the militia camp, she excitedly questioned them about the situation there. Their answer was alarming: all of the militia had been killed or captured and the Yankees were preparing to enter the city. Unable to keep the disastrous tidings to herself, she headed across the street toward the home of her neighbor, Jane Weddell, whose husband William had gone to Battery 27 with David Callender some hours before. Entering the house unannounced, she found the Reverend William A. Hall, chaplain of the Washington Artillery Battalion of New Orleans, seated at a table writing a letter. Hall and Mrs. Weddell were quickly informed of what Bessie Callender had seen and heard. Seeing the agitation of the women, Hall tried to reassure them: "Do not be alarmed, ladies; I will go out to the camp, and if I do not return you may be sure I am in camp with the 'boys.'" When

37 David Macrae, *The Americans at Home: Pen-and-Ink Sketches of American Men Manners and Institutions* (1870; New York, NY, 1952), 157; Callender, "Personal Recollections," 14; Archer, "Defense of Petersburg," 135-36; Petersburg *Daily Express*, June 13, 1864.

38 Archer, "Defense of Petersburg," 136.

Hall departed, Bessie Callender, only partially reassured, returned to her second-story vantage point and continued to watch for her husband.[39]

As Reverend Hall made his way toward Rives's farm, the news of the disaster that had befallen Archer's command spread rapidly through the city. On every hand the cry rang out that "The militia have been cut to pieces. The Yankees will be here directly." Citizens who earlier had been only vaguely apprehensive now began to focus more clearly upon what the arrival of the hated Federals would mean to them personally. In Erasmus Hinton's drugstore, Thomas Campbell had just pledged to rout every Federal in sight when Otway P. Hare, 61, dashed excitedly through the door with word from the front. "Gentlemen, h—l is to pay! The Yankees in considerable force have advanced to the toll-gate [near Rives's farm] on the Jerusalem plank road, have broken our lines, killed Geo. B. Jones, Wm. C. Banister and Jno. Friend, and will soon be here." Following Hare's announcement, the group dispersed in no little confusion as each man, including Thomas Campbell, ran off to look after his own affairs. As the names of known casualties spread throughout the town, their children were summoned home from school, and the resulting uproar caused at least one schoolmaster to call an end to classes. Heedless of the danger, relatives of men whose fate was not yet known rushed to Reservoir Hill. From that vantage point and others on the heights south of the city, the assembled citizens could see the Federal column preparing to make its final advance.[40]

North of the Appomattox River at Dunlop's, P. G. T. Beauregard could not hear the sounds of action at Rives's farm, but he was nevertheless aware that the battle was going badly. Around 1:00 p.m. he received a terse message from Henry Wise: "The enemy have taken the works on the Jerusalem plank road and are advancing into town. Send me reinforcements at once." Having already detached a cavalry regiment from Bermuda Hundred, Beauregard could send no more aid to beleaguered Petersburg without jeopardizing his position opposite Butler. Telegraphing Wise to "do the best possible with his present forces," Beauregard attempted once more to force the Confederate War Department to give him guidance. In a 1:00 p.m. telegram to Braxton Bragg, he reported Wise's situation and again stated that he could hold either Petersburg or Bermuda Hundred, but not both: what should he do? Thirty minutes later, with no answer from Richmond, Beauregard again telegraphed Wise: "I cannot furnish you at present with reinforcements. Defend the place to the last, and, if compelled, retire, fighting, in

39 Archer, "Defense of Petersburg," 142; Callender, "Personal Recollections," 14-15.

40 Glenn, "Cockade City," 12; Archer "Defense of Petersburg," 135, 142-43; Drewry, "Ninth of June," 292-93.

the direction of Swift Creek Bridge." The message to Wise notwithstanding, at the same time Beauregard ordered the 64th Georgia Infantry regiment to leave its position on Swift Creek and march southward toward Petersburg.[41]

In Richmond, 20 miles north of Dunlop's, Beauregard's morning telegrams had not aroused any particular anxiety. Braxton Bragg had acknowledged the early messages with a simple statement that the problem was being considered and that while waiting for a decision, Beauregard might telegraph directly to General Lee for support. Bragg had then discussed the situation with Secretary of War James A. Seddon, and Beauregard had been notified that neither reinforcements nor instructions would be forthcoming. Having decided that assistance was neither warranted nor possible, the Confederate War Department continued to cling to that position even after Beauregard's telegram of 1:00 p.m. reached Richmond. As far as Bragg and Seddon were concerned, both the problem and the responsibility remained Beauregard's. Seddon's endorsement on a later message bespoke his attitude toward Beauregard: "As commandant of the department he must decide on the proper employment of his forces under the emergency. This will place the responsibility where it properly belongs." Any further response to the crisis at Petersburg would have to come from the dapper little general pacing the floor at Dunlop's.[42]

Beauregard apparently did not contact Robert E. Lee, whom he regarded as a rival for Richmond's attention, but Bragg forwarded Beauregard's morning telegrams to the Army of Northern Virginia. In addition, President Jefferson Davis dispatched a letter of his own to Lee: "General Beauregard reports the enemy moving upon Petersburg, but our scouts give no information as to the arrival of troops from below, and if none have come I cannot believe the attack to be of much force." Although Lee's headquarters was not far from Richmond, he did not receive Bragg's message containing Beauregard's morning telegrams until 2:30 p.m. To Lee it seemed that Beauregard really had no problem at all, and he sent Beauregard a reassuring telegram, which closed: "The force seen by General Wise is small, truly—a reconnaissance to discover your operations." In a similar note to

41 OR 36, pt. 3, 885; OR 51, pt. 2, 1000; Roman, *Military Operations*, 2:566; P. G. T. Beauregard to J. H. Pearce, 1:00 p.m., June 9, 1864, P. G. T. Beauregard to Henry Wise, 1:30 p.m., June 9, 1864, and P. G. T. Beauregard to J. H. Pearce, 1:30 p.m., June 9, 1864, all in Official Telegrams, April 22-June 9, 1864, P. G. T. Beauregard Papers, Library of Congress; P. G. T. Beauregard to Commanding Officer, 64th Georgia Infantry regiment, June 9, 1864, Letter Book, May-July 1864, P. G. T. Beauregard Papers, Library of Congress.

42 Roman, *Military Operations*, 2:566; OR 51, pt. 2, 999-1000. According to Beauregard's biographer, the Confederate government did not take Beauregard's pleas seriously. T. Harry Williams, *P. G. T. Beauregard: Napoleon in Gray* (Baton Rouge, LA, 1955), 226.

Bragg, Lee offered to send reinforcements, even though he thought it unnecessary. Lee, Davis, Seddon, and Bragg all seemed to believe that Beauregard was overreacting and therefore sent him nothing but soothing messages. None of them would have considered it possible that at 1:30 p.m. a strong Federal force would be making its way into Petersburg, seemingly unopposed, yet that was exactly what was happening.[43]

43 Roman, *Military Operations*, 2:566; OR 51, pt. 2, 996; Dowdey and Manarin, *Wartime Papers*, 770. The relationship between Lee and Beauregard is described by one historian as follows: "Potentially and actually Lee and Beauregard were unequal collaborators, but because of Beauregard's ambition and the opportunities provided by the departmental system, he became in effect Lee's rival. The conflict between them began over which general would get the use of the spare troops." Clifford Dowdey, *Lee's Last Campaign* (Boston, MA, 1960), 245.

Chapter 5

"In the Midst of Life
We Are In Death"

In the midst of the Federal victory celebration at Rives's farm, August Kautz remembered his mission to destroy the Appomattox River bridges and began organizing a new advance to do so. Because neither Lt. Col. Conger nor his command had recovered control of themselves, Kautz assigned the task to Col. Samuel Spear's Second Cavalry Brigade. As usual, a squadron of Spear's old regiment, the 11th Pennsylvania, took the lead.

Skirmishers, preceding the column in open order, suddenly confronted Lt. Wayles Hurt, who was returning from his mission to Henry Wise's headquarters. In a brief melee the teenager was killed. Recognizing Hurt's mount (Raleigh Colston's mare) to be a valuable thoroughbred, a trooper seized the frightened animal as a prize of war. Resuming their advance, the cavalrymen next encountered Reverend William A. Hall, who was looking for the militia camp. Hall eventually found the militiamen when he joined them as a prisoner of war. Unhindered by any organized resistance, the squadron of the 11th Pennsylvania advanced effortlessly to an open plateau where New Road joined the Jerusalem Plank Road from the west. There the troopers halted to await reinforcements. To their left, New Road disappeared into a deep ravine before climbing Reservoir Hill, which appeared to be crowned by an earthen fortification.[1]

1 OR 36, pt. 2, 312; Kautz, "Siege of Petersburg," *National Tribune*, May 18, 1899; "Kautz in the Great Rebellion," August V. Kautz Papers, Library of Congress; Colston, "First Assault," 537n; Archer, "Defense of Petersburg," 119-20, 142; Glenn, "Cockade City," 8-9; Callender, "Personal Recollections," 15. Released in the subsequent confusion, Colston's mare was returned to him unharmed after the battle.

The Pennsylvanians were soon strengthened by the arrival of Kautz, Spear, the remaining gun of Lieutenant Morton's artillery section, and additional companies of the 11th Pennsylvania. No Confederates were visible on the hill beyond Lieutenant Run, so Kautz ordered a portion of the command to advance on Petersburg via New Road while the remainder of the column continued forward on the Jerusalem Plank Road toward the suburb of Blandford. As the advance guard of the 11th Pennsylvania, followed closely by Morton's gun, descended New Road into the ravine, there appeared to be nothing between them and their goal. The road was narrow and the banks of the ravine were high, but most of the troopers were not apprehensive. Reaching the bottom of the ravine and crossing Lieutenant Run, the cavalrymen drew their sabers and prepared to charge into the streets of Petersburg as soon as they gained the heights. The leading troopers were nearing the crest and Morton was approaching the stream with his piece when the top of the hill exploded with artillery and small-arms fire.[2]

Petersburg's saviors were two of her adopted sons, Brig. Gen. James Dearing and Capt. Edward Graham. Although neither was a native of the city, both had become identified with it through family connections. The son of a British army officer and a native of Northern Ireland, Edward Graham, 36, had come to Petersburg to join the business of his cousin, Archibald Graham McIlwaine. A lieutenant in the prewar Petersburg Artillery, he had enlisted with his company in 1861 and had risen to be its captain. James Dearing, a native of Campbell County, Virginia, had never been a resident of Petersburg, but had married a Prince George County woman. A cadet at West Point in 1861, Dearing had returned to Virginia to serve as an artillery commander in the Army of Northern Virginia. Transferring to the cavalry, Dearing had risen rapidly in rank. A brigadier general of cavalry since April 29, 1864, Dearing at the tender age of 24 now led the meager reinforcements Beauregard had been able to spare for the defense of the Cockade City.[3]

2   *OR* 36, pt. 2, 308-09, 312; *OR* 51, pt. 1, 1271; Colston, "First Assault," 537; Kautz, "Siege of Petersburg," *National Tribune*, May 18, 1899; "Kautz in the Great Rebellion," August V. Kautz Papers, Library of Congress.

3   Glenn, "Cockade City," 12-13; Scott and Wyatt, *Petersburg's Story*, 180; Boatner, *Civil War Dictionary*, 228; Warner, *Generals in Gray*, 69-70. Dearing's short life is chronicled in William L. Parker, *General James Dearing CSA* (Lynchburg, VA, 1990), but the brief June 9, 1864, section adds nothing new to the story of that day.

Brig. Gen. James Dearing
Centre Hill Museum

Upon receiving Beauregard's midmorning order to move to Petersburg, Dearing started Col. Dennis D. Ferebee's 4th North Carolina Cavalry and Graham's Petersburg Battery from their camp behind the right side of the Bermuda Hundred lines at Mary Dunn's farm, seven miles from the city. Crossing the Appomattox River on Pocahontas Bridge, Dearing led his command up Second Street. Sending a staff officer, Capt. William E. Hinton, Jr., to Henry Wise for deployment instructions, Dearing turned his men into Lombard (now Bank) Street and headed eastward, assuming he was needed at Battery 5. Hinton meanwhile learned from Wise's staff that Dearing should take his troops to the Wilcox farm, some distance west of Battery 27. Dearing's column had moved down Lombard Street as far as its intersection with Main Street (now Crater Road) in Blandford when Hinton appeared with the new instructions. At that point, Dearing was probably joined by Col. Valentine H. Taliaferro and part of his 7th Confederate Cavalry, the unit which had opened the battle against Gillmore many hours earlier. Rather than attempt to reverse the column in Petersburg's narrow streets, Dearing directed a left turn on Main Street to Bollingbrook Street, where another left turn would bring the column back to downtown Petersburg. There a final left turn on Sycamore Street would finally point the cavalrymen toward their destination.[4]

---

4 Archer, "Defense of Petersburg," 131-32; Glenn, "Cockade City," 13; Roman, *Military Operations*, 2:225; M. Clifford Harrison, "Petersburg's Ninth of June," in *Virginia Cavalcade* (Summer 1958), 8:13; Neil Hunter Raiford, *The 4th North Carolina Cavalry in the Civil War: A History and Roster* (Jefferson, NC, 2003), 69. There are two unresolved questions regarding Dearing's march. First, Dearing's staff officer Captain Hinton claimed that the command left the Bermuda Hundred works before daylight on June 9, which, if true, means that the command took approximately nine hours (from 4:30 a.m. to 1:30 p.m.) to travel a little over seven miles. It is unlikely, however, that Beauregard ordered Dearing's troops to Wise's aid until after hearing that the city was under attack around 9:00 a.m. Second, Butler's signalmen kept a constant watch from the tower at Point of Rocks upon the railroad and turnpike leading

Realizing the need for haste, Dearing ordered the movement to be executed at a gallop. Graham's artillery was in the lead, and once Bollingbrook was reached, the drivers lashed their teams. Even with the excitement of the morning's events, residents were unprepared for the sight of straining, foam-flecked teams galloping up the street with wildly careening limbers, guns, and caissons in tow. Miss Lossie Hill, "an old lady and quite a character," was just crossing the street when Graham's battery came charging into view and she barely escaped injury as they thundered past. Seeing her, and others in equally dangerous positions, Graham cried out, "D—n the women! Run over them if they don't get out of the way!" Influenced either by Graham's unchivalrous words or by the sight of the flashing hooves and churning wheels, the civilians scampered to safety while the battery continued its wild course downtown, closely followed by Ferebee's cavalrymen. Reaching Sycamore Street, the column slowed briefly to make the turn but soon accelerated again. Erasmus Hinton, who had stepped from his drugstore to watch the action, was appalled to see one of the guns break loose from its limber and slide to a halt in front of him. Fearing the worst, he was reassured when the artillerymen braked their team, raced back to the piece, re-coupled it to the limber, and charged up the street once more.[5]

As the column rolled up Sycamore Street the citizens realized that it was their own Petersburg Battery that was coming to their rescue. Bystanders cheered and shouted, "Here come our own men! Men who will defend us and drive the enemy back!" For some, the recognition was even more personal. Thomas Shanks, a member of the battery, saw the wife of William Baxter, a militiaman with Archer, and shouted as he passed, "Matilda, you'd better get home 'cause the Yankees are coming!" For everyone on the streets, the sight of Confederate reinforcements bravely dashing forward amid the joyful cheers

---

south into Petersburg and they saw no evidence of Dearing's approach. The tower not only provided a view of the surrounding countryside, but also a valuable glimpse into some of the streets of the city itself. Yet the movement of Graham's battery and Ferebee's cavalry regiment into Petersburg was apparently and inexplicably unobserved. *OR* 36, pt. 2, 279; *OR* 36, pt. 3, 718, 719. In some accounts, the Mary Dunn farm near Port Walthall Junction is identified as the Ruffin farm. See testimony of William E. Hinton, Jr. and John Trusheim in Archer, "Defense of Petersburg," 132.

5 Archer, "Defense of Petersburg," 132, 134, 135; Margaret Stanley Beckwith, "Reminiscences, 1844-1865," Virginia Historical Society, Richmond, Virginia.

and waves of the assembled women and children was an experience never to be forgotten.[6]

When Dearing's command had gone about halfway out Sycamore Street, it was met by Edmund Osborne, the militiaman who had "saved his things" at Rives's farm. Osborne told Dearing that the Federals were approaching on the Jerusalem Plank Road. Hearing Osborne's story, Capt. Hinton quickly pointed out that to continue to the Wilcox farm in light of the new information would render the command useless. Pausing a moment to consider the terrain relationships, Dearing then decided to divide his tiny force. He ordered Col. Taliaferro to take his detachment of the 7th Confederate Cavalry regiment and their small mountain howitzer back to Blandford and make a stand near the historic Blandford Church. As Taliaferro departed, Dearing, with Graham's battery and Ferebee's 4th North Carolina Cavalry regiment, continued south on Sycamore Street with redoubled effort.[7]

Previously, Graham's men had been riding on the limbers and caissons but, as the grade increased, they dismounted and ran alongside the pieces. Thus lightened, the guns fairly bounded up the incline, past the Southern Female College where the students waved their handkerchiefs in encouragement, past the convalescent hospital at Poplar Lawn where the recuperating veterans remarked that they had never seen artillery travel faster. Ahead of them dashed Edward Graham, seeking a site to emplace the guns. Returning to the column, he ordered the first two guns to turn left on Fillmore Street and then right on Jefferson, ending up on the crest of Reservoir Hill just south of the water works. The other two guns continued to the end of Sycamore Street, where William Cameron's residence "Mount Erin" stood. Behind all of them came a stream of women and children planning to watch the battle for their city.[8]

Standing at an upstairs window in company with her mother, Bessie Callender saw the first two of Graham's pieces go into position at the reservoir. As she watched, a small group of cavalrymen arrived to support the guns but seemed to hesitate and then to withdraw slightly. Appalled at such timid actions, the woman who hours earlier had not been alarmed at the ringing of the

6 Archer, "Defense of Petersburg," 132; "Historical Stories About Petersburg," Petersburg National Battlefield, Petersburg, Virginia.

7 Archer, "Defense of Petersburg," 131.

8 Archer, "Defense of Petersburg," 132-34, 136, 142-43; Glenn, "Cockade City," 13-14; Drewry, "Ninth of June," 292-93.

Capt. Edward Graham
Centre Mill Museum

warning bells now feared that Dearing's men were not going to fight. Turning to her mother, in anguished tones she blurted, "They are not going to make a stand, but are going to leave us in the Yankees' hands." Having seen much more tribulation than her daughter, the older woman calmly replied, "My child, God will be us just as much then as now."[9]

Not far from Bessie Callender's location, William Cameron never doubted that the Confederates would stand. Cameron had been watching the Federal advance for some time and had sent his family away to safety when Spear's cavalrymen began to move in his direction. He himself had remained standing at the gate of his property in an attempt to protect his belongings from destruction. While waiting for the Federals to arrive, he had been startled by the noise of Graham's guns ascending the incline in his rear. Now he watched with satisfaction as two of the pieces came directly toward him. The guns, under the command of Lts. Edward Pollard and William C. Butler, were speedily unlimbered, one on each side of Cameron's house. From that position they had a clear field of fire across the ravine to the plateau where New Road joined the Jerusalem Plank Road. Even before the guns at Cameron's could open, the other section of Graham's battery was in action, and not a moment too soon, because the leading Federal troopers were no more than 100 yards from the gunners. Quickly the drivers swung the teams around while some cannoneers unlimbered the guns and others prepared the first round. That shot stunned the Federals, halting them in their tracks.[10]

James Dearing, who had commanded George Pickett's artillery at Gettysburg and who remained an artilleryman at heart, personally supervised

---

9 Archer, "Defense of Petersburg," 143; Callender, "Personal Recollections," 15.

10 Archer, "Defense of Petersburg," 132-33, 136.

the location of the two guns at the reservoir and only then looked to his cavalry. He ordered Lt. Col. John L. Cantwell to charge the leading Federal squadron with a portion of the 4th North Carolina, while the remainder of the regiment deployed as skirmishers from the reservoir on the left to beyond Cameron's house on the right. Behind the cavalry skirmish line the shattered remnants of Archer's battalion gathered on the crest. Still at their posts, Raleigh Colston and Fletcher Archer halted the few militiamen that had escaped the Rives's farm debacle and formed them once more into line. With the situation stabilized and the militia rescued, Dearing resumed directing the fire of the guns at the reservoir.[11]

Unlike Graham's section at Cameron's house, which could only be brought to bear on the distant plateau, the guns at the reservoir could fire into the Federals milling about in confusion in the road cut just on the other side of Lieutenant Run. Dearing was clearly in his element as he directed fire first upon the Federals in the road cut, then upon a house on the plateau which he thought sheltered Federal officers, and finally upon what appeared to be another Federal battery trying to get into firing position. Watching Dearing's performance from his yard, William Cameron was astonished by the sight. Twenty-eight years later, the scene he witnessed on June 9, 1864, was still vividly imprinted on his memory: "I remember, too, that when seeing the rapid firing from the two guns on the reservoir hill, and the firing from the other two guns, and the bursting of their shells, I thought it looked as if almost the whole heavens were filled with the fire of blazing guns and exploding shells." Seeing the Federals waver, Dearing ordered a gradual advance by the 4th North Carolina under cover of Graham's fire. As the Confederate cavalrymen pushed forward, the Federals turned and departed the way they had come, hastened by two parting shots from the guns in Cameron's yard.[12]

The first blast from Graham's guns had thrown the advance guard of the 11th Pennsylvania into confusion, although it missed them completely. The aggressive charge by Lieutenant Colonel Cantwell's detachment, coupled with

11 Archer, "Defense of Petersburg," 120, 131-33, 143; Colston, "First Assault," 537; OR 36, pt. 2, 318.

12 Archer, "Defense of Petersburg," 133-34, 137. The Federal battery on the plateau may have been the mountain howitzers of one of the Pennsylvania regiments. More likely, Dearing's gunners shot at the mountain howitzer of Taliferro's 7th Confederate Cavalry regiment on the Baxter Road, which was firing on the portion of the 11th Pennsylvania Cavalry regiment that had reached the outskirts of Blandford.

the rapid fire of Graham's four guns, soon had the leading Federals in flight down Reservoir Hill. The troopers withdrew pell-mell down the slope to the bottom of the ravine, where they ran into Lieutenant Morton's single artillery piece. Many of Morton's men were caught up in the wild dash for safety and carried unwillingly to the rear. Left standing in the road without a visible support, Morton had no choice but to try to save his gun. Before the order to retreat could be executed, two of the horses of the gun team were shot down. As the drivers struggled to free the dying animals from the harness, another horse was felled by a shell fragment and the remaining three collapsed as well. Morton had no choice but to leave the gun or be captured with his remaining gunners. Nevertheless, Morton's men held fast until the gun was spiked, rendering it temporarily useless to the advancing Confederates. Only then did Peter Morton's artillerymen look to their own safety.[13]

On the far side of the ravine Colonel Spear labored to rally his shaken squadron. When the men regained their composure, he ordered a slow withdrawal to the plateau and the Jerusalem Plank Road. On the plateau he found August Kautz and reported his impressions of the Confederate position to the division commander. According to Spear, the Confederates had an inner line of earthworks on Reservoir Hill. He described the fortifications as very strong, and reinforced by a wooden stockade. As he approached to within 150 yards of the works, he had been fired upon by both infantry and artillery. Luckily, in Spear's opinion, the Confederates had sprung their trap too soon and he had been able to extricate his command. Otherwise, "the most fearful results . . . would have ensued." Whatever Kautz may have thought of Spear's report, it was seriously in error. Needless to say, the only earthworks facing Spear were the earthen retaining walls of the city reservoir.[14]

While Spear and Kautz discussed the situation on Reservoir Hill, the other prong of Kautz's thrust into the city also encountered resistance. Spear had led only one squadron of the 11th Pennsylvania along New Road; the remainder of

13 *OR* 36, pt. 2, 309; *OR* 51, pt. 1, 1271. In his after-action report, Lieutenant Morton complained bitterly about the cavalry, who "had not gone fifty yards when they wheeled and came back and passed me on a full run, taking off my cannoneers and left me entirely exposed."

14 *OR* 36, pt. 2, 312-14; Archer, "Defense of Petersburg," 147. Spear was not the only officer to be fooled by the Confederate "defenses." According to Lt. J. Frank Cummings, a staff officer, "The next line of defenses consisted of stockades on very high bluffs. The battery that opened on the Second Cavalry Brigade was behind the stockades. The stockade was defended by both infantry and artillery." No doubt the "stockades" were yard and garden fences.

Reservoir Hill
Battles and Leaders

the regiment had followed the Jerusalem Plank Road into the suburb of Blandford. While Dearing and Graham were decisively checking Spear, the other troopers were halted by an assemblage even more disparate in composition than Archer's battalion. During the morning the city's military hospitals had been scoured for any men able to walk and fire a weapon. Enough convalescents had been found to form a small company under a Captain Lockhart and a Lieutenant Lindsay. Another composite company had been formed from the military prisoners held in the city jail by Lt. Napoleon B. Hawes, the provost marshal, and they too had been sent forward. Initially, only these two groups, later styled "the patients and the penitents," faced the squadrons of the 11th Pennsylvania as they entered Blandford.[15]

Fortunately for the Confederates, the crippled and the sinful did not make their stand alone. Gillmore's departure had permitted Henry Wise to detach three companies of the 46th Virginia from Battery 9, and he now led the companies into position on the Federal right flank. The detachment of Taliaferro's 7th Confederate Cavalry which had left Dearing's column on Sycamore Street also joined the Blandford defenders, as did another gun from Sturdivant's battery. The aggressive front displayed by this heterogeneous force and its apparent arrival from all directions created consternation in the Federal ranks and caused them first to hesitate, then withdraw. The Federals were

---

15 OR 36, pt. 2, 312, 316; Petersburg *Daily Express*, June 13, 1864; Drewry, "Ninth of June," 292; Roman, *Military Operations*, 2:224-25; Wise, "Wise's Brigade," 12; "Manuscript of Gen. H. A. Wise Relative to Battle of Petersburg, Va. in June, 1864," P. G. T. Beauregard Papers, Library of Congress; Kenneth Radley, *Rebel Watchdog: The Confederate States Army Provost Guard* (Baton Rouge, LA, 1989), 271. For a graphic description of the "penitents," see the Charles Campbell Diary, 5-7 May, 1864, Charles Campbell Papers, Earl Greg Swem Library, College of William and Mary, Williamsburg, Virginia. Campbell found the prisoners to be filthy, profane, and generally disgusting, but some of them served the Confederacy well on June 9, 1864.

followed by a few shells from Sturdivant's gun and from a small mountain howitzer manned by another detachment of Taliaferro's men. Located on the Baxter Road in the Federal right-rear, the mountain howitzer gave a good account of itself as the Pennsylvanians passed across its front. In their haste to depart, the Federals made no attempt to capture the isolated piece, which encountered no fire except overshots from Graham's guns on the heights.[16]

With both elements of the 11th Pennsylvania momentarily checked, Kautz directed that the regiment rejoin the remainder of the command at Rives's farm. On returning to the scene of the militia's defeat, Samuel Spear entered the Gregory house where a number of the Confederate wounded had been taken. Questioning each of the Confederates separately, Spear summed up their testimony: "Beauregard had a large force (they could not state the number) between the Appomattox and Swift Creek, and that the town of Petersburg could be and was reinforced by him." From the prisoners' statements and from distant sounds which he took to be the arrival of trains, Spear concluded that it would require from 8,000 to 10,000 troops to occupy Petersburg. Having satisfied himself that the cavalry could do nothing further, Spear rewarded his informants with brandy from his personal supplies, washed his face, and took a short nap while waiting for further orders.[17]

While Spear took his ease, August Kautz pondered his options. Unlike Spear, he was not particularly impressed by the strength of Petersburg's defenders, but he knew that they could delay him for at least another hour. Nothing had been heard from Gillmore's columns, causing Kautz to conclude that the infantry was already marching back to Bermuda Hundred. Without pressure from Gillmore, the Confederate forces on the Dimmock Line could gather in Kautz's rear while he rode deeper into the town, thereby blocking his escape. By continuing the attack he might eventually reach the Appomattox bridges, but it would risk the loss of his entire command. Believing the safety of his 1,300 troopers to be paramount, Kautz reluctantly concluded that nothing more realistically could be achieved at Petersburg at the time. Consequently he ordered the bugler to sound recall, formed his division, gathered the prisoners

---

16 Roman, *Military Operations*, 2:224-25; Wise, "Wise's Brigade," 12; Petersburg *Daily Express*, June 13, 1864; "Manuscript of Gen. H. A. Wise Relative to Battle of Petersburg, Va. in June, 1864," P. G. T. Beauregard Papers, Library of Congress. In Colston, "First Assault," 537, Sturdivant was credited with having two guns present.

17 *OR* 36, pt. 2, 309, 313; Petersburg *Daily Express*, June 13, 1864.

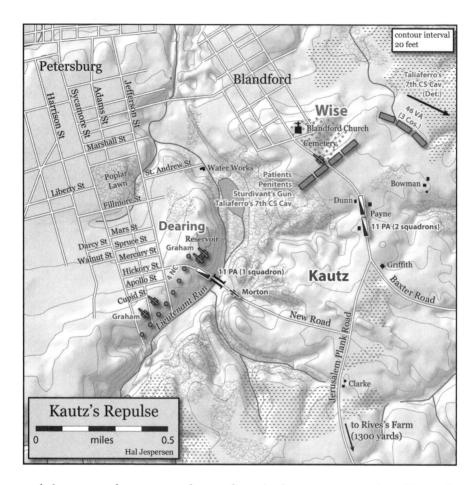

Kautz's Repulse

0   miles   0.5

Hal Jespersen

contour interval
20 feet

and the captured cannon, and started on the long return march to Bermuda Hundred.[18]

It was probably after 3:00 p.m. when Kautz's rear guard left the Dimmock Line. Four miles away at Thomas Baylor's clover field Quincy Gillmore's infantrymen were just finishing their dinner. By 3:30 p.m. Gillmore, too, was withdrawing to Bermuda Hundred with the brigades of Hawley and Hinks. The troops were exhausted, especially Hawley's men, who had marched or skirmished almost continually since 10:30 p.m. the previous night. During the afternoon the effects of the long hours in the swamp the night before and the bright midday sun on the open plain began to take their toll. Despite the risk of

18 OR 36, pt. 2, 309; Keiley, *In Vinculis*, 33; Kautz, "Siege of Petersburg," *National Tribune*, May 18, 1899; "Kautz in the Great Rebellion," August V. Kautz Papers, Library of Congress.

sunstroke, which cost more casualties in the 3rd New Hampshire than Confederate bullets, the officers allowed no rest periods whatsoever. Nevertheless, straggling was almost nonexistent. Usually during such a march men would surreptitiously fall out of the column for an unauthorized rest, then hasten to rejoin their unit before their absence was discovered, but this march was different. The Federals knew they were in Confederate territory and that a lone foot soldier separated from his unit risked spending the remainder of the war in a Confederate prison. Such fears kept the ranks full, leaving the men nothing to do but curse their officers and continue to place one foot before the other.[19]

As they tramped along, the infantrymen noticed their surroundings more closely than they had done on the approach march many hours before. Their impressions varied: some noted the verdant fields of corn and grain, while others were struck by the blackened chimneys dotting the countryside at intervals, evidence of forays by the City Point garrison. At last the Spring Hill fortifications came into view and then the pontoon bridge which had been so elusive on the previous night. For the 62nd Ohio in the rear of Hawley's brigade, Spring Hill was home, and there Lieutenant Colonel Taylor's regiment took leave of the expedition. Edward Hinks's men had already left the column for their own bivouac within the City Point fortifications. Just before sunset Hawley's brigade crossed the pontoon bridge, but it would be nearly 9:00 p.m. before his dirty, footsore, and disgusted men finally stumbled into their camps.[20]

Quincy Gillmore must have known he had failed to accomplish much, but he probably did not expect to be treated too harshly for his lapses. After crossing the pontoon bridge he stopped at Butler's headquarters to see if any word had come from Kautz, but Butler had no information about the cavalry. As he rode to his own camp, Gillmore must have realized that if Kautz and his men had gotten into trouble, his uncontested withdrawal of the infantry would not be viewed favorably. To ease his conscience and maintain his reputation,

19 OR 36, pt. 2, 289, 301, 303, 315; Eldredge, *Third New Hampshire*, 493-94; Little, *Seventh New Hampshire*, 264. According to the commander of the 5th Pennsylvania Cavalry, his unit left Battery 27 around 2:00 p.m., but if the works were entered at 1:15 p.m., this would leave only 45 minutes for the action at Reservoir Hill and the subsequent activity at Rives's farm. An additional hour, however, would encompass the actions known to have taken place.

20 Eldredge, *Third New Hampshire*, 493-94; Little, *Seventh New Hampshire*, 264-65; OR 36, pt. 2, 298, 301, 304-05.

Gillmore ordered his own escort to return to Butler and offer to search for the missing cavalry division. Unfortunately for Gillmore, the escort did not reach Point of Rocks until around 8:30 p.m., by which time Kautz himself had arrived. Butler's message returning the escort was tart: "General Kautz is at my quarters, having come from the inner line of intrenchments of Petersburg, having carried the outer and only line of intrenchments." Now aware that he probably would be called to account, Gillmore responded petulantly that he had remained near Petersburg until 3:15 p.m., and had heard nothing of Kautz to that time. Unknown to Quincy Gillmore, he would need a much stronger defense than that to ward off Butler's wrath, which increased in fury as Kautz's story unfolded.[21]

The chief exhibit damning Gillmore's performance was the bedraggled group of prisoners that Kautz brought back from Petersburg. After the defeat of Archer's battalion at Rives's farm, all of the captured militiamen who were able to travel were gathered together for removal to Bermuda Hundred. The severely wounded were left behind for want of transportation, but all those who could walk were taken. Before their departure a list of the prisoners' names was compiled for the benefit of the provost marshal at Bermuda Hundred. Just as the roll was being completed, the blast of Edward Graham's opening salvo put an end to the roll-taking. The dejected prisoners were hustled away without ceremony, past the overturned wagon blocking the road, past the body of Professor Staubly, and without a chance for Timothy Rives to say farewell to his daughters standing just a few yards away. Because the main body of Kautz's command did not immediately follow, the citizens could only imagine the fate of their city and their families as they trudged away.[22]

Satisfied that everything of potential military value in the vicinity had been destroyed, Kautz gave the final order to return to Bermuda Hundred. As the cavalrymen formed into column, Lt. Peter Morton prepared his lone remaining artillery piece for the retreat. Fearing that the damaged carriage could not stand the strain, Morton gingerly took his place in the column. Sure enough, it was not long before the wheels fell off and the carriage collapsed. Removing the tube from the now useless carriage, the cannoneers slung it under the limber and

---

21 OR 36, pt. 2, 282; OR 36, pt. 3, 719, 720. Perhaps Gillmore had been lulled into a sense of security because Butler's response to his message announcing his retreat had not been one of censure.

22 OR 36, pt. 2, 309; Keiley, In Vinculis, 26-27; Glenn, "Cockade City," 15.

resumed their march, leaving the carriage in the road where it fell. Morton thus had lost one of the guns and both of the carriages he had brought on the expedition. His unhappy state hardly matched that of the prisoners, however, who were on their way to an unknown fate. Somewhere along the way their number was increased by one when the column encountered a farmer, Daniel Lee Sturdivant, 24, and seized him as well. The prisoners' spirits momentarily rose when the main body of the cavalry passed them, indicating that Petersburg had not fallen, but generally the march was a gloomy one.[23]

Kautz's route back to Bermuda Hundred was essentially the same as that taken by the column during its morning approach and it proved an especially tiresome journey for most of the captives, who were on foot. Realizing the age and condition of the prisoners, some of the Federal troopers offered rides to several of them for a time, a kindness which was much appreciated. Equally accepted was the hospitality of Lt. W. E. Bird, the assistant provost marshal, who rode up and down the column, providing a surgeon to dress wounds here, a shot of whiskey there, and a kindly spirit everywhere. To anyone who would listen, Bird announced that he was the nephew of the late Henry D. Bird of Petersburg, and asked about local relatives. One of those sharing the contents of Bird's canteen was Anthony Keiley, who eventually struck up a conversation with Reverend William Hall. Hall expounded at great length on his unfortunate dealings with Benjamin Butler two years previously in New Orleans and how he feared to enter Butler's domain again. Telling Keiley that he planned to make a break for freedom after darkness fell, the minister was true to his word and eventually succeeded in eluding his captors.[24]

After a march of at least 16 miles, the column finally reached the pontoon bridge at Spring Hill, where it halted for the purpose of calling the roll of prisoners. To the anger of the Federals and the delight of the militiamen, in Keiley's expressive phrase, "the provost-marshal's bill of lading did not correspond with the consignment." One or more prisoners were absent from the column, causing the provost marshal to fly into a towering rage. While the tally sheet was being rechecked, the cavalry regiments passed over the bridge and headed for their respective camps, which they reached between 10:30 p.m. and midnight. It was nearer the latter hour when the prisoners crossed because

23 OR 36, pt. 2, 309; OR 51, pt. 1, 1271; Glenn, "Cockade City," 15; Compiled Service Records of Virginia Soldiers, National Archives.

24 Keiley, *In Vinculis*, 28-30; Glenn, "Cockade City," 15.

special precautions had to be taken to prevent further escapes. Horsemen lined the path to the bridge and sentries stood guard every few feet on the planking. None of the militiamen showed any inclination to follow Reverend Hall's example, however, and the prisoners marched uneventfully to Kautz's headquarters. There they were crowded into a dilapidated hut and allowed to rest for the remainder of the night. Unknown to them, Benjamin Butler had ordered that they be brought immediately into his presence. Samuel Spear passed the message to his regimental commanders, but someone neglected to implement it. The prisoners remained where they were, Butler fumed, and Spear received a reprimand in the morning.[25]

Kautz's return to Bermuda Hundred had been uneventful because there had been no pursuit. James Dearing's Confederates followed the withdrawing Federals no farther than the Gregory house, just beyond Battery 27. From there Dearing sent a victory message to Beauregard across the river. Entrusted to Roger A. Pryor, a former politician and general turned courier, the message read: "The enemy are repulsed and the city is safe. But should they attack it again more troops will be necessary for its defense." From her perch in the upstairs window Bessie Callender heard the firing die away. Hailing a passing courier for the reason, she too heard the glorious tidings, "the enemy have been repulsed and we have captured a gun and some prisoners."[26]

Unaware of Petersburg's reprieve, Beauregard spent the afternoon bombarding the War Department in Richmond with calls for aid. As the hours passed, the telegrams became more frantic, culminating in a 3:00 p.m. plea: "Enemy is now in possession of part of defensive works around Petersburg. Delay in sending reenforcements will be fatal to that city, and to Richmond for

---

25 Keiley, *In Vinculis*, 27, 29-30; *OR* 36, pt. 2, 310, 312; *OR* 36, pt. 3, 743-44; *OR* 51, pt. 1, 1270, 1271; Glenn, "Cockade City," 16. In addition to the escape of Reverend Hall documented by Keiley, Homer Atkinson and Daniel Gregory Claiborne Butts are listed as escapees in "Historical Stories About Petersburg," Petersburg National Battlefield, Petersburg, Virginia. Homer Atkinson, 16, was a member of Wolfe's Company, Second Class Militia. His Compiled Service Record shows him to be present for duty on June 30, 1864, so he could indeed have been captured briefly before making his escape. Daniel G. C. Butts, 15, received a Virginia Confederate pension in 1930, claiming to have been a member of R. F. Jarvis's Company of Junior Reserves and offering Homer Atkinson as a witness. He, too, could have been captured for a brief time before escaping. By 1870 he had become a Methodist minister. Federal Census of 1860, 1870, and 1880 (Virginia), National Archives; Compiled Service Records of Virginia Confederate Soldiers, National Archives; Confederate Pension Rolls, Veterans and Widows, Library of Virginia, Richmond, VA.

26 Archer, "Defense of Petersburg," 131, 143.

its supplies." Gradually the tone and volume of Beauregard's entreaties forced a reconsideration of the government's earlier position that no aid could be sent. In early afternoon Braxton Bragg requested Robert E. Lee to send Matt Ransom's North Carolina brigade to Beauregard, and he also released Archibald Gracie's Alabama brigade from the Richmond defenses to return to Bermuda Hundred. Both brigades headed for the pontoon bridge over the James River at Chaffin's Bluff, but it would be hours before they could join Beauregard. Unaware that Bragg had acted, at 4:00 p.m. Jefferson Davis advised Beauregard: "You will realize the impossibility of giving aid in time to save city by ordering troops to you from [other] commands. Even if they must be replaced, you should draw from Major-General Johnson the requisite assistance, concealing the movement so that their place may be supplied before their absence is discovered."[27]

By 6:00 p.m. General Beauregard was at last aware that the Federal attack on Petersburg had been repulsed. Sending the good news to General Bragg, he attempted to retain the troops returning to him by speculating that the Federal attack might be renewed. Unfortunately for Beauregard, when Bragg heard that Petersburg was safe he cancelled Archibald Gracie's orders to march his brigade across the James River and into Beauregard's area of command. Ransom's brigade, too, never moved toward Petersburg, although it was relieved from the front lines. When told that the reinforcements he had been expecting would not be forthcoming, Beauregard attempted to reverse the decision by wiring Bragg at 11:15 p.m.: "The force which attacked Petersburg is said to have come from Bermuda Hundred. It has retired from vicinity of city, but not known positively where gone to. The result of this reconnaissance will doubtless invite soon another attack. Gracie's brigade should be sent, as first ordered." The appeal went unheeded. It seemed as if the only way Beauregard was ever going to obtain reinforcements was if the Federals seized Petersburg—and that eventuality had been prevented by the heroic sacrifices of many of Petersburg's citizens.[28]

27 OR 36, pt. 3, 885, 887; OR 51, pt. 2, 997; Dowdey and Manarin, *Wartime Papers*, 772. Bragg's request for Ransom's brigade was sent at 1:00 p.m. but not received by Lee until 4:45 p.m. The time at which Gracie was dispatched is not known, but it must have been late in the afternoon because the brigade was already near Chaffin's Bluff and it had not moved far when the order was countermanded at 10:30 p.m.

28 OR 36, pt. 3, 885; OR 51, pt. 2, 997; Roman, *Military Operations*, 2:566; T. H. Pearce, ed., *Diary of Captain Henry A. Chambers* (Wendell, NC, 1983), 202.

In Petersburg itself the enormity of that sacrifice was just beginning to be apparent. After the Federals had begun to retreat, the remnants of Archer's battalion had been ordered to join the pursuit, which ended at Battery 27. Remaining at the fortifications only briefly, Archer's men soon returned to the heights and established a new camp. Although there was much to be done there, many of the men went home to their families. The city itself was filled with rumors about who had been killed, wounded, or captured. Relatives of several of the militiamen, hoping that the rumors would prove unfounded, hurried toward the scene of action. Bessie Callender was among those who could not wait for the news to reach them. Leaving her house, she hurried down the street toward Reservoir Hill. After only a few blocks she saw her husband and several other militiamen approaching in the distance. Knowing that David Callender would scold her for leaving home, she quickly retraced her steps and prepared a cool glass of buttermilk for his arrival.[29]

Unlike Bessie Callender, many residents were unable to learn the fate of their loved ones immediately. As a participant, David Callender was deluged with questions from anxious residents. Asked about George B. Jones, Callender could only say that Jones had been on the left where the fighting had been heaviest. Just as another citizen inquired about William C. Banister, word arrived that the dead were being brought in on wagons and that George B. Jones and William C. Banister were among them. At the Banister home on Franklin Street, Anne Banister stood with her mother and sister on their porch, seeking news of the head of the household from those who passed. As they stood, an uncle drove up to the front gate in a wagon carrying William Banister's lifeless body. Shot through the head, his blood-dappled gray hair presented a picture never to be forgotten by the youngsters gathered on the porch in the evening twilight. Instantly Mary Banister rushed to her husband's side and, kneeling, wept in uncontrollable grief. Later someone brought her Banister's glasses, which had been found undamaged at the battle site.[30]

As the bodies of the other dead were brought back from Rives's farm, people stood in the streets and watched silently while the wagons and ambulances passed. Residents of Union Street saw the body of young Wayles

29 Archer, "Defense of Petersburg," 121, 143; Callender, "Personal Recollections," 15-16; "Historical Stories About Petersburg," Petersburg National Battlefield, Petersburg, Virginia.

30 Archer, "Defense of Petersburg," 143; Banister, "Civil War Child," 2; "Historical Stories About Petersburg," Petersburg National Battlefield, Petersburg, Virginia.

Hurt carried to his home. Others saw John E. Friend's remains moved into a hotel. Ordnance Sgt. James W. Albright of Martin's Battery happened to be in Petersburg that day and helped recover the dead. A lady of his acquaintance inquired if he had seen her husband: "I told her no—*a brazen falsehood*—but my heart failed me, and I could not tell her he was dead. I shall never forget his white flowing beard and slender manly form as he lay cold in death." The list of the dead seemed endless: Godfrey Staubly, professor of French; John Crowder, 21-year-old from Matoaca; two militiamen from Prince George County; one of Sturdivant's cannoneers. Throughout the city the wails of the bereaved and the anguished could be heard at intervals as the bodies of the fallen were deposited at their homes.[31]

Four townsmen and another of Sturdivant's gunners were brought from the field with wounds that would prove mortal: Adj. George Guy Johnson, merchant William H. Hardee, dentist William Bellingham, tailor Henry A. Blanks, and Pvt. William F. Johnson of Albemarle County. At least 16 others were also wounded, many of them seriously, and nearly 40 of the militiamen did not return at all, being carried away as prisoners. There was little rejoicing over the city's rescue that night, for Petersburg's cup of grief was full to overflowing. One resident expressed the sentiments of many when she wrote in her diary: "Night closed in, and we sat down face to face with our woe—some to watch the dying, others to keep sad vigil beside their dead; while numberless hearts agonized in prayer for loved ones torn from home, and now on their way to pine, and perhaps die, in some Northern prison." Petersburg had been saved, but a dreadful price had been paid![32]

The next two days were filled with expressions of grief, both public and private. On Friday the *Daily Express* appeared late, and contained the funeral

31 "Historical Stories About Petersburg," Petersburg National Battlefield, Petersburg, Virginia; Archer, "Defense of Petersburg," 121; Macrae, *Americans at Home*, 158; Lee A. Wallace, Jr., *Surry Light Artillery and Martin's Wright's, Coffin's Batteries of Virginia Artillery* (Lynchburg, VA, 1995), 59.

32 Archer, "Defense of Petersburg," 121, 122n; OR 36, pt. 2, 309; Callender, "Personal Recollections," 16; Pryor, *Peace and War*, 277; Macrae, *Americans at Home*, 158. Lists of wounded can be found in Archer, "Defense of Petersburg," 121-22, the Petersburg *Daily Express* of June 10 and June 13, 1864, and the Richmond *Examiner* of June 14, 1864, but vary in their specifics. August Kautz claimed 42 prisoners were taken. For an exhaustive accounting of Archer's casualties, see Appendix 3. As for Petersburg's mood, according to William Cameron, in Archer, "Defense of Petersburg," 137, "there was great rejoicing that night in Petersburg." No other source mentions such rejoicing, and it seems odd that Cameron would do so because his brother George was among the prisoners.

notices of several of the dead. John E. Friend, 33, was buried at 10:00 a.m. that morning at St. Paul's Episcopal Church, the sanctuary being completely filled with mourners. Three hours later the funeral of Wayles Hurt, 16, was preached in the same building, to another crowded congregation. At 3:00 p.m. Godfrey Staubly, 41, professor of French at the Petersburg Female College, was buried from the Second Presbyterian Church on Washington Street, and at 5:00 p.m. services were held for George B. Jones, 42, druggist and father of six young children, at his home on Marshall Street. Sometime during the day, young John Crowder, 21, was laid to rest in Blandford Cemetery by surviving members of his family.[33]

Saturday was also a day of mourning in Petersburg. The funerals began early. At 9:30 a.m. Washington Street Methodist Church was the scene of the services for Henry A. Blanks, 52, a tailor and father of six. The procession included members of the Independent Order of Odd Fellows and the rites were conducted by the Reverends Wheelwright, Brown, and Blunt. Their text was Psalm 100:12: "So teach us to number our days, that we may apply our hearts unto wisdom." One hour later St. Paul's was filled, as on the previous day, when the Reverend Mr. Platt performed the Episcopal service over the remains of William C. Banister, 55, the father of four boys and two girls. After lunch the church was again opened for the funeral of Adj. George Guy Johnson, 59, who had died from his wounds the previous night. Again the Reverend Platt officiated. A smaller service took place on Lombard Street, where Reverend Mr. Campbell preached the funeral of young William Daniel, 18, at the home of his uncle.[34]

While the funerals were being held, the curious searched the battlefield at Rives's farm. Suddenly a swollen and partially decomposed body was found in the woods nearby. According to the June 13, 1864, edition of the Petersburg *Daily Express*, the remains were eventually ascertained to be those of William Crowder of the Petersburg suburb of Matoaca. He was the brother of John Crowder, already buried, and the son of Simon Crowder, missing in action. In the paper's telling, Crowder apparently had been badly wounded, but had had strength enough to leave the immediate vicinity of the fight. Collapsing after reaching the woods, he had died with no one to aid him. The Crowders were a

33 Petersburg *Daily Express*, June 10, 1864, and June 13, 1864; Richmond *Examiner*, June 14, 1864.

34 Petersburg *Daily Express*, June 12, 1864.

family of extremely modest circumstances from beyond the Appomattox River, but they had made their sacrifices along with the finest of Petersburg's citizens. Realizing this, the editor of the *Daily Express* was grateful: "Possessed of no means, that gallant father and his noble sons had nothing to lose pecuniarily, but actuated purely by motives of patriotism, they entered the fight cheerfully, struggled manfully, and the father only survives. Petersburg must protect and provide for the remaining portion of the family."[35]

A search of contemporary records regarding the Crowder family yields a somewhat different story from the newspaper account, but leaves a residual mystery of its own. The Census of 1850 found the Crowder family (Simon, age 30, wife Sarah, age 35, and five children, including John and William, age 7) living in the western part of Petersburg, with Simon working as a miller. In the 1860 Census, Crowder, age 43, was living with his wife Mary, age 42, and his two sons, John and William, age 17, in southern Chesterfield County, with Simon employed as a laborer. By that accounting, both young men would have been 21 in June 1864. The Compiled Service Record for John Crowder lists him as a member of Capt. Richard F. Jarvis's Company, Junior Reserves, and as killed on June 9, 1864. John Crowder's burial record in Blandford Cemetery indicates that he was buried on June 10, and was 17 when he died. The Compiled Service Record for William Crowder also lists him as a member of Capt. Richard H. Jarvis's Company, but as captured by the Federals on June 9. According to Federal army documents, William Crowder was taken to Bermuda Hundred, transferred to the Point Lookout prisoner of war camp in Maryland on June 13, and died there of unspecified causes on July 31, 1864. Thus he could not have been the unidentified body found in the woods on June 11. As for Simon Crowder, his Compiled Service Record shows him to have been a member of Capt. William H. Jarvis's Company, Petersburg Reserves, but makes no mention of June 9 activity. In July 1864 he was serving as a teamster detailed to the Army of Northern Virginia and was paroled with that army in the same capacity at Appomattox Court House on April 9, 1865. The Census of 1870 found him, age 58, living with wife Mary, 56, in Sussex County, Virginia, and working again as a miller. Thus no member of the Crowder family could have furnished the body found in the woods behind the position of Archer's

35 Petersburg *Daily Express*, June 13, 1864. In a section of the paper set in type earlier, William Crowder was reported to be among the missing. The Richmond *Dispatch* of June 14, 1864, reported that William Crowder was killed on June 9 and that John Crowder was the body found on June 11.

battalion on June 11. To date, that body remains unidentified. Nevertheless, the sacrifice of the Simon Crowder family on June 9 was greater than that of any other Petersburg family and fully merited the praise of the city's leading newspaper.[36]

On Sunday Dr. John Herbert Claiborne, Petersburg's secessionist delegate to the Virginia Convention in 1861 and in June 1864 director of the city's military hospitals, wrote to his wife of the recent events: "Yesterday was a gloomy day here—funerals all day & the enemy constantly looked for in force." Claiborne told of the recent death and funeral of William H. Hardee, whose leg had been amputated in a futile attempt to save his life. Once more St. Paul's was the site as an enormous congregation heard the Reverend Platt take as his text, "In the midst of life we are in death." Claiborne's letter continued:

> Poor Mr. Hardee's funeral was preached today at 2 o'clock but I could not go. Patty [Hardee's daughter] does not know of his death & Mr. Platt was to tell her this evening. There is sorrow again. I fear Dr. Bellingham will die—he is very dangerously wounded—the rest of the wounded are doing well. I have just been interrupted by being called to see Pattie to whom Mr. P. communicated the tidings of her Father's death. Poor thing she is greatly shocked but better than I could expect. If it does not bring on hemorrhage she will stand it. Her poor husband seems to have given up.[37]

Even after the death and burial of Dr. Bellingham, who finally succumbed to his injuries, the city's suffering was not over. There were still the wounded to be nursed back to health: young Willie Harwood, who had lost an arm; George V. Scott, shot in the jaw; C. L. Bartlett, professor of music, wounded severely in three places; Samuel Hall, shot in the thigh; William Griffith, wounded in both thighs; Richard Bagby, painfully wounded in the side; and 10 others. Also the loss of so many citizens as prisoners added to the sorrow: Capts. James Wolff and Peyton Alfriend, Lts. Berthier Bott and Thomas Chalkley, city councilman James Boisseau, city chamberlain John B. Stevens, William Cameron's brother

36 United States Federal Censuses of 1850, 1860, and 1870 (Virginia), National Archives; Compiled Service Records of Virginia Soldiers, National Archives. Archer, "Defense of Petersburg," 121, 122n, correctly reports the fate of the Crowder brothers. Simon Crowder was identified in previous editions of this work as Lawson Crowder because of a misreading of the handwritten manuscript returns of the Census of 1860.

37 John Herbert Claiborne to his wife, June 12, 1864, John H. Claiborne Papers, University of Virginia Library, Charlottesville, Virginia; Petersburg *Daily Express*, June 10, 1864, and June 13, 1864.

George, young Branch T. Archer and Joseph L. Peebles, Joseph D. Cooper, Anthony Keiley, John Glenn, and 27 others.[38]

Although it would be a long time before they would see their families and friends again, the prisoners were in no immediate danger. They were low in spirits, however, and except for Anthony Keiley who spent the night in Lieutenant Bird's tent, they were physically uncomfortable in their cramped quarters at Bermuda Hundred. The next morning, June 10, the captives received a meager breakfast of salt pork, hardtack, sauerkraut, and potatoes which they quickly consumed, so quickly that Keiley, who was being interrogated by Kautz, missed most of it. Guards then formed the prisoners into line and marched them to Butler's headquarters for interrogation by the commanding general himself. Once there, all of the captives except John Glenn and two wounded youngsters were forced to stand throughout the day under a hot sun while Butler quizzed a few of the prisoners individually. First to be called into Butler's presence was lawyer Anthony Keiley. When asked the number of Battery 27's defenders Keiley told the truth, but when asked the size of Petersburg's garrison, he declined to answer. Butler responded that he already knew that the city was virtually empty of soldiers. Puzzled, Keiley asked how Butler could know that, and he received the answer: "By this infallible induction: if there was a soldier in town, no lawyer would get into the trenches."[39]

After finishing with Keiley, Butler questioned several other prisoners, including Branch T. Archer, about conditions in Petersburg and the size of its garrison. Their answers were probably the same as Keiley's, because the militiamen all "had a little private understanding on this matter beforehand." Finding that he could learn little that he did not already know, Butler ended the interrogations. The guards then formed the prisoners into line again and marched them toward Bermuda Hundred Landing. As they filed down the dusty road, they passed the cannon of Sturdivant's Battery captured with them in Battery 28, which was being brought forward for Butler's inspection. As they trudged through the camps of the Army of the James, the old men and boys presented such a strange sight that many of the hardened veterans turned to stare at their passing. It was twilight when the forlorn militiamen reached the

38 Archer, "Defense of Petersburg," 121, 122n; Petersburg *Daily Express*, June 10, 1864; Richmond *Examiner*, June 14, 1864. See Appendix 3.

39 Keiley, *In Vinculis*, 30-31, 34-37, 40-42; Glenn, "Cockade City," 16-17.

landing, where the army's provost marshal took them in hand. They were placed in a frame building for the night and a guard of black cavalrymen was established outside.[40]

The next morning, June 11, the day Petersburg was burying many of their comrades, the prisoners were roused, fed, formed between two ranks of the 1st United States Colored Cavalry, and marched to the dock where the steamer *John A. Warren* awaited them. Placed aboard the vessel, the captives stood gaping at the bustle of activity in the makeshift port when word arrived from Butler's headquarters that three of the prisoners were to be retained at Bermuda Hundred. After removal of the three unfortunates, the *John A. Warren* cast off her lines and backed into the stream for the run down the James. As the ship passed down the wide river and the stately mansions of earlier and better times were left astern, many of the prisoners were in tears. Past City Point with its crowded wharves they went, past the pontoon bridge being readied for U. S. Grant's future crossing of the James, past steamships taking Federal reinforcements to the front. Soon Newport News and the large Federal fleet based in Hampton Roads appeared ahead, then dropped astern, and nothing was left but the long monotonous journey up Chesapeake Bay to the prison pen at Point Lookout, Maryland.[41]

Back in Petersburg, amidst all the pain and bereavement in the Cockade City, it soon became apparent that a wide spectrum of the city's population had taken part in the great victory. Because it had borne the brunt of the assault and had suffered nearly 60 percent casualties, Archer's battalion was singled out for special commendation. Two days after the battle when they were once more camped at Rives's farm, the surviving militia were visited by Beauregard himself. Beauregard asked Archer how the defense of the position had been conducted and when told, he exclaimed: "You have done well, sir; we cannot always be successful, but you have done well." Brigadier General Raleigh Colston also had kind words for the men whom he had led in their greatest fight. In his official report Colston wrote: "I wish to bear full and explicit

---

40 Glenn, "Cockade City," 17-18; Keiley, *In Vinculis*, 45-47, 49.

41 Glenn, "Cockade City," 18; Keiley, *In Vinculis*, 49-51. The three men retained by Butler (Lt. Thomas Chalkley, 45, Sgt. Thomas J. McCaleb, 44, and Pvt. Warren Russell, 42) later joined their comrades in prison. According to his Compiled Service Record, McCaleb "claimed to be a Union man," and in the Census of 1860, Russell was listed as a native of Maine. Compiled Service Records of Virginia Soldiers, National Archives; United States Federal Census of 1860 (Virginia), National Archives.

testimony to the steadiness and gallantry of the citizen soldiers who composed Major Archer's command. They stood to the breast-works like veterans. . . . The salvation of the city of Petersburg is undoubtedly due in the first place to the brave militia of the city; for had they retreated five or ten minutes sooner . . . the city would probably have remained in the enemy's hands."[42]

Even the irascible Brig. Gen. Henry A. Wise, the man who had earlier denigrated the fighting qualities of Archer's men, paid tribute in his congratulatory Special Orders No. 11 to the "mere handful of citizen soldiers, who stood firmly and fought bravely as veterans, until ordered to fall back." Wise was equally vigorous in his praise of Raleigh Colston's performance. Whatever Colston's reputation may have been in Petersburg prior to June 9, Wise altered it forever in an official letter of commendation:

> Your example was everything I could ask; you held the militia as long as regulars and veterans could have been held. . . . You did all that was possible with the men and means I had it in my power to place at your disposal. While Archer and his militia will ever be gratefully remembered, it must not be forgotton [sic] that they were led and commanded by you, that you shared their danger to the last and doubtless taught them how to win the glory and gratitude now shed upon their gallantry.[43]

The Petersburg *Daily Express* was equally profuse in its praise, and echoed by the Richmond *Dispatch* and the Richmond *Whig*, whose comments were reprinted in the Petersburg paper. The effusion reached its culmination on June 13, 1864, with the publication of Brigadier General Wise's Special Orders No. 11 in the newspapers. Indulging in soaring flights of rhetoric, Wise exhorted the citizens to remember forever what had happened at Rives's farm:

> Let the reserves and second-class militia of the surrounding counties now come in promptly, one and all, and emulate this bright and successful example; let it hotly hiss to blood-red shame the laggards and skulkers from the streets and alleys of the city to the lines, and let it proclaim aloud that Petersburg is to be and shall be defended on her outer walls, on her inner lines, at her corporation bounds, on every street, and around every temple of God and altar of man, in her every heart, until the blood of that heart is spilt. Roused by this spirit to this pitch of resolution, we will fight the enemy at every step, and Petersburg is safe.[44]

42 Petersburg *Daily Express*, June 13, 1864; Archer, "Defense of Petersburg," 122; *OR* 36, pt. 2, 318.

43 *OR* 36, pt. 2, 316, 319.

44 Petersburg *Daily Express*, June 13, 1864; *OR* 36, pt. 2, 317.

Chapter 6

"Petersburg Is to Be and
Shall Be Defended"

With the battle over and the troops once more within their camps an exact accounting of gains and losses could be made. Considering the number of men involved, the Federals had not suffered heavily. Hawley had lost 10 men, Hinks had lost five, and Gillmore's escort had lost one, for a total of 16 from Gillmore's combined infantry columns. Kautz's cavalry, on the other hand, had lost 36 troopers: four killed, 26 wounded, and six missing. Although he had lost none of his artillerymen, Lt. Peter Morton had left behind "one 3-inch rifled gun and limber complete, 20 rounds of ammunition, 1 gun carriage complete, seven horses, and 4 sets of double artillery harness complete." Confederate losses were somewhat higher, falling disproportionately upon Fletcher Archer's battalion of militia-reserves and Sturdivant's Battery. Out of approximately 130 men (125 militiamen and five artillerymen) who defended the entrenchments at Rives's farm or were in the vicinity, 74 became casualties. Fourteen men were killed, 17 wounded, and 43 captured, approximately 60 percent of the original force. The howitzer from Sturdivant's battery was also lost, but the gunners were given the newer and better piece left behind by Morton to replace it. Incorporated into Sturdivant's Battery for the remainder of the war, the gun performed exceptionally well in Wade Hampton's famous "Beefsteak Raid" in the fall of 1864.[1]

---

1 For Federal losses, see OR 36, pt. 2, 301, 305, 309, 310, 315; OR 51, pt. 1, 1270n, 1271; Eldredge, *Third New Hampshire*, 493; Marshall, *Butler's Correspondence*, 4:341-42; "Statement of Casualties of June 9 Affair," June 10, 1864, General Correspondence, 1864, Benjamin F. Butler Papers, Library of Congress. Slight discrepancies in the Federal reports prevent an exact accounting, but total Federal casualties amounted to either 52 or 55 men. Dyer, *Compendium*,

In addition to the losses sustained by both sides, a second result of the Federal defeat on June 9 was its effect on the reputations of the principal participants. For the Confederates, Raleigh Colston neutralized some of the ugly rumors circulating about him through his heroic performance at Rives's farm. Also, Fletcher Archer and his militia-reserves, and by inference all militia-reserves, were believed to have proven their value on June 9, a fact especially emphasized in the Richmond newspapers. On the Federal side, August Kautz received a brevet promotion to lieutenant colonel in the Regular Army for his actions on June 9 and had his reputation enhanced. Similarly, Joseph Hawley and Edward Hinks were also considered to have done well. Benjamin Butler's reputation, however, received another blow. For Butler's opponents, the failure to take Petersburg was just one more fiasco in a long line of blunders perpetrated by that incompetent officer. For Butler himself, Gillmore's defeat meant the loss of his last opportunity to accomplish something on his own before the arrival of U. S. Grant curtailed his semi-independent status. Even so, Quincy Gillmore was a greater loser than Butler.[2]

For the Federals, the most visible result of the unsuccessful expedition to Petersburg on June 9 was the virtual destruction of the Civil War career of Maj. Gen. Quincy Adams Gillmore. After hearing Kautz's story on the night of the battle, Butler commenced an investigation to discover the truth about the action. On the morning of June 10 he ordered both Hawley and Hinks to report to his headquarters. What Hawley may have reported to Butler is unknown, but his subsequent communications with Gillmore and others clearly indicate that Hawley vigorously supported Gillmore's decision not to assault the Dimmock Line. Unable to come to Point of Rocks at once, Hinks sent Capt. Thomas L. Livermore of his staff to explain Hinks's role in the affair. When Livermore

---

2:943, claimed a Federal total of 87, 20 killed and 67 wounded, but the basis of this statement is unknown, and it seriously conflicts with the official reports. Losses in Confederate units other than Colston's command are not extant, although at least two members of Batte's 44th Virginia Battalion were wounded on June 9 (James Bowie and James A. Cousins). For losses in Archer's battalion and Sturdivant's battery, see Petersburg *Daily Express*, June 10, 1864, and June 13, 1864; Richmond *Examiner*, June 14, 1864; Archer, "Defense of Petersburg," 121-22, 134; Glenn, "Cockade City," 12, 14; Compiled Service Records of Virginia Soldiers, National Archives. At least four civilians were included in the captured: John H. Lahmeyer, John McIlwaine, Timothy Rives, and Daniel Lee Sturdivant.

2 Petersburg *Daily Express*, June 13, 1864; Boatner, *Civil War Dictionary*, 449; Kautz, *August Valentine Kautz*, 130.

informed Butler that the Confederate works were heavy and extensive, and that two regiments had been seen joining the defenders facing Hinks's brigade, Butler strongly disputed the captain's account. As Butler continued, Livermore barely stifled a smile, because of "the manner and face of the general, who puffed out his cheeks at intervals, put on a portentous grin which one might suspect to be a sign of mirth until it dissolved into sobriety; and looked both ways until I was at a loss to know when he was looking at me. However, he was not, nor had he any reason to be, indignant with General Hinks nor me, nor otherwise than good-natured."[3]

Hawley's views notwithstanding, both Kautz and Hinks believed that Gillmore had performed poorly on June 9. Kautz was convinced that the Confederate garrison of Petersburg on that day did not exceed 1,500 men and that the cavalry could have accomplished more if Gillmore had remained longer in position. Kautz did not accept Gillmore's excuse that the cause of his departure was the lack of news of the cavalry's progress. In Kautz's words, "I found the distance to the enemy's lines on the Jerusalem Plank road greater than I expected and did not get to my destination as soon as we both expected. But Genl. Gillmore was hasty in returning." Hinks, too, thought an opportunity had been lost. On June 13 he again sent Captain Livermore to Butler with a message: "If you will return to me the detached brigade of my division, and Cole's cavalry, and give me the cooperation of Kautz's cavalry, I will place Petersburg or my position at your disposal."[4]

As the evidence mounted from both Federal and Confederate participants in the action that Petersburg had been ripe for the taking, Butler's anger at Quincy Gillmore grew in intensity. At 1:20 p.m. on June 10 Butler peremptorily demanded that Gillmore furnish a report of the operation by 5:00 p.m. The message specifically identified the categories of information required, and closed: "I have ordered a specific hour for this report because I have never yet received from you any report of your operations since you have been on this

3   OR 36, pt. 2, 301-02; OR 36, pt. 3, 743; John W. Shaffer to Joseph Hawley, June 10, 1864, Joseph Hawley to Gideon Welles, June 19, 1864, and Joseph Hawley to his wife, June 20, 1864, all in Joseph Hawley Papers, Library of Congress; Livermore, *Days and Events*, 353-54.

4   Cyrus B. Comstock Diary, entry for June 9, 1864, Cyrus B. Comstock Papers, Library of Congress; "Kautz in the Great Rebellion," August V. Kautz Papers, Library of Congress; Kautz, "Siege of Petersburg," *National Tribune*, May 18, 1899; Edward Hinks to Benjamin Butler, June 13, 1864, General Correspondence, 1864, Benjamin Butler Papers, Library of Congress; Marshall, *Butler's Correspondence*, 4:361; Livermore, *Days and Events*, 354-55.

line. This order is imperative. You will acknowledge receipt by telegraph." Hurriedly prepared by 5:20 p.m., Gillmore's report was a brief and rather inexact resume which unaccountably omitted most of the details specifically requested by Butler. Of course Gillmore was pressed for time, but clearly he could have complied more closely with Butler's demands if he had chosen to do so. Whether the form and content were intentional or not, the resulting document was a great mistake, because it played perfectly into Butler's hands.[5]

Butler's endorsement on Gillmore's effort was scathing. Calling the report "entirely unsatisfactory," Butler wrote: "The conduct of the expedition, as disclosed by it, and in fact, was dilatory and ill-judged. The demonstration, too feeble to be called an attack, was in direct disobedience to orders. The whole affair, in view of the forces known to be opposed, was most disgraceful to the Union arms." A copy of the endorsement was sent to Gillmore on June 11. On the same day, Butler wrote to his wife that "The Petersburg expedition was a most disgraceful failure owing to the incompetency of Gillmore. He thrust himself upon me, and then failed disgustingly." At 1:00 a.m. on June 12 Gillmore responded to Butler's endorsement with a verbal blast of his own. Calling Butler's charges "unmerited and unjust," Gillmore denied all of the allegations against him, demanded a copy of any written orders he had failed to obey, and stated his intention to seek a formal court of inquiry into his conduct while serving in Butler's department.[6]

Butler must have been delighted with Gillmore's retort, which was probably composed in the heat of anger, because it permitted him to use his considerable legal skills in an effort to destroy Gillmore once and for all. In a document of over 5,000 words, heavily laced with sarcasm, Butler granted the court of inquiry seemingly requested, then proceeded to indict Gillmore for almost everything he did in connection with the expedition to Petersburg. Much of the criticism was petty in nature, but the significant points, and there were many, were carefully drawn. In the document Butler reviewed the entire history of the operation from the time the original plan was conceived. In Butler's view, Gillmore's major derelictions were three in number: his tardy approach to the city, his failure to take the works facing him, and his failure to

5   *OR* 36, pt. 2, 273-74, 287-89, 291; *OR* 36, pt. 3, 742.

6   *OR* 36, pt. 2, 289-91; Marshall, *Butler's Correspondence*, 4:337. Butler's characterization of the operation as "disgraceful" is supported by the assessment of Edward Longacre, modern historian of Butler's command, who declared that it "probably constituted the sorriest performance ever turned in by the Army of the James." Longacre, *Army of Amateurs*, 135.

cooperate with Kautz. Like a prosecutor in a court of law, Butler demolished Gillmore's report of June 10 point by point. Gillmore received Butler's indictment on June 12, the same day that Butler wrote to his wife Sarah: "I am much dispirited and worn out with continual failures for which I see no remedy. True, I shall punish Gillmore, but that won't take Petersburg." By the following day Butler had decided on Gillmore's punishment and, in another letter to his wife, he confided, "I shall relieve Gillmore."[7]

On June 14 Butler forwarded the relevant correspondence and reports to U. S. Grant, and mentioned in passing that a court of inquiry would be convened. While Grant pondered the documents, Butler notified Gillmore that a supplementary statement made by Lieutenant Barnard (the courier to Hinks) could not be considered a part of Gillmore's official report. Further, Butler coldly informed Gillmore that a vessel was waiting to take him to Fort Monroe. The latter statement referred to a Special Order issued by Butler's headquarters that morning granting the court of inquiry, relieving Gillmore of his command, and ordering him to depart immediately for Fort Monroe. Upon receipt of the Special Order, Gillmore instantly replied, denying that he had specifically asked for a court, protesting his relief, and requesting that the Special Order be revoked. Maddeningly, Butler's chief of staff, John W. Shaffer, responded that if the charges lodged by Butler were true, Gillmore could not be continued in a position of such great responsibility. There was no connection at all between the order for relief and the granting of the court of inquiry; they were merely lumped together for convenience. After quoting the Articles of War relative to courts of inquiry, Shaffer pointedly asked Gillmore to state categorically whether or not he wanted such a court to be convened.[8]

While he waited for the matter of his relief and court of inquiry to be decided, Gillmore began to gather testimony from as many witnesses as possible about the state of Petersburg's defenses on June 9. Eventually at least 11 individuals provided Gillmore with written opinions of the strength of the

7 OR 36, pt. 2, 274-82, 290-91; Marshall, *Butler's Correspondence*, 4:357, 362. Butler's massive indictment is dated June 11, 1864, but it was written in response to a note from Gillmore dated June 12, 1864, 1:00 a.m.

8 OR 36, pt. 2, 282-86, 291-92. Once more, Gillmore's imprecise language had gotten him into trouble. His original reference on June 12 to a court of inquiry read: "It only remains for me to deny respectfully, but emphatically, all the charges therein set against me, to request a copy of the orders which I have disobeyed or have failed to obey, and then to demand of the President a court of inquiry to investigate all my official acts and conduct while serving in this department. I court a full investigation into the part I have taken in the campaign here."

Dimmock Line or a statement of the events preceding Gillmore's arrival in front of the works. Joseph Hawley, three of his regimental commanders, Samuel Spear, and Robert Foster all testified that Petersburg's defenses were formidable and most argued that an assault by Gillmore's force would have been folly. By the time three of the respondents answered Gillmore's query, the eastern end of the Dimmock Line had been successfully assaulted on June 15 and the Confederates had erected other fortifications nearer the city. Unaware of the weakness of Petersburg's garrison on June 9 and believing that the new Confederate works had existed on that date, Edward Hinks, Baldy Smith, and John G. Barnard all concurred with the prevailing opinion that the works were extremely strong and in some sections virtually impregnable. Barnard, Grant's chief engineer, unwittingly touched on the critical factor, however, when he stated that the works had to be "properly manned" to be considered impregnable.[9]

On June 16 Grant issued orders allowing Gillmore to remain at City Point until he had examined the case further, although Butler wrote to his wife on the same day that Gillmore "is come to his end. No army officers can uphold him." Also on June 16, Gillmore penned his answer to Shaffer's query about the court of inquiry and summed up his defense in a striking statement. Denying that Butler's estimate of the number and quality of Petersburg's defenders was accurate, Gillmore closed:

> No commander, except one of criminal rashness, would have ordered an assault on those works unless he ignored all the experience of this war. Your general authority to expend a certain number of lives to secure the destruction of certain property meant nothing really, for such things are not matters of barter. One word from my lips on that day would have caused the sacrifice, but in my opinion would not have secured the success. You say upon the subject of an assault and its probable success that it was not my business and that you had ordered it. I must respectfully take issue with you on both these points. The first I will not discuss; the second I most emphatically deny, and again request a copy of the order or the slightest proof of its ever having been given. . . . I shall apply for no court of inquiry that will take me from active service until all reasonable sources of prompt redress fail.[10]

Unwilling to submit to the scrutiny of a court of inquiry, Gillmore nevertheless had some success in portraying himself as the victim of a vendetta

9   *OR* 36, pt. 2, 294, 296-97, 301-02, 304-08, 312-14.

10   *OR* 36, pt. 2, 292-94; *OR* 40, pt. 2, 88; Marshall, *Butler's Correspondence*, 4:387.

by the army commander. Joseph Hawley especially defended his chief. In a private letter to Gideon Welles on June 19 Hawley wrote:

> I am satisfied that Gillmore was only wise and sound in not ordering a desperate assault when we had *no* reserves, a strong work in front, other lines behind that, and 2 ½ miles from the first works to any point of importance in the city. . . . Gen. Grant says he does *not* blame Gillmore. The difficulties that beset the operations of the last five or six days show whether or not Petersburg is a place that a brigade [could] walk into & out of at pleasure.

Such sentiments continued to be echoed in regimental histories of Hawley's brigade long after the war ended. No doubt aware of the personality clash of long standing between Butler and Gillmore, Grant moved cautiously. On June 17, the general in chief communicated gingerly with Butler, proposing to relieve Gillmore at his own request if Butler was agreeable. Butler had no objection and Grant accordingly issued Special Orders No. 36, which relieved Gillmore in the proposed manner and ordered him to report to the adjutant general in Washington for a new assignment. At the same time, Butler revoked his own orders for Gillmore's relief and at that juncture, the case appeared to be closed.[11]

Still unsatisfied, Gillmore interrupted his journey to Washington by making an impromptu visit on June 21 to the Point Lookout, Maryland, prison camp, where he tried to interview the members of Archer's battalion captured by Kautz. He was refused permission to see them by the commandant, who notified Butler. Regarding Grant as Gillmore's protector, Butler wired the general in chief: "What action shall I take in this matter, if any? General Gillmore refuses to demand a court of inquiry, and yet is preparing his case." His patience exhausted, Grant signaled an end to the affair by drafting a peremptory telegram to Quincy Gillmore: "General: You will proceed at once to Washington in obedience to your order." As a final irony, the telegram was transmitted through the headquarters of Maj. Gen. Benjamin F. Butler, commanding the Department of Virginia and North Carolina.[12]

Satisfying as it was to Butler, Quincy Gillmore's downfall did nothing to make the fall of Petersburg more likely. In fact, Gillmore's failure to seize the

---

11 OR 36, pt. 2, 286-87; OR 40, pt. 2, 120, 142, 148; Joseph Hawley to Gideon Welles, June 19, 1864, Joseph Hawley Papers, Library of Congress; Walkley, *Seventh Connecticut*, 146.

12 OR 40, pt. 2, 293, 302.

city on June 9 simply gave P. G. T. Beauregard a stronger argument for demanding the return of the troops he had loaned to the Army of Northern Virginia. After the Federal repulse on June 9, Beauregard concluded that the affair had been only a reconnaissance to test the strength of his defenses and that the result would be another, stronger attempt to take the city. Also expecting the Federals to return soon, Henry Wise on June 10 issued a contingency plan to be implemented if the main fortifications of the Dimmock Line were lost. That night Beauregard received a report from pickets that Federal troops were again gathering south of the Appomattox River. Informing Braxton Bragg, Beauregard speculated that another attack on Petersburg was imminent and he again pled for reinforcements to be sent. Hardly expecting that Bragg would comply, Beauregard notified Bushrod Johnson at Bermuda Hundred to be prepared again to denude his lines if Petersburg was the Federal target.[13]

Receiving Beauregard's telegram at 11:30 p.m. on June 10, Braxton Bragg decided that he could not risk Petersburg a second time without taking remedial action. Not long after midnight on June 11 Bragg telegraphed Robert Ransom, commander of the Department of Richmond, to send Archibald Gracie's Alabama brigade to Bermuda Hundred. Notified that Gracie was to be sent, Beauregard decided to reinforce Petersburg with the remainder of Henry Wise's Virginia brigade as soon as Gracie's men entered the Bermuda Hundred trenches. During the afternoon most of Gracie Alabamians finally reached the northern sector of the Bermuda Hundred lines and reported to Bushrod Johnson. In turn, Johnson relieved Wise's 26th and 34th Virginia Infantry regiments and started them toward Petersburg. In the city itself, Henry Wise formally assigned Raleigh Colston to command the southeastern sector of the Dimmock Line.[14]

13 *OR* 36, pt. 2, 885, 889, 895-96; *OR* 51, pt. 2, 1002; "Special Orders No. 10, 1st Military District," June 10, 1864, Raleigh Edward Colston Papers, Southern Historical Collection, University of North Carolina; P. G. T. Beauregard to Bushrod Johnson, 10:45 p.m., June 10, 1864, Letter Book, May-July 1864, P. G. T. Beauregard Papers, Library of Congress.

14 *OR* 36, pt. 2, 896-97; *OR* 51, pt. 2, 1003-04; P. G. T. Beauregard to Bushrod Johnson, June 11, 1864, Letter Book, May-July 1864, P. G. T. Beauregard Papers, Library of Congress; Luther Rice Mills, "Letters of Luther Rice Mills, a Confederate Soldier," in *North Carolina Historical Review* (1927), 4:302.

On the same day that Bragg finally granted Beauregard's request for reinforcements, Maj. Gen. Daniel Harvey Hill, an unofficial aide of Beauregard's, counseled his chief:

> I am so much disturbed about our condition, but especially about our relations to Petersburg, that you must excuse me for a suggestion. It seems to me that there is but one way to save the country, and bring the authorities to their senses, and that is to say, 'I cannot guard Bermuda Hundred and Petersburg both with my present forces. I have decided that Petersburg is the important point and will withdraw my whole command to that place to-night.' . . . Grant can get 10,000 or 20,000 men to Westover and Lee know nothing of it. What then is to become of Petersburg? Its loss surely involves that of Richmond—perhaps of the Confederacy. An earnest appeal is called for now, else a terrible disaster may, and I think will, befall us.

Reviewing the events of the last few days, Beauregard gently endorsed on the paper, "I fully concur in the above views, which have been already communicated to the Government in substance if not in words. I consider it useless again to do so, as it would produce no good results and my records are already 'all right.' I shall continue to hold 'the lines' as long as there is the slightest hope of being able to do so with success and without endangering Petersburg."[15]

Beauregard's pessimism notwithstanding, Quincy Gillmore's abortive thrust on June 9 and the response of the Confederate War Department had ensured that Petersburg's garrison would be larger the next time the Federal army came to town. By June 15, when the XVIII Corps assaulted Petersburg, Henry Wise's command had more than doubled in size. Present on that day were the same units that had faced Hawley, Hinks, and Kautz: Batte's and Hood's battalions of reserves, the 46th Virginia Infantry regiment, Taliaferro's 7th Confederate Cavalry regiment, Sturdivant's and Young's Virginia Batteries, and Archer's battalion of militia-reserves. Also present, as a direct result of the action on June 9, were James Dearing, the 4th North Carolina Cavalry regiment, Graham's Virginia Battery, and the 64th Georgia Infantry regiment, none of which had returned north of the Appomattox River. In addition, Beauregard's entreaties had caused Bragg to send additional forces to Bermuda Hundred, freeing the 26th and 34th Virginia Infantry regiments for duty at Petersburg. The presence of these last two regiments, therefore, could also be considered a result of the Federal failure on June 9. Whereas Henry Wise on June 9 could

15 *OR* 36, pt. 2, 896.

deploy approximately 1,200 troops, a quarter of whom were citizen soldiers, on June 15 he defended Petersburg with approximately 2,800 men, 90 percent of whom were veterans.[16]

The possibility that a premature strike at Petersburg might cause the Confederate government to reinforce the Cockade City occurred to U. S. Grant as soon as he decided to transfer the Army of the Potomac south of the James River. Notifying Butler on June 11 that he was returning Baldy Smith's XVIII Corps to Bermuda Hundred, and probably unaware of the events of June 9, Grant advised Butler on future moves:

> Expecting the arrival of the Eighteenth Corps by Monday night, if you deem it practicable from the force you now have to seize and hold Petersburg, you may prepare to start on arrival of troops to hold your present lines. I do not want Petersburg visited, however, unless it is held, nor an attempt to take it unless you feel a reasonable degree of confidence of success. If you should go there, I think troops should take nothing with them except what they carry, depending upon supplies being sent after the place is secured.

Unfortunately for the Federals, by the time Grant warned Butler not to alarm the Confederates about Petersburg, the deed had already been done and reinforcements for the Cockade City were already in motion.[17]

In retrospect, the failure of Quincy Gillmore's expedition to Petersburg on June 9, 1864, did much to shape the course of the war in central Virginia for the next 10 months. Even a temporary occupation, such as envisioned by Butler, would have caused serious damage to the Confederate war effort. Petersburg was the home of an important lead smelter and a powder mill, as well as the South Side Railroad shops, numerous clothing mills, and two small foundries. All of these could easily have been wrecked at leisure after the rail and highway bridges over the Appomattox River were destroyed. With the railroad bridge down, Lee's direct supply line to Wilmington, North Carolina, would have been

---

16 Confederate strength on June 15 is derived from *OR* 51, pt. 2, 999. The list of units present on June 15 can be found in G. T. Beauregard, "Four Days of Battle at Petersburg," in Robert U. Johnson and Clarence C. Buel, eds., *Battles and Leaders of the Civil War*, 4 vols. (New York, NY, 1884), 4:540. Beauregard includes the 23rd South Carolina Infantry regiment as being at Petersburg, but no other source corroborates him. Apparently Company F of the 23rd South Carolina was at Petersburg on June 9 (*OR* 36, pt. 2, 316), but the regiment most likely remained with its parent unit at Bermuda Hundred. Beauregard's strength figure of 2,200 men is also too low.

17 *OR* 36, pt. 3, 755; Grant, *Personal Memoirs*, 2:571.

severed. If the bridges had not been restored by the time Grant crossed to the south side of the James River six days later, the entry of Lee's veterans into Petersburg's defenses would have been seriously hindered. The delay of the Army of Northern Virginia by just a few hours would have been of incalculable value to Grant's assaulting divisions. Instead of lying in ruins, the bridges stood unharmed on June 15. In addition, Baldy Smith and the XVIII Corps had to contend with a Petersburg garrison that, while still woefully weak, was far stronger than it had been on June 9. As it was, Smith captured more than a mile of the Dimmock Line and was barely kept out of Petersburg. A different outcome on June 9 might have facilitated Smith's entry and spared Petersburg the agony of 10 months of siege.[18]

Even with a reinforced Petersburg garrison, the Confederates almost lost the Cockade City on June 15-16. For several days prior to Smith's appearance, Beauregard had noted ominous Federal preparations and had called for even greater assistance, but to no avail. It is possible that the events of June 9 may have had some bearing on Richmond's response. On June 9 Beauregard had called all day for reinforcements and threatened the direst consequences if denied them, yet by evening the situation had been stabilized without any assistance from outside Beauregard's own command. Such an overwrought response to an apparently minor Federal probe may have caused the Confederate government to discount the magnitude of the threat when similar messages began to arrive from Dunlop's on June 14 and 15. On the other hand, such considerations may not have been operative in the highest Confederate councils at all. Robert E. Lee usually based his judgments on hard information received from a variety of sources, while Jefferson Davis, with a long-standing dislike of Beauregard, may have been swayed by his own prior analysis of Beauregard's character. At this remove, the role played by the events of June 9 in the deliberations of the principal characters six days later is impossible to determine with certainty. Nevertheless, the government's response to Beauregard on June 15 mirrored that of June 9, with nearly fatal consequences for the Confederacy.[19]

18 For the most recent study of Grant's initial assaults on Petersburg, see Thomas J. Howe, *The Petersburg Campaign: Wasted Valor, June 15-18, 1864* (Lynchburg, VA, 1988).

19 Clifford Dowdey, in *Lee's Last Campaign*, 327, 331-32, argues that Jefferson Davis was not concerned about affairs at Petersburg during the time in question. As for Braxton Bragg, Dowdey speculates: "Sharing Davis' dislike of Beauregard, he was inclined to extend him the same type of incivility.... It is also possible that he had ceased to pay attention to Beauregard's

Two days before the massive Federal attack on June 15, the editor of the Petersburg *Daily Express* voiced the hope of most residents of the Cockade City when he wrote: "The heroes and martyrs all now sleep quietly in Blandford Cemetery. We hope no farther [sic] sacrifice of life remains to be made. May our city never pass through such another season, and may the determination of the living to defend their homes be doubly increased, by the sacrifices which have already been made." Yet June 9, 1864, was not the end of Petersburg's ordeal, only the beginning. The assault on Petersburg on June 15 was the opening event in a campaign that would come to be known as the 10-month siege of Petersburg. The Cockade City was destined to be the object of the longest siege ever conducted against an American city and would be the largest battle site in area on the continent. Names such as the Crater, Weldon Railroad, Peebles's Farm, Hatcher's Run, Burgess's Mill, Fort Stedman, Five Forks, and Fort Gregg would be written with blood into the annals of American military history. There would be bombardment of the residential districts, starvation rations, countless refugees, and everywhere, death in the streets and in the environs. But throughout the long night of suffering the Cockade City would remember June 9, 1864, as its most tragic day.[20]

For a time Fletcher Archer's remaining militia-reserves continued to take part in the defense of their homes. The same issue of the *Daily Express* that carried the editor's plea for an end to sacrifice also contained a brief announcement retaining the citizen soldiers for another 30 days of service. On June 16 Archer and his battalion were once again in the trenches when U. S. Grant's veterans resumed the hammer blows against the Dimmock Line that had begun the previous day. As before, the militia-reserves suffered severely. This time three members of the command were killed, 14 wounded (including Archer, shot in the left arm), and several more taken prisoner. Initially unwilling to leave the field, at last Archer relinquished command to Capt. W. H. Jarvis and allowed himself to be led to the rear. After the battle, at the behest of the men, Charles F. Collier asked General Beauregard to release the militiamen from active duty in the lines. Praising the services of Archer's battalion in the highest

---

unending stream of desperate telegrams. Since he first began his resistance to releasing troops to Lee, Beauregard had repeatedly alerted the war office to impending crisis.... When, on June 14th, Bragg received a somewhat more specific telegram from Beauregard, he made no distinction between it and the routine calls for help."

20 Petersburg *Daily Express*, June 13, 1864; Scott and Wyatt, *Petersburg's Story*, 167; Harrison, "Ninth of June," 12-13.

terms, Beauregard graciously assigned the unit to guard duty within the city. The active service and the sacrifice of Archer's battalion were at last at an end.[21]

The prisoners taken on June 16 eventually joined the group captured on June 9 in prison. There for the first time men like John Glenn and Anthony Keiley learned of Dearing's and Graham's providential rescue of their adopted city and of Petersburg's bereavement at the loss of so many of her sons. For most, their record of incarceration was the same: transfer from Bermuda Hundred to the Point Lookout, Maryland, prison camp for a month, then an ocean voyage to New York City, followed by a trip by rail to the newly established prison camp at Elmira, New York, with arrival on July 12, 1864. As conditions at Elmira deteriorated rapidly, 17 of the militiamen were paroled on October 11, 1864, and returned via Baltimore, Maryland, to Point Lookout for exchange. Two other Petersburg defenders joined the group at Point Lookout. After their names were formally placed on the exchange rolls, they traveled with 3,005 others by sea to Venus Point, Savannah River, Georgia. There, on November 15, 1864, they returned once more to Confederate hands. Virtually all were badly malnourished and suffering from disease. Sadly, one member of this group, Robert H. Daniel, 52 and father of seven, died at Baltimore while being transferred from the prison train to a waiting ambulance.[22]

Officers captured on June 9 followed a different path from their enlisted comrades. Captain Peyton Alfriend, 50, Capt. James E. Wolff, 51, and First Lt. Berthier Bott, 46, remained only briefly at Point Lookout until being transferred to Fort Delaware on Pea Patch island in the Delaware River on June 25. Bott was the first to be freed, returning to the Confederacy at Cox's Wharf on the James River on October 15, 1864. Wolff languished at Fort Delaware until February 27, 1865, when he was exchanged at City Point. Of the three, Peyton Alfriend had the most unusual experience, being randomly selected to participate in a curious experiment in retaliation. Because captured Federal officers were incarcerated in the city of Charleston, South Carolina, under fire

---

21 Petersburg *Daily Express*, June 13, 1864; Archer, "Defense of Petersburg," 138.

22 Compiled Service Records of Virginia Soldiers, National Archives; OR 7, ser. 2, 894; Archer, "Defense of Petersburg," 122n; Michael Horigan, *Elmira: Death Camp of the North* (Mechanicsburg, PA, 2002), 33-43, 114-16. Providentially, the Petersburg contingent barely missed being part of the horrific Shohola, Pennsylvania, prison train wreck of July 15, 1864, which claimed the lives of 48 Confederate and 17 Federal soldiers. For an extended account of the militiamen's journey from Elmira to the Savannah River, see Keiley, *In Vinculis*, 189-210, 213-15.

from Federal batteries on Morris Island that were shelling the city, the Federal War Department sent approximately 600 captured Confederate officers to Morris Island to be exposed to the return fire of Confederate artillery. Alfriend was one of the "Immortal Six Hundred," as the group came to be called. The unlucky prisoners were billeted in a stockade on Morris Island and were under fire for approximately six weeks before being transferred to Fort Pulaski, Georgia, in October. Although most of the prisoners were retained in Federal custody well into 1865, Alfriend was exchanged at Charleston, South Carolina, on December 15, 1864. As of March 1865 he remained in a Petersburg hospital because of his ordeal. A final officer, Second Lt. Thomas Chalkley, 45, was one of those prisoners retained for several weeks at Bermuda Hundred by Butler's order. Pretending to be only an enlisted man, Chalkley was sent to Point Lookout, where he was paroled for exchange on October 11 and transferred to the Confederacy at Varina on the James River on October 15, 1864.[23]

The experiences of other prisoners varied widely. Alexander Vaughan, 16, arrived at Point Lookout on June 13 with the others, but was released five days later to join Company F, 1st United States Volunteers (the "Galvanized Yankees"). Samuel H. Cuykendall, 17, a native New Yorker wounded and captured on June 9, was treated at the X Corps hospital at Bermuda Hundred on June 10 and admitted to Hampton Hospital on June 11. During his recovery he worked as a nurse in that hospital. On January 11, 1865, he returned to City Point to take the oath of allegiance and was then sent to Skaneateles, New York, on January 16, 1865, for release. Death released William Crowder, 21, from Point Lookout on July 31, 1864. Warren Russell, 42, a native of Maine and another of the men retained for a time by Butler, eventually arrived at Elmira on July 26 but secured his freedom on August 25, 1864. Thomas J. McCaleb, 44, the final man detained by Butler, traveled to Elmira with Russell in July but was not released until after taking the oath of allegiance on November 30, 1864. Three militiamen, Thomas W. Clements, 46, John F. Glenn, 26, and Joseph L. Peebles, 16, all either wounded or desperately ill, were paroled at Point Lookout and repatriated to the Confederacy at Varina on the James River on September 22, 1864. Several others also returned home via James River exchange points on January 21, February 14, March 14, and March 23, 1865. Whenever they

23 Compiled Service Records of Virginia Soldiers, National Archives. For a first-person account by one of the "Immortal Six Hundred," see John Ogden Murray, *The Immortal Six Hundred: A Story of Cruelty to Confederate Prisoners of War* (Roanoke, VA, 1911).

returned home, they found Petersburg to be far different from the city they had left months earlier. Walking the deserted, shell-damaged streets of the beleaguered Cockade City, the militiamen could only remember with regret a bright Thursday morning in June, when William Banister had been in his bank and George Jones had been in his drugstore, and there had been less sadness in the world.[24]

In regard to the Federals who struggled at Petersburg on June 9, 1864, some went on to greater fame while others returned to the relative obscurity from whence they had come. In Butler's expressive phrase, Quincy Gillmore's "active service with the Armies of the United States during the remainder of the war was desultory in character, and migratory in detail and assignment." After returning to Washington, Gillmore took command of two divisions of the XIX Corps chasing Jubal Early in the Valley of Virginia. On July 14 he fell from his horse while campaigning, suffering painful foot and ankle injuries. Upon his recovery, he was a member of several military boards and commissions, then the commander of the Department of South Carolina in June 1865. After the war Gillmore remained in the Regular Army, where he produced a number of technical works on engineering and served a term as president of the Mississippi River Commission. By his death at Brooklyn, New York, in 1888 he had reached the permanent rank of colonel.[25]

Of Gillmore's subordinates, Joseph Hawley was the most successful. Continuing in brigade command, Hawley was promoted to brigadier general in September 1864. In the following year he commanded both a division and the District of Wilmington. Ending the war as a brevet major general, Hawley returned home in 1866 to become active in Connecticut politics. Elected governor in that year, he served as president of the Republican national convention in 1868 and went on to represent Connecticut in both the House of Representatives and Senate until his death in 1905. Edward Hinks also finished the war as a brevet major general, although his wounds forced an end to his combat service in July 1864. Resigning his commission in 1865, Hinks rejoined the army in 1866 and served until 1870, retiring as a colonel. Before he died in 1894 he supervised soldiers' homes in several states. August Kautz retained

---

24 Compiled Service Records of Virginia Soldiers, National Archives; Glenn, "Cockade City," 21-23; Keiley, *In Vinculis*, 215-16.

25 Butler, *Butler's Book*, 679; Boatner, *Civil War Dictionary*, 343; Warner, *Generals in Blue*, 177; Eicher and Eicher, *High Commands*, 255.

command of his cavalry division until March 1865, when he was given a division of the XXV Corps, which he led into Richmond. Brevetted several times, Kautz served (with Robert S. Foster) on the commission that tried those accused of conspiring in Abraham Lincoln's assassination. In later years Kautz held commands on the frontier and in the Pacific Northwest, retiring as a brigadier general in 1892, three years before he died.[26]

Henry A. Wise continued to serve around Petersburg and Richmond with his brigade for the remainder of the war. During Lee's final retreat to Appomattox Court House, Wise was appointed to command a division but did not receive major general's rank. After the war he built a law practice in Richmond, but never applied for amnesty from the Federal government. Wise died in 1876, unreconstructed to the end. His personal gallantry on June 9 notwithstanding, Raleigh Colston continued to hold minor posts until April 1865, which found him commanding the defenses of Lynchburg, Virginia. After briefly operating a military school in North Carolina, Colston accepted a commission as colonel in the Egyptian army. He served his new employers faithfully until a fall from a camel paralyzed him during an exploration trip in the Sudan. Undaunted, Colston continued the expedition in a litter until relieved several months later. Discharged in 1879, he returned to America destitute and permanently disabled. For 11 years he labored as a clerk in the War Department, but the two years before his death in 1896 were spent in the Confederate Soldiers' Home in Richmond. Unlike Wise and Colston, James Dearing did not survive the war. Commanding his brigade throughout the siege of Petersburg, he was mortally wounded at High Bridge, Virginia during the retreat to Appomattox. Two days short of his 25th birthday when he died on April 23, 1865, Dearing was the last general officer of the Confederacy to die as a result of battle.[27]

Fletcher H. Archer remained in command of his battalion of militia-reserves until the end of the war. Recovering from a wound sustained on June 16, he was again wounded at Sayler's Creek on the retreat to Appomattox. A graduate of the University of Virginia Law School, Archer returned to his original profession after the surrender. In 1882 he was elected mayor of

26 Boatner, *Civil War Dictionary*, 387-88, 402-03, 449; Warner, *Generals in Blue*, 159, 219-20, 230, 258; Eicher and Eicher, *High Commands*, 288-89, 298, 327-28.

27 Boatner, *Civil War Dictionary*, 166-67, 228, 944; Warner, *Generals in Gray*, 59, 69-70, 342; Eicher and Eicher, *High Commands*, 181, 576-77, 593; Robert K. Krick, "James Dearing," in Davis and Hoffman, *Confederate General*, 2:56.

Petersburg by the Common Council to complete the unexpired term of William E. Cameron (not the June 9 eyewitness), who had become Governor of Virginia. Like Archer, most of the men of his battalion returned to their customary occupations in 1865 and lived out the remainder of their lives in peace. Only one of their number achieved any notoriety and he had not technically been a militiaman at all. Following the war, Anthony Keiley turned from the law to newspaper work and later entered Richmond politics. Elected mayor of Richmond, Keiley filled that office for five years. While serving as Richmond City Attorney, Keiley was appointed ambassador to Italy in 1885 by President Grover Cleveland. Rejected by Italy because of his wife's Jewish heritage, Keiley was then appointed to the same position for Austria-Hungary, with similar results. Unreceived abroad, Keiley lived out the rest of his days in Virginia.[28]

Although the privations of the siege took precedence for a while, Petersburg did not forget her heroes of June 9, 1864. On May 8, 1866, following the adjournment of the Society for Resuscitation of the Library, a group of devoted Petersburg women organized the Memorial Society of the Ladies of Petersburg. The organization flourished and at the meeting on May 30, 1866, the following resolutions were proposed and adopted:

> As the 9th of June, the anniversary of the defense of our city, approaches therefore, be it Resolved, That we devote that day to the renewing and decorating the graves of the soldiers in the neighborhood of Petersburg, as a grateful and beautiful testimonial of the memory of their heroism. Resolved, that the Standing Committee be requested to wait on the Committee of the Confederate Memorial Society to solicit their cooperation, in the commemoration of the 9th of June, and that the citizens generally be requested to unite in this holy and grateful task.

An additional resolution that called for the placing of floral tributes first on the graves of the dead from the June 9 action was adopted on June 6, 1866.[29]

Three days later, on the second anniversary of the action at Rives's farm, the ladies' work bore fruit. A great procession formed at the Washington Street Methodist Church at 8:00 a.m. and the ladies, veterans, and residents sorted themselves out by divisions. At 9:00 a.m. Brig. Gen. David Weisiger, grand

28 Bernard, *War Talks*, xvi, xviii; Louis Ginsberg, *History of the Jews of Petersburg, 1789-1950* (Richmond, VA, 1954), 35.

29 William H. Baxter Scrapbook, Petersburg National Battlefield, Petersburg, Virginia.

Blandford Church, Petersburg, Virginia
Library of Congress

marshal for the day, gave the signal and the precession began its journey up Sycamore Street to Weeks's Cut and thence to Blandford Cemetery. The city's businesses were closed and thousands joined the throng, all carrying bouquets and wreaths of flowers. At the cemetery, after appropriate ceremonies, the procession split into groups which proceeded to all parts of the burial ground, decorating the graves of the Confederate dead. The ceremony was repeated the next year and the next, until it was established as an annual affair in the life of the city.[30]

In March 1868, Mrs. John A. Logan, wife of the prominent Federal general who then commanded the veterans' organization known as the Grand Army of

30 William H. Baxter Scrapbook, Petersburg National Battlefield, Petersburg, Virginia. For an exhaustive analysis of the postwar Ladies' Memorial Associations, including the one in Petersburg, see Caroline E. Janney, *Burying the Dead but Not the Past: Ladies' Memorial Associations and the Lost Cause* (Chapel Hill, NC, 2008), especially Chapter 2.

the Republic, visited the battlefields of Virginia. Touring the cemeteries of Richmond and Petersburg, she was especially impressed by the remains of the floral tributes on the graves at Blandford Cemetery in Petersburg. Touched by the sentiment embodied in the small sun-bleached Confederate flags and wilted bouquets decorating the soldiers' graves, Mary Logan informed her husband of what she had seen at Petersburg. John A. Logan found merit in the idea and concluded that a universal day of tribute would be a worthwhile national project. In May 1868 he issued an order for G.A.R. chapters everywhere to emulate the Petersburg example, and from these modest beginnings the veterans' day of remembrance grew into the present national Memorial Day. For the nation at large June 9 had no special significance and Logan's choice of late May was eventually adopted by the nation. Although Petersburg may not have been the first city to decorate its Confederate graves, Mary Logan's testimony gives some credence to the Blandford ceremony's claim to have been the inspiration for the national day of remembrance.[31]

Throughout the years the residents of the Cockade City continued to revere "The Ninth of June" as their own Memorial Day. At one time the day was Petersburg's largest holiday, when all the stores would be closed and everyone would follow a massive parade to Blandford. At the cemetery the Petersburg Grays, the city's militia company, would be drawn up in formation outside old Blandford Church, where the assembled throng would hear an orator recount the events of June 9, 1864. As part of the ceremony, either an old man or a young boy would read the names of those who died in defense of their city. When the speeches and the calling of the roll of honor were concluded, a bugler would sound Taps and a firing party from the Grays would render the traditional salute of three volleys. The graves of the thousands of Confederate dead in the cemetery would then be decorated.[32]

31 Mrs. John A. Logan, *Reminiscences of a Soldier's Wife: An Autobiography* (New York, NY, 1913), 242-46; Scott and Wyatt, *Petersburg's Story*, 334; "Memorial Day at Petersburg, Va.," *Confederate Veteran* (August 1924), 32:292. For other claimants to the first memorial day, see Virginius Dabney, *Richmond: The Story of a City* (Garden City, NY, 1976), 203; Mrs. James R. Armstrong, "The Origin of Memorial Day," *Confederate Veteran* (December 1927), 35:475, 478; and John R. Neff, *Honoring the Civil War Dead: Commemoration and the Problem of Reconciliation* (Lawrence, KS, 2005), 136-37, 148-49, 153-54. Perhaps not surprisingly, the official G.A.R. account of the origins of Memorial Day omits Mrs. Logan's (and Petersburg's) role entirely. Neff, *Civil War Dead*, 137, 154.

32 Harrison, "Ninth of June," 14-15.

In 1904 a plaque honoring the "gray haired sires and beardless youths" was placed in Blandford Church by the Petersburg Chapter of the United Daughters of the Confederacy. Five years later a large commemorative stone was erected at the site of Battery 27 and inscribed:

THIS STONE MARKS THE SPOT WHERE
THE OLD MEN AND BOYS OF PETERS-
BURG UNDER GEN. R. E. COLSTON AND
COL. F. H. ARCHER
125 STRONG
ON JUNE 9TH, 1864
DISTINGUISHED THEMSELVES IN A
FIGHT WITH 1300 FEDERAL CAVALRY
UNDER GEN. KAUTZ, GAINING TIME FOR
THE DEFEAT OF THE EXPEDITION

As the years passed, the rites of remembrance so proudly established in 1866 and etched in stone by 1909 gradually began to erode. By the time Homer Atkinson, the last survivor of Archer's battalion, passed away on March 31, 1945, at the age of 96, lack of interest and the intervention of two other great conflicts had served to sharply curtail the commemoration of "The Ninth of June." The stores no longer closed, the great procession no longer formed on Sycamore Street, and only a few score of the elderly continued the commemoration in their hearts. Little by little the crowd at the services in Blandford Cemetery dwindled to a fraction of those who had once stood with bowed heads long years before.[33]

Today little remains in the way of physical reminders of the battle of June 9, 1864. Battery 5 still stands atop its commanding ridge, but it is remembered more for events of the siege than for the time Joseph Hawley stared up from the plain and declared that the works could not be taken. The plaque still hangs in Blandford Church and the commemorative stone still stands on the site of Battery 27, but the latter is now surrounded by commercial establishments. Places like Rives's farm, the Gregory house, and Battery 27 itself have been gone for many years. In their places are paved streets, most of them with unfamiliar names, although behind the shopping center, near where Timothy

33 Glenn, "Cockade City," 12; Harrison, "Ninth of June," 12, 14-15.

Rives once lived, runs Colston Street, intersected by Beauregard Avenue. New Road is still a well-traveled route into the inner city, but it now fittingly bears the name Graham Road. In the city museum can be found a large portrait of Raleigh Colston, photographs of James Dearing, Edward Graham, and G. Guy Johnson, and a few mementos of the men of Archer's battalion. But that is all, except for the sparsely attended annual memorial service and the silent graves. Petersburg still remembers, faintly, what happened at Rives's farm on June 9, 1864, but 150 years have passed since that bright June day so long ago, and there are so many other things to do.[34]

34 The author personally attended the Memorial Service on at least three occasions: June 9, 1968; June 9, 1989; and June 9, 2013. On all three occasions, the order of events was essentially the same, with the same hymns ("Onward Christian Soldiers" and "How Firm a Foundation"), the same reading of the names of the killed, the same type of brief inspirational address, the sounding of "Taps," and the firing of a volley from period rifles to salute the Confederate dead. While there has been no modification of the ceremony or growth of the audience in the author's admittedly limited sample of dates, there has not been a diminution in participation either, and the diversity of those attending in 2013 bodes well for the future of both the Memorial Service and the city.

Expedition to Petersburg, June 9, 1864

Major General Quincy A. Gillmore

Infantry
Major General Quincy A. Gillmore
4th Massachusetts Cavalry (detachment)
Captain Lucius Richmond

Hawley's Brigade
Colonel Joseph R. Hawley
6th Connecticut Infantry
Lieutenant Colonel Lorenzo Meeker
7th Connecticut Infantry
Captain Theodore Bacon
3rd New Hampshire Infantry
Lieutenant Colonel Josiah I. Plimpton
7th New Hampshire Infantry
Colonel Joseph C. Abbott
62nd Ohio Infantry
Lieutenant Colonel Samuel B. Taylor
Battery D, 1st United States Artillery (two sections)
Lieutenant Joseph P. Sanger

Hinks's Provisional Brigade,
Brigadier General Edward W. Hinks
1st United States Colored Troops
Colonel John H. Holman
6th United States Colored Troops
Colonel John W. Ames
Battery B, 2nd United States Colored Light Artillery
Captain Francis C. Choate

Cavalry Division, Army of the James
Brigadier General August V. Kautz

1st Brigade
Lieutenant Everton J. Conger
1st District of Columbia Cavalry (six companies)
Lieutenant Colonel Everton J. Conger

3rd New York Cavalry (detachment)

2nd Brigade
Colonel Samuel P. Spear
5th Pennsylvania Cavalry regiment,
Lieutenant Colonel Christopher Kleinz
11th Pennsylvania Cavalry
Lieutenant Colonel George Stetzel
8th Battery, New York Light Artillery (one section)
Lieutenant Peter Morton

Appendix 2

Defenders of Petersburg, June 9, 1864

Brigadier General Henry A. Wise

Petersburg Garrison
Brigadier General Henry A. Wise
46th Virginia Infantry
Colonel Randolph Harrison
44th Virginia Battalion
Major Peter V. Batte

Hood's Battalion
Major William H. Hood

Archer's Battalion
Major Fletcher H. Archer

Company F, 23rd South Carolina Infantry
Captain Johnson M. Woods

7th Confederate Cavalry
Colonel Valentine H. Taliaferro

Sturdivant's Virginia Battery
Captain Nathaniel A. Sturdivant

Young's Virginia Battery
Captain Edward R. Young

Brigadier General Raleigh E. Colston

Reinforcements
Brigadier General James Dearing
4th North Carolina Cavalry
Colonel Dennis D. Ferebee

Graham's Virginia Battery
Captain Edward Graham

Provisional Company (hospitals)
Captain Lockhart

Provisional Company (prisons)
Lieutenant Hawes

Confederate Casualties at Rives's Farm, June 9, 1864

No two lists agree fully on the names of the Confederate casualties on the Jerusalem Plank Road on June 9, 1864. A consolidated listing published in the first edition of this work found a total of 78 names, when killed, wounded, and captured categories were combined. Since that time, the availability of disparate online sources, such as the Compiled Service Records of Virginia Troops and the various records of the Federal Census, makes it possible to create a more accurate list through electronic cross-referencing. The list of names below is the result of such a process. Even though the list is believed to be the most comprehensive available, given the many variables at play, it remains tentative at best.

Killed and Mortally Wounded (14)

William Constable Banister—Private, Wolff's Company Second Class Militia, age 55, bank officer, wife and six children, killed June 9.

J. William Bellingham—Sergeant, Rogers's Company, Petersburg Reserves, age 45, dentist, no family, native of Delaware, wounded in side, died of wounds June 23.

Henry A. Blanks, Sr.—Private, Wolff's Company Second Class Militia, age 52, merchant tailor, wife and five living children, died of wounds (body and arm) June 10.

Edward P. Brown—Private, Sturdivant's Battery, age 21, farmer, parents and five siblings, native of Albemarle County, killed June 9.

George R. Conway—Private, Hare's Company, Prince George Reserves, age 46, overseer, wife and three children, killed June 9.

John G. Crowder—Private, R. F. Jarvis's Company, Junior Reserves, age 21, no occupation listed, parents and one sibling, killed June 9.

William B. Daniel—Lieutenant, Hare's Company, Prince George Reserves, age 18, farmer, mother and four siblings, killed June 9.

John E. Friend—Private, Wolff's Company, Second Class Militia, age 33, contractor, wife and one child, killed June 9.

William H. Hardee—Private, Wolff's Company, Second Class Militia, age 50, merchant, one child, right leg amputated below knee, died June 12.

Wayles Hurt—Lieutenant, R. F. Jarvis's Company, Junior Reserves, age 16, mother and two brothers, killed June 9.

George Guy Johnson—Adjutant, Petersburg Reserves, age 59, tobacconist, no living family, native of Connecticut, severely wounded, died of wounds June 10.

W. F. Johnson—Private, Sturdivant's Battery, age 17, native of Albemarle County, wounded in head, died of wounds June 16.

George Benjamin Jones—Private, Wolff's Company, Second Class Militia, age 42, druggist, wife and six children, killed June 9.

Godfrey Staubly—Private, Wolff's Company, Second Class Militia, age 41, professor, wife and one son, native of Switzerland, killed June 9.

Wounded (17)

Richard Bagby—Corporal, Rogers's Company, Petersburg Reserves, age 30, no occupation listed, wife, wounded painfully but not dangerously in side June 9.

Charles Loomis Bartlett—Private, Wolff's Company, Second Class Militia, age 55, professor of music, wife and four children, wounded severely in three places June 9.

James Cain—Private, Hare's Company, Prince George Reserves, age 44, farmer, wife and four children, wounded in leg June 9.

Richard M. Cary—Corporal, Wolff's Company, Second Class Militia, age 39, school teacher, wife and two children, wounded in both thighs June 9.

William Griffith—Civilian, formerly Private, Company F, 3rd Virginia Cavalry, age 46, farmer, wife and five children, native of Pennsylvania and Prince George County resident, wounded in both thighs June 9.

Samuel Hall—Private, Wolff's Company, Second Class Militia, age 49, hatter, wife and two sons, wounded severely in thigh June 9.

A. C. Harrison—Second Lieutenant, Wolff's Company, Second Class Militia, age 47, carriage dealer, wife and five children, wounded slightly in arm June 9.

Richard A. Harrison—Private, Prince George Reserves, age 42, farmer, wife and one son, wounded in hand June 9 (tentative identification).

William E. Harwood—Private, Wolff's Company, Second Class Militia, age 17, bookstore clerk, parents and one sister, wounded in arm (amputated at shoulder) June 9.

Robert A. Martin—Private, Wolff's Company, Second Class Militia, age 39, merchant, wife and four children, member of Petersburg Common Council, wounded in arm June 9.

William Meanly—Private, Alfriend's Company, Petersburg Reserves, age 41, farmer/carpenter, wife and four children, wounded severely in three places June 9.

Norborne T. Page—Private, Wolff's Company, Second Class Militia, age 51, tobacconist, wife and six children, wounded in hand June 9.

David Hamilton Payne—Private, Wolff's Company, Second Class Militia, age 51, lumber merchant, wife and six children, wounded June 9.

Nathan Brooks Prichard—No Compiled Service Record on file, age 16, parents and 10 siblings, wounded slightly June 9.

Hiland Rushmore—Private, Rogers's Company, Petersburg Reserves, age 38, master carpenter, wife and one son, native of New York, wounded severely June 9.

George V. Scott—First Lieutenant, Wolff's Company, Second Class Militia, age 52, ship chandler, wife and two children, wounded severely in face and thigh June 9.

A. S. Shafer—Private, Wolff's Company, Second Class Militia, age 53, clothier, wife and three children, wounded slightly in leg June 9.

Captured (43)

Peyton Alfriend—Captain, Alfriend's Company, Petersburg Reserves, age 50, saddle maker, one sister, captured June 9 (Point Lookout; Fort Delaware; Hilton Head, South Carolina, one of the "Immortal 600;" Fort Pulaski; exchanged at Charleston, South Carolina, December 15, 1864, and in hospital thereafter).

Branch Tanner Archer—Private, Wolff's Company, Second Class Militia, age 19, clerk, father and five siblings, captured June 9 (Point Lookout; Elmira, July 12; paroled October 11, exchanged October 29, 1864; transferred to CSA at Savannah River, Georgia, November 15, 1864).

Homer Atkinson—Private, Wolff's Company, Second Class Militia, age 16, occupation unknown, parents and three siblings, captured June 9 (escaped same evening).

James Boisseau—Private, Wolff's Company, Second Class Militia, age 45, grocer/commission merchant, wife and five children, member of Petersburg Common Council, captured June 9 (Point Lookout; Elmira, July 12; paroled October 11, exchanged October 29, 1864; transferred to CSA at Savannah River, Georgia, November 15, 1864).

Berthier Bott—First Lieutenant, Prince George Reserves (in command on June 9), age 46, farmer, wife and three children, captured June 9 (Point Lookout; Fort Delaware; exchanged October 15, 1864).

E. A. Broadnax—Private, Wolff's Company, Second Class Militia, age 42, dry goods merchant, wife and two children, captured June 9 (Point Lookout; Elmira, July 12; paroled October 11, exchanged October 29, 1864; transferred to CSA at Savannah River, Georgia, November 15, 1864).

Benjamin H. Butts—Private, Prince George Reserves, age 34, farmer, wife and two children, captured June 9 (Point Lookout; Elmira, July 12; paroled October 11, exchanged October 29, 1864; transferred to CSA at Savannah River, Georgia, November 15, 1864).

Daniel Gregory Claiborne Butts—Private, R. F. Jarvis's Company, Junior Reserves, age 15, occupation unknown, parents and one brother, captured June 9 (escaped same evening).

George Cameron—Private, Rogers's Company, Petersburg Reserves, age 25, tobacconist, citizen of Scotland, one brother, captured June 9 (Point Lookout; Elmira July 12; paroled October 11, exchanged October 29, 1864; transferred to CSA at Savannah River, Georgia, November 15, 1864).

Thomas Chalkley—Second Lieutenant, Alfriend's Company, Petersburg Reserves, age 45, master painter, wife and three children, captured June 9 (Bermuda Hundred; Camp Hamilton; Point Lookout, June 30; paroled for exchange, October 11; transferred to CSA as private soldier at Varina on James River, October 15, 1864).

Thomas W. Clements—Private, Rogers's Company, Petersburg Reserves, age 46, grocer, wife and eight children, captured June 9 (Point Lookout; paroled and transferred to CSA at Varina on James River, September 18, 1864; in hospital thereafter for debility and diarrhea).

Joseph D. Cooper—Private, Wolff's Company, Second Class Militia, age 16, parents and two siblings, captured June 9 (Point Lookout; Elmira, July

12; paroled October 11, exchanged 29 October 1864; transferred to CSA at Savannah River, Georgia, November 15, 1864).

William Crowder—Private, R. F. Jarvis's Company, Junior Reserves, age 21, occupation unknown, parents and one brother (John Crowder), captured June 9 (Point Lookout, June 13; died at Point Lookout prison camp, July 31, 1864).

Samuel Cuykendall—Corporal, R. F. Jarvis's Company, Junior Reserves, age 17, occupation unknown, parents and three siblings, native of New York, wounded in right leg and heel, captured June 9 (treated at X Corps Hospital Point of Rocks; admitted Hampton Hospital, June 11, 1864; transferred to City Point, January 11, 1865; oath of allegiance taken January 13, 1865; transferred to Washington, DC, then to Skaneateles, New York, for release, January 16, 1865).

Robert H. Daniel—Private, Wolff's Company, Second Class Militia, age 52, farmer, seven children, captured June 9 (Point Lookout, June 13; Elmira, July 12; paroled October 11, 1864, and sent to Point Lookout for exchange; died at Baltimore, Maryland, en route).

John Davidson—Private, Wolff's Company, Second Class Militia, age 43, leather and hides merchant, wife and four children, captured June 9 (Point Lookout; Elmira, July 12; paroled October 11, exchanged October 29, 1864; transferred to CSA at Savannah River, Georgia, November 15, 1864).

Thomas D. Davidson—Private, Wolff's Company, Second Class Militia, age 37, school teacher, wife and five children, captured June 9 (Point Lookout; Elmira, July 12; paroled October 11, exchanged October 29, 1864; transferred to CSA at Savannah River, Georgia, November 15, 1864).

John L. Emory—Private, Hare's Company, Prince George Reserves, age 42, farmer, wife and seven children, captured June 9 (Point Lookout, June 13; paroled at Point Lookout Hospital and exchanged February 10, 1865; transferred to CSA at Cox's Landing on James River, February 14, 1864; admitted Chimborazo Hospital, Richmond, February 15, 1865, with chronic rheumatism; admitted Jackson Hospital, Richmond, April 9, 1865).

Joseph L. Evans—Private, Alfriend's Company, Petersburg Reserves, age 36, shoe maker, wife and two children, captured June 9 (Point Lookout; Elmira, July 12; paroled February 20, 1865, and transferred for exchange, March 23, 1865, at Dutch Gap on James River; admitted Chimborazo

Hospital, March 24, 1865, with chronic diarrhea; furloughed March 27, 1865).

John F. Glenn—Private, Wolff's Company, Second Class Militia, age 26, occupation unknown, mother and sister, wounded and captured June 9 (Point Lookout; paroled and transferred to Aiken's Landing on James River for exchange, September 18; at Chimborazo Hospital, Richmond, with chronic diarrhea, September 23, 1864).

William A. Hall—Chaplain, Washington Artillery of New Orleans, age 30, Presbyterian minister, unmarried, native of New Jersey, captured June 9 (escaped same evening).

John A. Jefferson—Sergeant, Wolff's Company, Second Class Militia, age 36, Methodist minister, wife and one son, captured June 9 (Point Lookout; Elmira, July 13; paroled, October 11, exchanged, October 29, 1864; transferred to CSA at Savannah River, Georgia, November 15, 1864).

Joseph R. Johnson—Private, Alfriend's Company, Petersburg Reserves, age 21, printer's apprentice, no family, captured June 9 (Point Lookout; Elmira, July 12; paroled October 11, exchanged October 29, 1864; transferred to CSA at Savannah River, Georgia, November 15, 1864).

Samuel H. Jones—Private, Hare's Company, Prince George Reserves, age 46, farmer, wife and two children, captured June 9 (Point Lookout; paroled and exchanged, November 1, transferred to CSA at Savannah River, Georgia, November 15, 1864).

Anthony M. Keiley—Civilian, age 30, attorney, no family, native of Paterson, NJ, First Lieutenant in 12th Virginia Infantry until wounded at Malvern Hill; member of Virginia House of Delegates, captured June 9 (Point Lookout; Elmira, July 12; paroled October 11, exchanged October 29, 1864; transferred to CSA at Savannah River, Georgia, November 15, 1864).

James Kerr—Corporal, Wolff's Company, Second Class Militia, age 50, china/glass merchant, widower with six children, native of Scotland, wounded and captured June 9 (Point Lookout, June 13; exchanged November 1; transferred to CSA at Savannah River, Georgia, November 15, 1864).

John H. Lahmeyer—Civilian, age 38, harness maker, native of Hanover, wife and two children, captured June 9 (testimony of Reverend William A. Hall, Richmond *Examiner*, June 14, 1864, no Federal prisoner of war record).

William W. Lecture—Private, R. F. Jarvis's Company, Junior Reserves, age 18, no occupation, father a member of Alfriend's Company, captured June 9 (Point Lookout; paroled and transferred to Aiken's Landing on James River for exchange, March 14, 1865; admitted to Chimborazo Hospital, Richmond, with catarrh, March 17, 1865; furloughed, March 22, 1865).

Thomas J. McCaleb—Sergeant, Rogers's Company, Petersburg Reserves, age 44, cabinet maker, wife and three children, captured June 9 (Bermuda Hundred, Camp Hamilton; Point Lookout, July 1; Elmira, July 26; oath of allegiance taken, November 30, 1864; released).

Robert McCandlish—Private, Wolff's Company, Second Class Militia, age 44, express agent, wife and three children, captured June 9 (Point Lookout; Elmira, July 12; paroled October 11, exchanged, October 29, 1864; transferred to CSA at Savannah River, Georgia, November 15, 1864).

William Taliaferro McCandlish—Private, Wolff's Company, Second Class Militia, age 52, merchant, wife, wounded in hand and captured June 9 (Point Lookout; Elmira, July 12; paroled October 11, exchanged, October 29, 1864; transferred to CSA at Savannah River, Georgia, November 15, 1864).

James R. McCann—Sergeant, Hare's Company, Prince George Reserves, age 48, carpenter, wife and seven children, captured June 9 (paroled, no further information).

John McIlwaine—Civilian, age 29, boot and shoe merchant, wife and one child, native of Ireland, discharged from 12th Virginia Infantry in April 1862 by furnishing a substitute, captured June 9 (testimony of Reverend William A. Hall, Richmond *Examiner*, June 14, 1864, no Federal prisoner of war record).

William Mann—Private, R. F. Jarvis's Company, Junior Reserves, age 23, clerk, parents, captured June 9 (listed as being at Chimborazo Hospital, Richmond, in September 1864 with old gunshot wound, no further information).

Joseph L. Peebles—Private, R. F. Jarvis's Company, Junior Reserves, age 16, farmer, mother and one brother, captured June 9 (Point Lookout; paroled and transferred for exchange, September 18, 1864; transferred to CSA at Varina on James River, September 22, 1864; admitted Chimborazo Hospital, Richmond, September 22, 1864).

Timothy Rives—Civilian, formerly Captain, 3rd Virginia Infantry to 1862, age 57, attorney/farmer, four children, delegate to Virginia Convention of

1861 (conditional Unionist, ultimately voted for secession), captured June 9 (no Federal prisoner of war data).

John N. Roper—Private, Wolff's Company, Second Class Militia, age 49, tailor, wife and six children, captured June 9 (Point Lookout; paroled and transferred for exchange, January 17, 1865; transferred to CSA at Boulware's Wharf on James River, January 21, 1865).

Warren Russell—Private, Alfriend's Company, Petersburg Reserves, age 42, boot and shoe maker, wife and six children, native of Maine, captured June 9 (Bermuda Hundred; Camp Hamilton; Point Lookout, July 1; Elmira, July 26; released, August 25, 1864).

John E. Smith—Corporal, Rogers's Company, Petersburg Reserves, age 47, hardware merchant, wife and three children, captured June 9 (Point Lookout; Elmira, July 12; paroled October 11, exchanged, October 29, 1864; transferred to CSA at Savannah River, Georgia, November 15, 1864).

John B. Stevens—Private, Wolff's Company, Second Class Militia, age 44, Petersburg City Chamberlain, wife and five children, captured June 9 (Point Lookout; Elmira, July 12; paroled, October 11, exchanged, October 29, 1864; transferred to CSA at Savannah River, Georgia, November 15, 1864).

Daniel Lee Sturdivant—Civilian (discharged for disability, 5th VA Cavalry, late 1861), age 24, farmer, wife, captured June 9 during Federal retreat (Point Lookout; Elmira, July 12; paroled, October 11, exchanged October 29; transferred to CSA at Savannah River, Georgia, November 15, 1864; not on roles of Wolff's Company or Archer's Battalion).

Alexander Vaughan—Sergeant, R. F. Jarvis's Company, Junior Reserves, age 16, no occupation, parents and three siblings (father in Alfriend's Company), captured June 9 (Point Lookout, June 13; released June 18, 1864, by joining Company F, 1st United States Volunteers).

James E. Wolfe—Captain, Wolff's Company, Second Class Militia, age 51, hat and cap merchant, widower with three children, captured June 9 (Point Lookout, June 13; Fort Delaware, June 25; paroled and sent to City Point for exchange, February 27, 1865).

Grand Total of Confederate Casualties at Rives's Farm and Vicinity (74)

Note: Many casualty lists for Rives's Farm include the names below, none of whom appear to have become a casualty at that place on June 9, 1864.

Captured June 15, 1864:

Peyton Fuqua—Private, Hood's Battalion, Virginia Reserves.
Wiliam C. Lumsden—Second Lieutenant, Hood's Battalion, Virginia
    Reserves.
James Smith—Hare's Company Prince George Reserves.

Casualties at Battery 5, June 9, 1864:

James Bowie—Company A, 44th Virginia Battalion (lost an arm).
James A. Cousins—Company A, 44th Virginia Battalion (wounded in breast
    and face).

Present at Rives's Farm but erroneously listed as casualties:

Simon Crowder—Private, W. H. Jarvis's Company, Petersburg Reserves, age
    43, miller/laborer, wife and sons John and William. Serving as a teamster
    in July 1864, present at Appomattox C.H., April 9, 1865, according to
    Compiled Service Record.
Frank Maddox (or Mattox)—Private, R. F. Jarvis's Company, Junior
    Reserves, age 16, occupation unknown, parents. Present for duty on June
    30, 1864, and March 1865 muster rolls in Compiled Service Record.
William B. Carr—Private, Wolff's Company, Second Class Militia, age 43,
    mathematics professor, wife and one son. Status "not stated" on June 30,
    1864, muster roll in Compiled Service Record, no Federal prisoner of war
    data, no mention of prisoner of war status in his own published account.
Williams Thomas Davis—Private, Wolff's Company, Second Class Militia,
    age 47, college president, widower with six children. Status "not stated"
    on June 30, 1864, muster roll in Compiled Service Record, no Federal
    prisoner of war data.

Appendix 4

An Interview with
Author William Glenn Robertson

SB: How did you become interested in the Petersburg Campaign, and especially the Battle of June 9?

WGR: I grew up in the western part of Tidewater Virginia, approximately sixty miles southeast of Petersburg. The Siege of Petersburg was my first battlefield to explore, both on the ground and in the books. My first war relics were two bullets purchased by my mother for me at the "Fort Hell" gift shop in the late 1950s, so the Petersburg interest was there from the beginning.

SB: And this stayed with you into college.

WGR: Yes. When I was in graduate school at the University of Virginia, I needed a topic for a Master's Thesis that would be large enough to meet the requirements and small enough to be manageable, yet told a complete story. The Battle of June 9 was just the right scale, had some potential war-changing consequences, highlighted controversial senior leaders, and included the timeless theme of citizens defending their homes. So it was the right size and embodied dramatic and emotional events. It fit my needs perfectly at the time.

SB: What sources were the most useful to you in telling your story?

WGR: The Official Records provided the most information on the Federal side, especially because the conflict between Benjamin Butler and Quincy Gillmore generated a great deal of additional communications beyond the normal after-action reports. For the Confederates, most of my information came from personal accounts of the citizen soldiers and townspeople of the city of Petersburg. Individual accounts by Raleigh Colston, Fletcher Archer, John Glenn, Anne Banister, and Bessie Callender were especially useful. The 1860 Census and the

Compiled Service Records of the reserve and militia formations fleshed out the lives of individual Confederate participants.

SB: Which Federal leaders performed well?

WGR: For the Federals, Benjamin Butler had a good plan, based upon extraordinary intelligence, but when seniority issues placed Quincy Gillmore in overall command, the plan was doomed to failure.

SB: It is interesting to hear that Butler, who is usually never credited with anything positive, had crafted a "good plan." Who on the Federal side performed poorly or at least not as well as hoped or expected?

WGR: Edward Hinks and August Kautz performed acceptably, but Joseph Hawley allowed the terrain to overawe him completely. Samuel Spear fully lived up to his reputation as a reckless and ignorant cavalryman.

SB: Interesting. And I know all the details are set forth in your book. How did General Beauregard and others in the Southern high command perform?

WGR: Senior leaders like P. G. T. Beauregard and Henry Wise had little to do but funnel pitifully small reinforcements to the front, but they did the best they could. The real heroes were Raleigh Colston, Fletcher Archer, and men like William C. Banister in the militia ranks, men who saw their duty clearly and stood up to the challenge, whatever the cost.

SB: What do you think was the key to Confederate success in this critical battle?

WGR: If the Federals had been led by a competent and bold field commander, there would have been no Confederate success—the Petersburg bridges would have been destroyed and thus unavailable for Lee's army to use a week later. But Quincy Gillmore was neither competent in field operations nor bold. On the other hand, Petersburg's handful of defenders could not have done more. They stood their ground at all points, masked their utter weakness, and bought enough time to win the day. They paid a heavy price, but saved their town for nine more months.

SB: And that in and of itself is really extraordinary. What was the impact of the Confederate June 9 victory?

WGR: Not only did the Confederates preserve the critical bridges over the Appomattox River, but their stand also alerted Beauregard and the Richmond authorities to the weakness of Petersburg's garrison. Although the reinforcements sent to Henry Wise in the week ahead were small, they may have provided the margin of victory on June 15 when William "Baldy" Smith and the XVIII Corps came to town in strength.

SB: So the fighting demonstrated to the Richmond authorities just how weak it was. You don't think the additional Southern reinforcements would have even been provided but for the June 9 battle?

WGR: Those Confederate reinforcements were unlikely to have been there if the June 9 battle hadn't occurred.

SB: What other impacts flowed from this little-known battle?

WGR: In the postwar period, Petersburg's memorialization of the citizen-soldiers who died in the Battle of June 9 may have had a lasting effect on the nation. Petersburg's may not have been the first Memorial Day, but its connection to the current national commemoration through Mr. and Mrs. John A. Logan and the Grand Army of the Republic is a salient fact.

SB: That is quite fascinating. Does this study provide any insights for 21st Century readers?

WGR: I think so. The story of the Battle of June 9 highlights several enduring lessons for us all. First, it represents a case study in how the personalities of senior leaders can interact in significant ways to negate a good plan and make competent troops fail. Second, it indicates what individuals bonded into a true community can accomplish against all odds. Finally, it illuminates the human cost of war to such a community, and how that cost still resonates more than 150 years later. Through their courage and self-sacrifice, William Banister, George Jones, the Crowder boys, Wayles Hurt, and the rest of Petersburg's "old men and young boys" have provided a timeless example of how to act when the odds are long, and the cost is great. May we never face such a horrendous event as they did, but if we do, may we perform as they did on June 9, 1863.

SB: Thank you for your time, Mr. Robertson.

WGR: You're welcome.

Bibliography

Unpublished Material

College of William and Mary Library, Williamsburg, VA
    Charles Campbell Diary
Library of Congress, Washington, DC
    P. G. T. Beauregard Papers
    Benjamin F. Butler Papers
    Cyrus B. Comstock Papers
    Joseph R. Hawley Papers
    August V. Kautz Papers
Library of Virginia, Richmond, VA
    Confederate Pension Rolls, Veterans and Widows
National Archives and Records Administration, Washington, DC
    Compiled Service Records of Confederate General and Staff Officers,
        and Non-Regimental Enlisted Men
    Compiled Service Records of Confederate Soldiers Who Served in
        Organizations From the State Of Virginia
    Compiled Service Records of Former Confederate Soldiers Who Served
        in the 1st Through 6th U.S. Volunteer Infantry Regiments, 1864-1866
    United States Federal Census for the years 1850, 1860, 1870, and 1880
North Carolina Office of Archives and History, Raleigh, NC
    Julia Ward Stickley Collection
Petersburg National Battlefield, Petersburg, Virginia
    Anne A. Banister, "Incidents in the Life of a Civil War Child"
    William H. Baxter Scrapbook
    Bessie Callender, "Personal Recollections of the Civil War"
    "Historical Stories About Petersburg"
Southern Historical Collection, University of North Carolina, Chapel Hill,
    North Carolina
    Raleigh Edward Colston Papers
University of Virginia Library, Charlottesville, Virginia
    George S. Bernard Diary
    J. H. Claiborne Papers
    Gilliam Family Papers
Virginia Historical Society, Richmond, Virginia
    Margaret Stanly Beckwith, "Reminiscences, 1844-1865"
    Jeremy Francis Gilmer Map Collection

Newspapers

Petersburg *Daily Express*
Richmond *Daily Dispatch*
Richmond *Examiner*

Published Material

Archer, Fletcher H. "The Defense of Petersburg on the 9th of June, 1864." *War Talks of Confederate Veterans.* Petersburg, VA: Fenn and Owen, 1892.

Armstrong, Mrs. James R. "The Origin of Memorial Day." *Confederate Veteran* 35 (December 1927).

Badeau, Adam. *Military History of Ulysses S. Grant, From April 1861, to April 1865.* New York, NY: D. Appleton, 1885

Beauregard, G. T. "Four Days of Battle at Petersburg." *Battles and Leaders of the Civil War.* New York, NY: Century, 1884.

Black, Robert C., III. *The Railroads of the Confederacy.* Chapel Hill, NC: University of North Carolina Press, 1952.

Boatner, Mark Mayo, III. *The Civil War Dictionary.* New York, NY: David McKay, 1959.

Brock, Robert Alonzo. *Virginia and Virginians.* Richmond, VA: 1888.

Bruce, George A. "General Butler's Bermuda Campaign." *Papers of the Military Historical Society of Massachusetts.* Boston, MA: Military Historical Society of Massachusetts, 1912.

Butler, Benjamin F. *Autobiography and Personal Reminiscences of Major General Benjamin F. Butler: Butler's Book.* Boston, MA: A. M. Thayer, 1892.

Cadwell, Charles K. *The Old Sixth Regiment, its War Record, 1861-5.* New Haven, CT: Tuttle, Morehouse and Taylor, 1875.

Carr, William N. [B.]. "Battle Of The 9th Of June." *Civil War Talks.* Charlottesville, VA: University of Virginia, 2012.

Catton, Bruce. *Grant Takes Command.* Boston, MA: Little, Brown, 1969.

———. *Never Call Retreat.* Garden City, NY: Doubleday, 1965.

Chambers, Henry A. *Diary of Captain Henry A. Chambers.* Wendell, NC: Broadfoot, 1983.

Claiborne, John H. *Seventy-Five Years in Old Virginia.* New York, NY: Neale, 1904.

Colston, Raleigh E. "Repelling the First Assault on Petersburg." *Battles and Leaders of the Civil War.* New York, NY: Century, 1884.

Cowles, Calvin D., compiler. *Atlas to Accompany the Official Records of the Union and Confederate Armies.* Washington, DC: Government Printing Office, 1891-1895.

Cutchins, John A. *A Famous Command: The Richmond Light Infantry Blues.* Richmond, VA: Garrett and Massie, 1934.

Dabney, Virginius. *Richmond: The Story of a City.* Garden City, NY: Doubleday, 1976.

Davidson, Nora F. M. *Cullings From the Confederacy.* Washington, DC: Rufus H. Darby, 1903.

Davis, William C., and Julie Hoffman, eds. *The Confederate General.* 6 vols. Harrisburg, PA: National Historical Society, 1991.

Dowdey, Clifford. *Lee's Last Campaign.* Boston, MA: Little, Brown, 1960.

———, and Louis Manarin, eds. *The Wartime Papers of R. E. Lee.* Boston, MA: Little, Brown, 1961.

Drewry, Patrick H. "The Ninth of June 1864." *Confederate Veteran* 35 (August 1927).

Dyer, Frederick H. *A Compendium of the War of the Rebellion.* 1908. Reprint, New York, NY: Thomas Yoseloff, 1959.

Eicher, John H., and David J. Eicher. *Civil War High Commands.* Stanford, CA: Stanford University, 2001.

Eldredge, Daniel. *The Third New Hampshire and All About It.* Boston, MA: E. B. Stillings, 1893.

Fox, William F. *Regimental Losses in the American Civil War, 1861-1865.* 1889. Reprint, Dayton, OH, Morningside, 1974.

Freeman, Douglas Southall. *Lee's Lieutenants: A Study in Command.* New York, NY: Charles Scribner's Sons, 1943.

Ginsberg, Louis. *History of the Jews of Petersburg, 1789-1950.* Richmond, VA: Williams, 1954.

Glenn, John F. "Brave Defence of the Cockade City." *Southern Historical Society Papers* 35 (1907).

Grant, Ulysses S. *Personal Memoirs of U. S. Grant.* New York, NY: Charles L. Webster, 1886.

Greene, A. Wilson. *Civil War Petersburg: Confederate City in the Crucible of War.* Charlottesville, VA: University of Virginia, 2006.

Harrison, M. Clifford. "Petersburg's Ninth of June." *Virginia Cavalcade* 8 (Summer 1958).

Harrison, Walter. *Pickett's Men: A Fragment of War History.* New York, NY: D. Van Nostrand, 1870.

Henderson, William D. *Petersburg in the Civil War: War at the Door.* Lynchburg, VA: H. E. Howard, 1998.

History of the Eleventh Pennsylvania Volunteer Cavalry, Together with a Complete Roster of the Regiment and Regimental Officers. Philadelphia, PA: Franklin, 1902.

Hood, W. H. "The Defense of Petersburg." *Civil War Talks.* Charlottesville, VA: University of Virginia, 2012.

Horigan, Michael. *Elmira: Death Camp of the North.* Mechanicsburg, PA: Stackpole, 2002.

Howe, Thomas J. *The Petersburg Campaign: Wasted Valor, June 15-18, 1864.* Lynchburg, VA: H. E. Howard, 1988.

Humphreys, Andrew A. *The Virginia Campaign of '64 and '65.* New York, NY: Charles Scribner's Sons, 1883.

Janney, Caroline E. *Burying the Dead but Not the Past: Ladies Memorial Associations and the Lost Cause.* Chapel Hill, NC: University of North Carolina, 2008.

Johnston, Angus James, II. *Virginia Railroads in the Civil War.* Chapel Hill, NC: University of North Carolina, 1961.

Kautz, August V. "The Cavalry Division of the Army of the James." *National Tribune,* September 21, 1899.

———. "First Attempts to Capture Petersburg." *Battles and Leaders of the Civil War.* New York, NY: Century, 1884.

———. "The Siege of Petersburg." *National Tribune,* May 18, 1899.

Kautz, Lawrence G. *August Valentine Kautz, USA: Biography of a Civil War General.* Jefferson, NC: McFarland, 2008.

Keiley, Anthony M. *In Vinculis; or, The Prisoner of War.* New York, NY: Blelock, 1866.

Little, Henry F. W. *The Seventh Regiment New Hampshire Volunteers in the War of the Rebellion.* Concord, NH: Ira C. Evans, 1896.

Livermore, Thomas L. *Days and Events, 1860-1866.* Boston, MA: Houghton Mifflin, 1920.

Logan, Mrs. John A. *Reminiscences of a Soldier's Wife: An Autobiography.* New York, NY: Charles Scribner's Sons, 1913.

Longacre, Edward G. *Army of Amateurs: General Benjamin F. Butler and the Army of the James, 1863-1865.* Mechanicsburg, PA: Stackpole, 1997.

Lykes, Richard W. *Petersburg Battlefields.* Washington, DC: Government Printing Office, 1951.

Macrae, David. *The Americans at Home.* New York, NY: E. P. Dutton, 1952.

Marshall, Jessie Ames, ed. *Private and Official Correspondence of Gen. Benjamin F. Butler During the Period of the Civil War.* Norwood, MA: Plimpton, 1917.

McAuley, John D. *Civil War Breech Loading Rifles.* Lincoln, RI: Andrew Mowbray, 1987.

"Memorial Day at Petersburg, Va." *Confederate Veteran* 32 (August 1924).

Merrill, Samuel H. *The Campaigns of the First Maine and First District of Columbia Cavalry.* Portland, ME: Bailey and Noyes, 1866.

Mills, Luther Rice. "Letters of Luther Rice Mills, a Confederate Soldier." *North Carolina Historical Review* 4 (1927).

Neff, John R. *Honoring the Civil War Dead: Commemoration and the Problem of Reconciliation.* Lawrence, KS: University of Kansas, 2005.

Newsome, Hampton, John Horn, and John G. Selby. *Civil War Talks*. Charlottesville, VA: University of Virginia, 2012.

Owen, William Miller. *In Camp and Battle with the Washington Artillery of New Orleans*. Boston, MA: Ticknor, 1885.

Parker, William L. *General James Dearing CSA*. Lynchburg, VA: H. E. Howard, 1990.

Pryor, Mrs. Roger A. *Reminiscences of Peace and War*. New York, NY: Macmillan, 1904.

Radley, Kenneth. *Rebel Watchdog: The Confederate States Army Provost Guard*. Baton Rouge, LA: Louisiana State University, 1989.

Raymond, Harold B. "Ben Butler: A Reappraisal." *Colby Library Quarterly* 6 (September 1964).

Raiford, Neil Hunter. *The Fourth North Carolina Cavalry in the Civil War*. Jefferson, NC: McFarland, 2006.

Robertson, William G. *Back Door to Richmond: The Bermuda Hundred Campaign, April-June 1864*. Newark, DE: University of Delaware, 1987.

Rockwell, Alfred P. "The Tenth Army Corps in Virginia, May 1864." *Papers of the Military Historical Society of Massachusetts*. Boston, MA: Military Historical Society of Massachusetts, 1912.

Roman, Alfred. *The Military Operations of General Beauregard in the War Between the States, 1861 to 1865*. New York, NY: Harper, 1883.

Scott, James G., and Edward A. Wyatt, IV. *Petersburg's Story: A History*. Richmond, VA: Whittet and Shepperson, 1960.

Scott, John. "A Ruse of War." *The Annals of the War Written by Leading Participants North and South*. Philadelphia, PA: Times, 1879.

Thompson, S. Millet. *Thirteenth Regiment of New Hampshire Volunteer Infantry in the War of the Rebellion, 1861-1865*. Boston, MA: Houghton Mifflin, 1888.

Turner, George Edgar. *Victory Rode the Rails*. Indianapolis, IN: Bobbs-Merrill, 1953.

Vandiver, Frank E. *Ploughshares into Swords: Josiah Gorgas and Confederate Ordnance*. Austin, TX: University of Texas, 1952.

Walkley, Stephen. *History of the Seventh Connecticut Volunteer Infantry*. Southington, CT: 1905.

Wallace, Lee A., Jr. *A Guide to Virginia Military Organizations, 1861-1865*. Lynchburg, VA: H. E. Howard, 1986.

———. *Surry Light Artillery and Martin's, Wright's, Coffin's Batteries of Virginia Artillery*. Lynchburg, VA: H. E. Howard, 1995.

War of the Rebellion: A Compilation of the Official Records of the Union and Confederate Armies. Washington, DC: Government Printing Office, 1880-1901.

Warner, Ezra J. *Generals in Blue: Lives of the Union Commanders*. Baton Rouge, LA: Louisiana State University, 1964.

———. *Generals in Gray: Lives of the Confederate Commanders*. Baton Rouge, LA: Louisiana State University, 1959.

West, Richard S., Jr. *Lincoln's Scapegoat General: A Life of Benjamin F. Butler, 1818-1893*. Boston, MA: Houghton Mifflin, 1965.

Williams, T. Harry. *P. G. T. Beauregard: Napoleon in Gray*. Baton Rouge, LA: Louisiana State University, 1955.

Williamson, J. Pinckney. *Ye Olden Tymes, History of Petersburg*. Petersburg, VA: Frank A. Owen, 1906.

Wills, Brian Steel. *The War Hits Home: The Civil War in Southeastern Virginia*. Charlottesville, VA: University of Virginia, 2001.

Wise, Barton H. *The Life of Henry A. Wise of Virginia, 1806-1876*. New York, NY: Macmillan, 1899.

Wise, Henry A. "The Career of Wise's Brigade, 1861-5." *Southern Historical Society Papers* 25 (1897).

Wise, Jennings C. *The Long Arm of Lee*. 1915. Reprint, New York, NY: Oxford, 1959.

Index

Bermuda Hundred, described, 12; Federal landing at, 13-14; mentioned, 16-21, 24, 27-29, 31, 33-34, 36-37, 45, 59-60, 70-71, 77, 100, 104, 105n, 112-113, 115-118, 122, 124-125, 135-136, 137-137n, 140-141, 155, 158-159

Bermuda Hundred campaign, 29, 38, 42, 75

Bermuda Hundred Landing, 13, 39-40, 124

Big Bethel, Battle of, 7, 9

Bird, Henry D., 116, 124

Bird, W. E., 116

Blackwater River, 7, 14-14n

Blandford, Virginia, 104-105, 107, 109n, 110-111, 146

Blandford Cemetery, 121-122, 139, 144, 146-147

Blandford Church, 107, 146-147; *photo*, 145

Blanks, Henry A., Sr., 85-86, 120-121, 152

Blunt, Reverend, 121

Board of Relief, 6

Boisseau, James, 51, 56, 85, 123, 155

Bollingbrook Street, 4, 105-106

Bott, Berthier, 84, 123, 140, 155

Boulware's Wharf, Virginia, 159

Bowen, Edwin N., 64

Bowie, James, 129n, 160

Bragg, Braxton, 60, 76-77, 100-102, 117, 118-118n, 135-136, 138n

Branch, Thomas, 1

Broadnax, E. A., 85, 155

Broadway Landing, 43

Brooklyn, New York, 142

Brown, Edward P., 152

Brown, Reverend, 121

Bryant, Henry T., 71

Bryant's house, 71

Burgess's Mill, 139

Burnside, Ambrose E., 11

Butler, Benjamin F., department commander, 9; previous career, 9; relations with Grant, 11; instruct-ions from Grant, 12; operations in Bermuda Hundred campaign, 13-14, 16-19; problems with Gillmore, 13, 17, 32, 33n; military reputation, 11; proposes attack on Petersburg, 21, 22-22n; loses troops, 21-22, 27n; proposes second attack on Petersburg, 27-28; proposes third attack on Petersburg, 30; plan of attack, 33; prepares expedition, 34; waits for news, 58-59; interrogates prisoners, 124; reputation dam-aged, 129; post-battle controversy with Gillmore, 114, 130-134; mentioned, 13, 16, 20, 29, 35, 39-41, 43-44, 46, 60, 67, 70-72, 75-77, 81, 100, 105n, 115n, 116-117, 125-125n, 131n, 132n, 141; *photo*, 10

Butler, Sarah, 131-132

Butler, William C., 108

Butterworth's Bridge, 25

Butts, Benjamin H., 155

Butts, Daniel G. C., 117n, 155

Cain, James H., 85, 153

Callender, Bessie, 51, 55-56, 98-100, 107-108, 117, 119

Callender, David, 51, 55, 99, 119

Cameron, George, 57, 120n, 123, 155

Cameron, William, 51, 57-58, 98-99, 107-109, 120n, 123

Cameron, William E., 144

Cameron's house (Mount Erin), 57, 107-109

Camp Hamilton, Virginia, 155, 158-159

Campbell, Charles, 51, 56, 111n

Campbell, Reverend, 121

Campbell, Thomas H., 57, 99-100

Campbell County, Virginia, 104

Cantwell, John L., 108-109

Carr, William B., 51, 85, 89n, 160

Cary, Richard M., 153

Catton, Bruce, 11-12

Cavalry Bureau, 79